D0944535

GILBERT RYLE

An Introduction to his Philosophy

GILBERT RYLE

An Introduction to his Philosophy

WILLIAM LYONS
Lecturer in Philosophy, University of Glasgow

THE HARVESTER PRESS · SUSSEX
HUMANITIES PRESS · NEW JERSEY

First published in Great Britain in 1980 by
THE HARVESTER PRESS LIMITED
Publishers: John Spiers and Margaret A. Boden
16 Ship Street, Brighton, Sussex

and in the USA by
HUMANITIES PRESS INC.,
Atlantic Highlands, New Jersey 07716

British Library Cataloguing in Publication Data
Lyons, William
  Gilbert Ryle. –(Harvester studies in philosophy; 21).
  1. Ryle, Gilbert
  192   BI649.R964
  ISBN 0-85527-477-8

Humanities Press
ISBN 0-391-01800-0

Photoset in Great Britain by
Rowland Phototypesetting Limited, Bury St Edmunds, Suffolk
and printed by
St Edmundsbury Press, Bury St Edmunds, Suffolk

TO ANNIE

CONTENTS

PREFACE

Ryle will always be linked with Austin and, especially, Wittgenstein as the founding fathers of Linguistic Analysis which, for better or for worse, has set the style and developed the methods of philosophising in much of the English-speaking world for the past forty years or more. In the introduction to his conversation with Gilbert Ryle on BBC radio during the winter of 1970–71, Bryan Magee suggested that 'the first clear public statement of the view of philosophy that has come to be known as Linguistic Philosophy or Linguistic Analysis was made by the young Gilbert Ryle in 1931 at the end of his paper on "Systematically Misleading Expressions".' (Bryan Magee, *Modern British Philosophy*)

Both Ryle and Wittgenstein were products of Positivism but in different ways. Wittgenstein was influenced by nineteenth-century Austro-German Positivism, as well as by the new logic of Frege, Peano and others, and wrote one of the classics of Logical Positivism, the *Tractatus Logico-Philosophicus*, though he later reacted strongly against this phase of his philosophical thinking. Ryle saw Positivism as claiming to supplant philosophy with science and so to render philosophy, all philosophy, obsolete. In answer to this challenge, Ryle tried to delineate what was the unique task of philosophy and derived a view of philosophy as the activity of laying bare the logical categories which underlie and are often distorted by the surface grammar of our ordinary speech or scientific speech. Thus this programme, along with Wittgenstein's of untying the knots in our thinking and displaying the correct language games in which our words are to be used, set the tone and the content for philosophy in the English-speaking world in this century. Wittgenstein and Ryle sowed the seeds in our minds of distrust of ordinary language, making us realise that it must be negotiated very carefully as it is pitted with logical and

x   *Gilbert Ryle: An Introduction to his Philosophy*

ontological howlers, and eroded by obsolete theories. Philosophy in this century has been fixated with language and the pitfalls in its use, and this has been due as much to Ryle as to Wittgenstein. A great many of the idioms in which the twentieth-century philosopher philosophises— 'philosophical analysis', 'the analysis of concepts', 'mapping the logical geography of concepts', 'category mistakes', 'dispositional analyses', 'adverbial analyses', 'systematically misleading expressions'—were first coined by Ryle.

But Ryle also began another major movement in modern philosophy, anti-Cartesianism. Until Ryle came on the scene, Cartesian mind-body dualism had easily held the day against the few attacks that had been launched against it since the seventeenth century. But since his 'hatchet job' on the Cartesian doctrine of 'the ghost in the machine', as Ryle called it, in his masterpiece *The Concept of Mind*, Cartesian dualism has lost ground to such an extent that, in philosophy if not yet in the world at large, one would be hard put to find someone who believes that mind or spirit is a substance. Ryle's decimation of Cartesian dualism has now threatened to become an annihilation with the appearance of positive materialist theories built on the ground cleared by his demolition work. Already, Bryan Magee suggests, *The Concept of Mind* is 'one of the best-known works of philosophy in the English language' and 'one of the small handful that the serious student of the subject simply must read'. Moreover, Stuart Hampshire, in his review of the book in the journal *Mind*, wrote that 'it has the distinction of style and the large simplicity of purpose which have always made the best philosophical writing a part of general literature', and compared him in this respect with Hume. Yet Ryle's work, by and large, has not been read by the general public any more than Hume's was, and one begins to wonder how often it is now read by philosophers. For, while still acknowledged to be a major influence in twentieth-century philosophy, on the whole, discussion of Ryle's work has been negligible in the last twenty years, and there still remains no single book, introductory or advanced, solely on his philosophy other than a collection of essays. Part of the reason for this

neglect may be the feeling that there was no central theme
or themes running through his work. I have tried to show
that this feeling is unjustified and that Ryle was very much
preoccupied in his early work with a single problem, the
nature of philosophy, and in his later years mainly with
applying what he thought to be the correct method of
philosophising to one very definite target, Cartesian
dualism.

Part of the reason for this neglect of Ryle's work may
also lie in the way Ryle philosophised. For while Ryle
writes with literary fluency, he also writes with a deliberately allusive style which all too often makes his arguments and conclusions elusive as well. When one has read
through a paper, a chapter, or even a whole book of his,
one is puzzled, provoked, and usually charmed by the
epigrams and analogies, yet, on reflection, one is not able
easily to say exactly what his arguments have been and
what conclusions one should draw from them. I have tried
to lay bare the central themes in his work, and his central
arguments when pursuing those themes, and in a way that
is digestible by a tyro in philosophy.

This book is intended as an introduction to the work of
Gilbert Ryle. It concentrates on the central issues in Ryle's
philosophy and makes no claim to be an exhaustive
account of the many topics which Ryle wrote about. While
disputed areas are pointed out, lines of criticism suggested, and some of the ways in which his work has been
or might be developed outlined, it is intended that the
book be primarily a simple, clear and basically sympathetic
introduction to his work.

ACKNOWLEDGEMENTS

I would like to thank Margaret Boden, Tony Pitson, Flint Schier, John Skorupski and Geoffrey Warnock for their kind and helpful comments on draft versions of various parts of this book. I would like also to thank George Weir for his generous assistance in checking quotations and references. Finally, I should acknowledge the permission granted by the editor and publishers of the *International Philosophical Quarterly* to make use of my article 'Ryle's Three Accounts of Thinking' which appeared recently in their journal.

Chapter 1
A SHORT BIOGRAPHY OF GILBERT RYLE

In his obituary in *The Times* it was said of Ryle that 'because of his energy, judgment, sympathy, and out-standing intellectual power, Ryle was the most influential figure in British philosophy in the middle years of the twentieth century.'

Gilbert Ryle was born in 1900 in Brighton. Clearly, one of the most formative influences was his father, who was a general practitioner, but had an abiding interest in both astronomy and philosophy, and helped found the Aristotelian Society. It is hardly surprising then that Gilbert became a philosopher, and it may not be a complete coincidence that one of his nephews is Sir Martin Ryle F.R.S., the famous radio astronomer. And Ryle tells us in his 'Autobiographical', the Introduction to the Modern Studies in Philosophy collection of critical essays on his work, that his father's library 'contained many philosophical and semi-philosophical works' and that he was 'an omnivorous reader'.

Ryle was educated at Brighton College and went up to The Queen's College, Oxford, as a Classical Scholar in 1919. While he believed that he lacked the requisite flair for being a classicist, he nonetheless gained a First Class in Classical Honour Moderations, the first part of his Literae Humaniores B.A. But, he says, 'I took greedily to the off-centre subject of Logic. It felt to me like a grown-up subject, in which there were still unsolved problems. This was not my impression of the Classics in general, as they were then taught.' ('Autobiographical'—hereafter *A*—p. 2) Ryle enjoyed both the ancient and modern philosophy segments of 'Greats', the second part of Literae Humaniores, as well as the extra-curricular Jowett Society, an undergraduate society for philosophical discussion.

At this time his philosophical reading ranged widely. Under the influence of his tutor, H. J. Paton, he read some Italian philosophy, chiefly Croce and Gentile, but he was also dipping into Russell's *Principles of Mathematics* at a time when Russell was definitely not officially approved of at Oxford. At the end of his fourth year Ryle gained a First Class in Greats. In his fifth year he worked for the new school of 'Modern Greats', Philosophy, Politics and Economics, intending to take the final examination in this school at the end of the year. Anticipating that most of the examiners for Modern Greats would be expecting 'post-Cartesian pabulum' from other candidates, Ryle made a point of studying some medieval philosophy. At any rate at the end of the year, 1924, he again gained First Class honours, though at the time he was also actively interested in rowing, being Captain of The Queen's College Boat Club and was in the University Trial Eights. In this same year he was made a lecturer in philosophy at Christ Church.

Ryle describes Oxford philosophy at this time in the following terms:

During my time as an undergraduate and during my first few years as a teacher, the philosophic kettle in Oxford was barely lukewarm. I think that it would have been stone cold but for Prichard, who did bring into his chosen and rather narrow arenas vehemence, tenacity, unceremoniousness, and a perverse consistency that made our hackles rise, as nothing else at that time did. The Bradleians were not yet extinct, but they did not come out into the open. I cannot recollect hearing one referring mention of the Absolute. The Cook Wilsonians were hankering to gainsay the Bradleians and the Croceans, but were given few openings. Pragmatism was still represented by F. C. S. Schiller, but as his tasteless jocosities beat vainly against the snubbing primnesses of his colleagues, even this puny spark was effectually quenched.

Logic, save for Aristotelian scholarship, was in the doldrums. Little was heard now even of the semi-psychological topics discussed in Bradley's mis-titled *Principles of Logic*. Russell's *Principles of Mathematics* had been published when I was three; twenty-five years later it and *Principia Mathematica* were still only the objects of Oxonian pleasantries. The names of Boole, De Morgan, Venn, Jevons, McColl, Frege, Peano, Johnson, and J. M. Keynes did not crop up in lectures and discussions. In the bibliography of the Kneales' *The Development of Logic* no Oxford entries, save contributions to scholarship, belong to the half century from Lewis Carroll (1896). (*A*, p. 4)

Ryle went on to describe how this provincialism was only broken down by the next generation of philosophers, his generation, importing into Oxford the ideas of Moore,

Russell and Wittgenstein from Cambridge, and Ryle himself was at this time reading Wittgenstein's *Tractatus* as
well as Russell's logic papers and was particularly influenced by Russell's work on the theory of types.

But at the same time, again under the influence of
Paton, Ryle deliberately set out to gain some knowledge of
what was going on in continental Europe. He taught
himself German and read Husserl's *Logische Unter-
suchungen*, as well as Meinong, Brentano, Bolzano and
Frege, and made some of this reading the subject matter,
as he himself put it, of 'an unwanted course of lectures,
entitled Logical Objectivism: Bolzano, Brentano, Husserl
and Meinong', which became known as 'Ryle's three
Austrian railway stations and one Chinese game of
chance'. Ryle's first published pieces of philosophical
writing were book reviews of works by the Polish philosopher, Ingarden, a follower of Husserl, and by the
German existentialist, Heidegger.

As with the Cambridge school, so with the Continentals,
Ryle was principally interested in their philosophical
logic, and his first philosophical papers were entitled
'Negation' (1929), 'Are there Propositions?' (1930), and
'Systematically Misleading Expressions' (1932).

In the 1930s Ryle, along with most of his generation,
was influenced by the doctrines of Logical Positivism.
Indeed it was Ryle's most famous pupil A. J. Ayer who, on
Ryle's suggestion, went to Vienna to find out about
Logical Positivism, and it was through Ayer's book which
resulted from this trip, *Language, Truth and Logic*, that
the English-speaking world became aware of Logical
Positivism. The particular form that the Logical Positivist
influence took in Ryle's case was that, while 'most of us
took fairly untragically its demolition of Metaphysics' (*A*,
p. 10), Ryle realised that Logical Positivism also inadvertently raised the awkward question 'What is the
nature of philosophy itself?' for Logical Positivism made
the paradigms of meaningful utterances to be those of
science, yet it was clear that philosophy was not science.

Ryle felt that the solution to this problem might lie in
returning to the history of the subject to find out what in
fact philosophers had accomplished when their more

vacuous metaphysical speculations were excised. He makes it clear, however, that this regard for the history of the subject was not one of the more usual by-products of Logical Positivism or similar views. As Ryle put it:

In my own case this reaction was strengthened by my occasional visits to the Moral Sciences Club at Cambridge. At its meetings veneration for Wittgenstein was so incontinent that mentions, for example my mentions, of other philosophers were greeted with jeers. Wittgenstein himself not only properly distinguished philosophical from exegetic problems but also, less properly, gave the impressions, first, that he himself was proud not to have studied other philosophers—which he had done, though not much—and second, that he thought that people who did study them were academic and therefore unauthentic philosophers, which was often but not always true. This contempt for thoughts other than Wittgenstein's seemed to me pedagogically disastrous for the students and unhealthy for Wittgenstein himself. It made me resolve, not indeed to be a philosophical polyglot, but to avoid being a monoglot; and most of all to avoid being one monoglot's echo, even though he was a genius and a friend. This resolve was all the easier to keep because, for local curricular reasons, I and my colleagues had as students had to study, and had now as teachers to teach in considerable detail some of the thoughts of, *inter alios*, Plato, Aristotle, Descartes, Hume, and Kant. (*A*, p. 11)

It was at about this time, 1933, that Ryle delivered one of the John Locke Tercentenary Addresses, and wrote reviews of books on Hume and Meinong. But, though the last of these appeared in print in 1940, from 1935 to 1939 Ryle returned to his central concern of this period, philosophical logic or, as it was beginning to be called, logical analysis. He wrote, among others at this time, the papers 'Unverifiability by Me' (1936), 'Induction and Hypothesis' (1937), 'Categories' (1938) and 'Conscience and Moral Convictions' (1940), and was reviewing books like *Communication* and *Language and Reality*. But also he was still *the* obvious choice for reviewing books on German philosophy and Plato, and it was during this period that he made his first of many contributions to Platonic studies in 'Plato's Parmenides' (1939). His other articles at this time fall into the category of local disputes with 'the older generation', *en masse* in 'Taking Sides in Philosophy' (1937), with particular members, Bradley and Collingwood, in 'Internal Relations' (1935) and 'Mr Collingwood and the Ontological Argument' (1935).

It is also worth noting that, in the late twenties and early thirties we find the beginning of what was a lifelong disposition of Ryle's, his willingness and even eagerness to take part in philosophical discussion at conferences and congresses. Ryle's first published paper, 'Negation' (1929), was delivered to the then still quite fledgling Joint Session of the Mind and Aristotelian Societies, and many of his subsequent papers were printed either with the Joint Session papers or as a contribution to the Proceedings of the Aristotelian Society. In 1938 he was called upon to make the welcoming speech to the Fourth International Congress for Unified Science which met that year in Cambridge,* and Ryle attended all the International Congresses of philosophy until the thirteenth one held in Mexico in 1963.

In his 'Introduction' to *The Revolution in Philosophy*— BBC Third Programme lectures—Ryle suggested that the

new professional practice of [philosophers] submitting problems and arguments to the expert criticism of fellow craftsmen [at the then recently inaugurated Aristotelian Society or in the fairly recently founded journal *Mind*] led to a growing concern with questions of philosophical technique and a growing passion for ratiocinative rigour . . . From both these causes transcendental dictions were becoming unidiomatic at the same time as the technicalities of logical theory and scientific method were stiffening the working parlance of philosophers. (pp. 3–4)

Then came the Second World War, and Ryle volunteered. He was commissioned in the Welsh Guards and was engaged in intelligence work. When the war was over Ryle was elected in 1945 to the Waynflete Chair of Metaphysical Philosophy which had lain vacant since R. G. Collingwood's death in 1943. The irony of his holding a chair of that title would not have been lost on him. His Inaugural Lecture was entitled 'Philosophical Arguments', and it is significant that it was reprinted later as part of a collection of papers edited by Ayer and entitled *Logical Positivism* (1959), for Linguistic Analysis was still not

---

* The unification of science, by reducing the multiplicity of confusing concepts in the various sciences to some fewer fundamental concepts, was one of the platforms of the early Logical Positivists.

formally separated from its chief progenitor, Logical Positivism.

The next ten years saw Ryle's major contribution to philosophy, the publication of his first book *The Concept of Mind* (1949). The impact was immediate and established him as a philosopher of the first rank. As Stuart Hampshire wrote in his review of the book in *Mind*, 1950:

This is probably one of the two or three most important and original works of general philosophy which have been published in English in the last twenty years. Both its main thesis and the mass of its detailed observations will certainly be a focus of discussion among philosophers for many years to come; and it has the distinction of style and the large simplicity of purpose which have always made the best philosophical writing a part of general literature.

J. L. Austin's review of the book for *The Times Literary Supplement* in 1950 included the following comment: 'In short, it stands head and shoulders above its contemporaries; it will deservedly enjoy a success, and even a vogue.' The book, as Ryle himself put it, was 'a sustained piece of analytical hatchet-work' (*A*, p. 12) on Cartesian dualism, or, as Ryle would say, the Cartesian myth that there is a ghost in the human machine, that is a mind or soul inhabiting and piloting the body. The book employed the logical tactics which Ryle had been working up over the previous twenty years, and was his finest display of these tactics in the full heat of battle.

His other major contribution to philosophy in these years was the beginning of his term of editorship of *Mind*, which was probably the leading philosophical journal in those days. He succeeded Moore who had been editor for the previous quarter century, and was himself to be editor for most of the next quarter century. Besides maintaining the highest standards of scholarship and critical debate within its pages, Ryle maintained a policy of deliberately encouraging those just beginning their philosophical career. Under his editorship the contents of *Mind* certainly reflected the new tone of philosophy in the post-war years. The contributions were not long systematised accounts of theories but shorter papers on a particular point or discussions about particular arguments. It was the beginning of the style of careful undramatic analysis which is still prevalent today. The contributors to *Mind* also reflected the growing importance of philosophers in America and other parts of the New World. This reflected Ryle's consistent dislike of provincialism and insularity in philosophy.

In 1954, under the title *Dilemmas*, were published the Tarner Lectures which Ryle had delivered in the Lent Term of 1953 at Trinity College, Cambridge. These lectures were a further working out, though less spectacularly than in *The Concept of Mind*, of his view that many philosophical problems can be solved if we realise that the key terms of these problems are being misused, because their logic, that is the way they should be connected with other expressions, is not understood. Between 1949 and 1954 Ryle wrote a further series of influential papers on philosophical logic, for example his '"If," "So" and "Because"' (1950), 'Heterologicality' and 'Thinking and Language' (1951) and 'Ordinary Language' (1953).

The first in the series of papers on a theme which was to occupy Ryle on and off right up to the year of his death appeared in 1953, namely the theme of the nature of thinking, particularly reflective or contemplative thinking, for Ryle believed that an inadequate account of this latter aspect was one of the major gaps in *The Concept of Mind*.

The other major work of Ryle's after *Dilemmas* was a series of articles on Plato which culminated in his book *Plato's Progress*, a reappraisal of the chronology of Plato's dialogues, which outraged some Platonic scholars by its unorthodoxy but intrigued and amused all.

While Ryle was not interested in university administration as such, he was interested in the university processes and structures through which philosophy was taught. He is credited with the introduction of the new postgraduate degree, the B.Phil., which by contrast with the dissertation-based D.Phil. and B.Litt., was partly examinable course work. And Ryle's obituarist in *The Times* wrote that 'the expansion and vitality of postgraduate philosophical studies in Oxford in those years gave Ryle an uncommon indirect influence on the university appointments in the subject throughout Britain.' In short, Ryle was undoubtedly something of a philosophical 'kingmaker' in the fifties and sixties.

Ryle retired from his chair at Oxford in 1968 but he remained philosophically active, writing articles, delivering papers and attending conferences. He died in October 1976 at the age of 76.

Chapter 2
RYLE AND THE NATURE OF PHILOSOPHY

It is now fashionable among professional philosophers to be reluctant to say what philosophy is. In much the same spirit as one might reply to questions about what love is, we reply to questions about what philosophy is by saying 'I know till you ask me.' But it is worth seeing some of these replies themselves:

This is a book for newcomers to philosophy, though I have made no attempt to say what philosophy is or what makes a problem philosophical. I believe the only way to find out what philosophy is, is to do it rather than talk about it.
(L. Goddard, *Philosophical Problems*, 1977)

Books like this one usually begin with an attempt to define their subject. But in the case of moral philosophy, defining the subject is itself a controversial philosophical problem. Therefore no short definition can be satisfactory, and a detailed explanation here would be premature since it could be assessed only by someone already familiar with the subject. So the best way, and really the only way, to find out what moral philosophy is, is to plunge right in it.
(J. Glickman ed., *Moral Philosophy: An Introduction*, 1976)

However, in this essay I wish to avoid discussion based on pre-selected definitions; and I do not pretend to offer any slick statement about the nature of philosophical knowledge. I intend to proceed in an empirical manner by selecting for examination certain discussions and enquiries which are generally thought of as pertaining to 'philosophy'.
(F. Copleston, *Philosophers and Philosophies*, 1976)

Nowadays a newcomer to philosophy might be forgiven for thinking that philosophy is some sort of arcane craft, its practices passed on within the guild from master to apprentice, but its aims and rules unwritten and immune from outside scrutiny. While the enemies of philosophy will be quick to point out that philosophers refrain from a scrutiny of their craft because they are afraid they will find out it is useless and obsolete, its friends may want to shield the fraternity by suggesting that such scrutinies are avoided for much the same reasons that scientists usually do not engage in any enquiry into the nature of science or its methods, namely that it is far less interesting or important than getting on with the task itself.

But things were not always so, even in our own century. In the twenties and thirties philosophers were only too eager to tell us what did and what did not constitute philosophy, for those were the heady days of the birth of Linguistic Analysis when philosophers were confident that they had carved out a subject which was exclusively theirs. Gilbert Ryle was one of those who were not only very interested in the question 'What is philosophy?' but could be said to have been fascinated by this question, at least in the thirties. His answer to this question is not only very revealing about the nature of philosophy at that time, but also about the nature of his own work and its influence on subsequent philosophy.

In the 'Introduction' to his *Collected Papers*, Volume 2, 'Collected Essays 1929–1968' Ryle writes that,

There was in me, from quite early days, an ulterior concern. In the 1920's and the 1930's there was welling up the problem 'What, if anything, is philosophy?' No longer could we pretend that philosophy differed from physics, chemistry and biology by studying mental as opposed to material phenomena. We could no longer boast or confess that we were unexperimental psychologists. Hence we were beset by the temptation to look for non-mental, non-material objects—or Objects—which should be for philosophy what beetles and butterflies were for entomology. Platonic Forms, Propositions, Intentional Objects, Logical Objects, perhaps, sometimes, even Sense-Data were recruited to appease our professional hankerings to have subject-matter of our own.

I had learned, chiefly from the *Tractatus Logico-Philosophicus*, that no specifications of a proprietary subject-matter could yield the right answer, or even the right sort of answer to the original question 'What is Philosophy?'

(*Collected Papers*, Vol. 2—hereafter *CP* 2—p. vii)

The nineteen twenties and nineteen thirties were marked by the radical manifesto of the Logical Positivists, the clearest version of which, in English, is in A. J. Ayer's *Language, Truth and Logic* (1936). The Positivists declared that the paradigms of meaningful sentences were the empirical statements of the natural sciences, that is, sentences whose truth or falsity was to be tested by observation or experiment. But the Logical Positivists also made it clear that philosophical statements were not empirical ones testable by observation or experiment. However, they did allow that there was one other sort of meaningful statement which a person could make, an analytic statement, such as 'A bachelor is an unmarried man' or '2 + 2 = 4', where the statement could be seen to be true or false merely by a consideration of the meanings of the words or symbols used. Such analytic statements could be generated in any language, code or calculus. It was to this second sort of statement that Ryle looked as the most likely area where philosophical statements could legitimately be placed.

But Ryle did not think that philosophical statements were principally lexicographical ones like 'Bachelors are unmarried men' or mathematical ones like '2 + 2 = 4', but second-order statements about a certain aspect of language rather than ones made within the language.

For Ryle, philosophical statements 'are condemned to be uninformative about the world and yet able, in some important way, to be clarificatory of those propositions that are informative about the world, reporting no matters of fact yet correcting our mishandlings of reported matters of fact.' (*The Revolution in Philosophy*, p. 5) So for Ryle, as for Wittgenstein, philosophy was analysing ordinary language in order to correct its mishandlings, not, as many who misunderstand the nature of linguistic analysis believe, appealing to ordinary language as the touchstone of truths about the world or anything else. Ryle's view of philosophy was that it was a method of revising misuses of ordinary language and revising the theories that we derived incorrectly from the surface structure or logic, and so the surface meaning, of ordinary language. Thus Ryle tells us that 'philosophical problems are problems of a special sort; they are not problems of an ordinary sort about special entities.' (*CP* 2, 'Introduction', p. vii) The problem is that of getting past the surface grammar or surface logical structure of ordinary language and its apparent meaning, to its fundamental grammar or, as Ryle put it, to its 'true logical form'.

Wittgenstein, at least in his early philosophical days,

had an almost identical view. He wrote in the posthumously published *Notebooks 1914–1916*:

In philosophy there are no deductions; it is purely descriptive. The word 'philosophy' ought always to designate something over or under, but not beside, the natural sciences. Philosophy gives no pictures of reality, and can neither confirm nor confute scientific investigations . . . Distrust of grammar is the first requisite for philosophizing. Philosophy is the doctrine of the logical form of scientific propositions (not primitive propositions only). (Appendix 1, p. 93)

And in the *Tractatus Logico-Philosophicus* which grew out of those notebooks, and was published first in German in 1921 and translated for the first time into English the following year, Wittgenstein writes even more explicitly of the role of philosophy:

Philosophy is not one of the natural sciences.
(The word 'philosophy' must mean something whose place is above or below the natural sciences, not beside them.)
Philosophy aims at the logical clarification of thoughts.
Philosophy is not a body of doctrine but an activity.
A philosophical work consists essentially of elucidations.
Philosophy does not result in 'philosophical propositions', but rather in the clarification of propositions.
Without philosophy thoughts are, as it were, cloudy and indistinct: its task is to make them clear and to give them sharp boundaries.
                                    (*Tractatus* 4.111, 4.112)

Both Wittgenstein and Ryle would say that philosophy is not the propounding of theories but an activity of clarifying and sharpening the meaning of ordinary language and correcting misuses of it, though this process may reveal theories underlying our use of language. Wittgenstein has sometimes been interpreted as suggesting that philosophy's clarificatory role could be described as a kind of therapy in which one's muddled thinking is cured. This interpretation was derived from some of Wittgenstein's more aphoristic remarks on the nature of philosophy, such as that 'philosophy unties the knots in our thinking.' (*Philosophische Bemerkungen*) Thus both Wittgenstein and Ryle maintained that philosophy was not in the business of discovering new empirical truths but of rearranging our language, or at least analysing it, so as to display its correct logical form or real meaning. This was to be done, in Ryle's view, by excising or at least having our attention drawn to pseudo-referring expressions, category mistakes, and the incorrect use of various words, phrases and sentences. As Ryle put it in 'Taking Sides in Philosophy' (1937):

I have said that there is no philosophical information. Philosophers do not make known matters of fact which were unknown before. The sense in which they throw light is that they make clear what was unclear before, or make obvious things which were previously in a muddle. And the dawning of this desiderated obviousness occurs in the finding of a logically rigorous philosophical argument. (*CP* 2, p. 166)

And the way philosophical argument functions is to point out internal contradictions in the alleged meaning of ordinary propositions or their incompatibility with other well-grounded beliefs, that is, to point out the need for clarification. It continues by exposing the bad arguments or misunderstandings that generate the contradictions and incompatibilities, and concludes by attempting to replace the bad arguments and misunderstandings with good arguments aimed at a new and correct understanding.

Ryle's most explicit and informative discussion of what he took to be the nature of philosophy is, fittingly, his Inaugural Lecture as Waynflete Professor of Metaphysical Philosophy in 1945. But this lecture seemed at the same time to herald a shift or at least an expansion of his view of philosophy. In a passage reminiscent of the Logical Positivists' programme for a Unified Science, the role of philosophy is now seen not merely as clarifying ordinary language propositions but as questioning and clarifying, and then coordinating the underlying conceptual assumptions of various scientific disciplines and their theories. For Ryle writes: 'The philosopher may, perhaps, begin by wondering about the categories constituting the framework of a single theory or discipline, but he cannot stop there. He must try to co-ordinate the categories of all theories and disciplines.' (*CP* 2, p. 195) In this lecture, after having again stressed that philosophy is not scientific induction, and so not in the business of discovering facts, he stresses that, 'On the other hand philosophical arguments are not demonstrations of the Euclidian type, namely deductions of theorems from axioms or postulates. For philosophy has no axioms and it is debarred from taking its start from postulates. Otherwise there could be alternative philosophical doctrines as there are alternative geometries.' (*CP* 2, pp. 196–7) While it seemed that philosophical statements, if they are to be meaningful statements, must be placed in that other category of statement which the Positivists allowed had meaning, the category of analytic statements, previously Ryle had warned us that philosophy's analytic statements were not of the lexicographical sort, or should not be. Now he warns us that they are not of the mathematical sort, that is, they are not the deriving, by deduction from axioms, of analytically true theorems.

So it remained for Ryle to reveal exactly in what philosophy's analytic activity consisted. Ryle's example of paradigmatic philosophical analysis is the philosopher's use of the *reductio ad absurdum* argument, namely the drawing out of conclusions or entailments from some statement or theory to show that these conclusions are absurd. They might show, for example, that these conclusions clash with such very basic and well-grounded beliefs which we already hold, or that they involve such practical impossibilities as the negotiation of an infinite series of steps, that the conclusions seem absurd with the result that the initial statement or theory is to be rejected.

In general, then, philosophy tests statements or theories, not by observation or experiment, that is, not by testing it against the facts, but by showing that it contains latent contradictions or entails infinite regresses or that it is incompatible with well-grounded beliefs which we already hold. Thus philosophy's first, and perhaps prime task is to take the propositions uttered in the normal course of speech or postulated by theorists in some discipline or other, and to see whether they are really understood, that is whether their real meaning or logical form is grasped. The philosopher does this by seeing whether or not these propositions or their inherent ideas or concepts 'lead directly to logically intolerable results', or not. (*CP* 2, pp. 200–01) Thus views or theories which have not been grasped properly will be put into language by those who hold the views or theories in such a way as to create paradoxes or give rise to absurd conclusions. This is the sign that these views or theories need to be revised or tightened up. As Ryle himself put it:

Philosophical arguments of the type described [i.e. ones like *reductio ad absurdum* arguments] have something in common with the destruction-tests by which engineers discover the strength of materials . . . In somewhat the same way, philosophical arguments bring out the logical powers of the ideas under investigation, by fixing the precise forms of logical mishandling under which they refuse to work. (*CP* 2, pp. 197–8)

The philosopher's task is to work back from these paradoxes or absurdities so as to find their exact source in a particular concept which, say, may turn out to be ambiguous or internally contradictory or, especially, supposed to have a logical form which it has not, or else appears in a series of concepts which, taken together, are incompatible.

Finally, his task is the rehabilitation of the concept or theory in question. But the rehabilitation of the theory or concept cannot be done *in vacuo*, for a concept is only logically healthy if it fits in with other well-established concepts with which it is or ought to be connected.

The problem, that is, is not to anatomize the solitary concept, say, of liberty but to extract its logical powers as these bear on those of law, obedience, responsibility, loyalty, government and the rest. Like a geographical survey a philosophical survey is necessarily synoptic. Philosophical problems cannot be posed or solved piecemeal. (*CP*2, p. 202)

Thus Ryle's view of philosophy came to be known as mapping the logical geography of concepts. This was not entirely an accurate description, for, strictly speaking, it encapsulated only one aspect of his view, the second stage in the philosophical process. The first stage of a philosopher's task was to scrutinise and test a theory or concept to see whether it led to 'logically intolerable results' or not. If it did, the philosopher's task became that of working out, if it was a proposition, its true logical form, and if it was a concept, its logical powers, by carefully mapping it on to theories and concepts already accepted and understood.

Part, perhaps even the major portion, of this second stage was making sure that, in seeking out the correct logical form of propositions or logical powers of concepts, one was not misled by grammar or the surface look of the words and the way they were arranged in a sentence or utterance. As Ryle wrote: 'Concepts and propositions carry with them no signal to indicate the logical types to which they belong. Expressions of the same grammatical patterns are used to express thoughts of multifarious logical sorts.' (*CP*2, p.200) For example, says Ryle, we would be wrong to conclude, from the fact that we use one and the same verb 'exists' for all the nouns in the sentence 'There exists a cathedral in Oxford, a three-engined bomber, and a square number between 9 and 25', that there are three existents: a building, a brand of aircraft and a number. Only the building exists in the sense of 'is an observable material object in the world' for the other two only 'exist' as concepts, the class concept of 'a three-engined bomber', and the concept of 'a square number between 9 and 25', i.e. 16.

So Ryle believed that there was no special entity which philosophers studied in the way that entomologists studied beetles and butterflies, but that philosophers asked unusual questions about very ordinary things. The ordinary things were the utterances or sentences of ordinary people, or the more basic theoretical utterances and sentences of scientists and other specialists. The unusual questions asked of these utterances and sentences were, What is the true logical form of the proposition they expressed? and, What are the logical powers of the concepts they made use of?

Thus Ryle believed that he had answered the Positivists' unsettling question 'What is the nature of philosophy?' by agreeing with them that it was not a science and therefore its statements did not fall into that category of meaningful statements called 'empirical'. The only other alternative— and Ryle seemed to agree with the Positivists that there was only one alternative—was that the statements of philosophy were, if not strictly speaking analytic in the narrow Positivist's sense, at least *a priori*. Ryle did not hold that philosophical statements were lexicographical ones, nor did he believe that they were analytic in the way that mathematical statements were, that is, derivable by valid rules of inference from axioms, but that they were statements about a sentence which statement was not licenced by observation but by reference to the logical properties (the logical implications) of concepts and the proposition expressed in the sentence. For example, for Ryle, a paradigm philosophical statement would be of the form 'The sentence S is misleading in that its grammar suggests that the phrase X which is in S, is an expression of logical type LT when it is not'. A particular example, illustrating this form, might be the complicated sentence ' "Jones hates the thought of going to hospital" is a sentence which is liable to mislead, in that its grammatical structure suggests that the phrase "the thought of going to hospital" is a referring expression like the expression "Smith" in the sentence "Jones hates Smith" when in fact it is not.' Another typical philosophical statement might be one which leads on from this one, namely 'The sentence "Jones hates the thought of going to hospital" should be restated as "Whenever Jones thinks of going to hospital he is distressed", if one wants the sentence to reveal its correct logical form.'

Thus paradigm philosophical statements are ones which restate the grammatical form of sentences so as to reveal their true logical form (that is, the correct logical categories or types of the expressions used in the sentences), and ones which display the ensuing arguments used to show that the grammatical form of a sentence is misleading. That is, paradigm philosophical statements are comments about the logical form of sentences and *a priori* arguments in support of them. Paradigm philosophical statements are not statements about the world, but statements about statements about the world; or philosophy is talk about talk about the world, that is, a second-order enterprise.

That the philosophical statements which display the arguments in support of the initial statements about the logical form of sentences are themselves *a priori* can be seen by working out a simple example. To pursue our example of Jones hating the thought of going to hospital, a philosopher might argue that, if hating the thought of going to hospital was really on a par with hating Smith, as it *appears* to be, then it should be impossible to restate the proposition concerned in such a way that any reference to the putative direct-object, a thought, is eliminated while the meaning of the original proposition is preserved. But such a restatement is possible. 'Jones dreads going to hospital' means the same as 'Jones hates the thought of going to hospital.'

Finally, Ryle would say that paradigm philosophical statements were not merely those which brought to light contradictions revealing a misunderstanding about the logical form of propositions, and those which restated the logical form correctly, and gave arguments in support of the restatement, but also those which tried to describe the logic of concepts brought to light in such restatements. In short, philosophy also had the positive task of mapping the logical geography of concepts, that is showing their connection with other concepts, particularly basic ones which are tested and no longer in dispute.

But in the very spelling out of Ryle's view of philosophy in this way one is immediately struck by the possibility of construing Ryle's account of the activity of philosophy as including reference to a proprietary subject matter, namely the logical form of propositions and the logical powers of concepts or, in general, the logical features of propositions and their inherent concepts. After all, an atomic physicist might say that his area of investigation was the micro-world of atomic particles and their relations which underlie the surface of the macro-physical world. Might not a philosopher engaged in Ryle's programme say that what he was dealing with were the concepts and propositions and the relations between them which underlie the surface grammar of our sentences and utterances? Perhaps sentences, and their meaning components, propositions and concepts, could be said to be to philosophy what beetles and butterflies are to entomologists.

Ryle might reply that what is distinctive of philosophy is not that it deals with propositions or concepts, or even with their logical features, for one could say that a philologist, a lexicographer, or someone engaged in theoretical linguistics might also be concerned, at least on occasion, about propositions and concepts and their logical features. Ryle would want to argue that what was distinctive of philosophy was *what* it did in regard to the logical features of propositions and concepts, namely correct mishandlings of ordinary language traceable to mishandlings or misunderstandings of these logical features. To put it another way, philosophy alone was seeking to correct mishandlings of ordinary language which led people to populate the world with entities which did not exist. Though Ryle would not have used the word 'ontological' without a wince, one could say that Ryle's view was that philosophy corrected mishandlings and misunderstandings of ordinary language which led to incorrect ontological beliefs.

Another basic puzzle about this view of the task of philosophy is its own status as a view. Is it a descriptive thesis purporting to be an account of how in fact philosophy has been carried out? Or is it, as seems more likely, a normative thesis telling us what, irrespective of what philosophers in the past have done, we should now be doing?

It is unlikely to be a descriptive thesis because Ryle was well aware that, in its infancy, philosophy was barely distinguished from natural philosophy or the natural sciences. Then, in the not so distant past, philosophers such as the Phenomenologists have seen their task not as analysing language but as being a descriptive enterprise in which one described the phenomena or essences one intuits only in the direct awareness of imagination. Existentialists see philosophy in almost the opposite manner, as neither descriptive nor analytic nor even systematic but as the enterprise of confronting one's existence and so realising what it is for a human person to exist, in particular in moments such as those of choice, especially agonising choice, or during certain emotional states such as those of the objectless emotions, anxiety and dread. Indeed most of the philosophers of other centuries would not have recognised what Ryle describes as the enterprise of philosophy. Descartes, Hobbes, Leibniz, Spinoza, Malebranche, for example, would have seen the task of philosophy as working out some definite first principles from which one could deduce a whole system of theorems or conclusions pertaining to many areas of knowledge. Ryle's philosophical ancestors, Locke and Hume, would have described philosophy as, by and large, the empirically based examination of the faculties and principles governing all aspects of the human mind but especially its powers of knowing and perceiving.

So it seems clear that Ryle's position must be the normative one that, no matter what philosophers have previously thought philosophy was about, what philosophers nowadays ought to be doing is what he suggests. This view does not entail that the philosophers of previous eras were wrong to pursue philosophy in the way they did. Ryle would probably say that their methods were appropriate for their time but that now they are no longer appropriate. The natural and social sciences have usurped all or most of the tasks in which these philosophers engaged, indeed, their work often helped to give birth to these sciences. But the clock cannot be put back; that is one of the messages of Positivism. Philosophy is no longer the matriarch of the sciences. Descriptive enterprises are the province of science and cannot be taken back again by philosophy. To do so would be to engage in scientific work in an amateur way, for a philosopher is not trained in any particular science.

But granted all this, one can still ask why Ryle settled on analysis, or the discovering of the correct logical form of propositions, as the *sui generis* task of philosophy. One reason is that Ryle felt that if philosophy had no special territory of its own then it must be a special way of mapping or examining someone else's territory. And this special way must be connected with the special tools of the philosopher, namely logic. What has been a constant throughout all periods of philosophy has been its use of logic. In Ryle's time this use was going through an important phase where the tools used were themselves being subjected to a new scrutiny and reappraisal. Ryle's early years in philosophy coincided with one of the richest periods in the history of the study of logic itself. So clearly Ryle saw the task of philosophy as, not merely the study of logic itself, but the employment of its rules and principles as tests. Influenced by the new logic and by Positivism, Ryle believed that the task of philosophy was to test our sentences, whether drawn from theory or ordinary converse, for their underlying logical form, which in turn would help clarify their meaning at the deepest level. This testing was to be done by the rules of logic and logical argument, particularly the *reductio ad absurdum* argument. It was because Ryle saw logic, and discussion about its nature, as the one enduring and inalienable bit of philosophy that he felt that the central task of philosophy must always be closely connected with this.

But one could question this view of the fundamental nature of philosophy by arguing, for example, that one of the enduring glories of philosophy is that it has been the source of so many new areas of enquiry, such as natural science, theology, economics, political science, psychology and sociology. It is only because philosophers have engaged in tasks other than just pure analysis of existing usages, and have formed theories of their own from basic empirical data—data that is available to everyone—or from more sophisticated data gained as a result of a more than amateur acquaintance with some area of knowledge, that they have formed the theories which became the basis of these new areas of enquiry. That is, one fairly persistent view of philosophy has seen its basic task as asking fundamental questions about areas where such fundamental questions have not been asked before. As Ryle himself has written:

Genius shows itself not so much in the discovery of new answers as in the discovery of new questions. It influences its age not by solving its problems but by opening its eyes to previously unconsidered problems. So the new ideas released by genius are those which give a new direction to enquiry, often amounting to a new method of thinking. (*CP*2, p. 210)

Indeed, just as the genius can begin new areas of enquiry, he can give old ones new direction, and there is no reason to think that philosophy is immune from this. Just as Ryle and others gave philosophy new directions by redefining its task, so there is no good reason to doubt that the same will happen again, that a new Ryle will come along to tell us that now philosophy should be doing something else.

Ryle would probably reply that the two roles of philosophy, the corrective cum clarificatory, and the breaking

new ground, are not separate, and that it is in seeking to
make sense of what we now say about some area—in
seeking clear concepts and unequivocal propositions—
that we may be forced to derive new concepts and so new
theories which extend the area to such an extent that it
really defines a new area of investigation. By broaching the
question about the clarity of certain concepts or questions
in some area, philosophical analysis might point out that
in fact there is really more than one area under investigation, or, rather, that there should be.

At first sight it might appear that there are contemporary
philosophers who would disagree with Ryle's delineation
of the nature of philosophical enquiry in a very fundamental way. Of course, as we have seen, contemporary
Existentialists and Phenomenologists would. But there
are also those who see themselves as working in the same
philosophical tradition as Ryle who would disagree. As
Kai Nielsen writes in his article 'On Philosophic Method':

Quine with his wholistic approach is well-known for refusing to make a
sharp division between science and philosophy and for stressing that
there is no domain or approach that is distinctively philosophical . . .
Many philosophers, less relativistic than Quine, but influenced by
his approach and in agreement with the attitudes I have just articulated,
take it as a working goal that philosophy need not carry on as a matter of
warring of mutually disinterested schools or postures with essentially
contested approaches, but should in unity with science, and indeed as
part of a 'scientific conception of the world,' theoretically elaborate
such a conception of the world. A ruling assumption here is that there
are no clearly demarcated divisions—let alone methodological barriers
—between scientific and philosophical activities.
      (*International Philosophical Quarterly*, Vol. 16, 1976, p. 359)

On this view, philosophy would always be chiefly *philosophy of*. Its subject matter would be the concepts,
arguments and theories of the first-order empirical
sciences. Philosophy's role would be to exercise its
expertise in making clear and tight distinctions, formulat-
ing valid arguments, and constructing coherent propositions and hypotheses. Its role would be a second-order
one of scrutinizing the findings of these first-order
sciences as regards their logical and conceptual under-
pinnings. The subject-matter of philosophy would be the

more theoretical pronouncements of the first-order sciences and their theoretical tools.

I suspect that this aspect of the holistic view is not the one that really constitutes a fundamental disagreement with Ryle's view, for Ryle might say that this account agrees with his contention that philosophy has no *subject-matter* of its own but is chiefly a method or activity, namely the special one of correcting and clarifying propositions as regards their logical form, and correcting and clarifying concepts as regards their logical powers. Nor would Ryle disagree that this method could and should be applied to the propositions and concepts of the sciences, though Ryle would not limit philosophy's activity to second-order work on the propositions and concepts of science. Ryle would want to say that this activity can also be carried out, with profit, in regard to the propositions and concepts of the ordinary man in the street, the theologian, the politician and so on. Indeed, he would want to say that philosophy should primarily work in these latter areas rather than in the provinces of the sciences, and that it is when scientific concepts become part of ordinary parlance that the philosopher should scrutinise them.

But I think the holist's chief criticism of Ryle's view of philosophy, of the pure Linguistic Analyst's view of philosophy, will always be that it took too seriously the Positivist's dichotomy between empirical scientific knowledge and analytic knowledge. Given that philosophy ought not to be amateur science, it was assumed that it must be totally unconnected with empirical investigation and so must be some purely *a priori* enterprise. Ryle suggested that this enterprise was the mapping of concepts and the correction of any misuse of them. But nowadays many, even of those brought up strictly in the Analytic tradition, would deny that the enterprise of correcting and mapping concepts was purely *a priori*. Let us first take a simple example from philosophy of science. If one is to examine the concept, electron, and decide what logical type the concept belongs to, one would have to refer not merely to how scientists have used the term, which is itself arguably an empirical survey, one would also have to refer to the experimental work on which the concept of an electron, and the usage of the term 'electron', is based. *A fortiori*, if one were to dispute some particular interpretation of the logical powers of the concept or arbitrate between conflicting concepts of electron, one would need to refer to the classical experiments that revealed the properties of the electron.

To take another example, from Ryle's home territory, philosophy of mind, if one were to examine the concept of emotion and then postulate, say, that it was a disposition to behave in a certain way or react physiologically in accordance with certain discernible patterns, then it would be germane to refer to empirical psychological data when arriving at or criticising such a view. If, for example, one considered as solid and sound the work of empirical psychologists who say that their experiments show that there are no distinguishably different physiological re-actions for the putatively different occurrent emotional states, then one would have to rule out the possibility that 'emotion X' and 'emotion Y' were just labels for certain distinguishable physiological reactions. Again, if experi-mental psychology supplied evidence that what we in-tuitively distinguish as fear, love and anger cannot be distinguished in terms of behavioural patterns, then this would rule out a pure behaviourist interpretation of the logical powers of the concepts, fear, love, anger and emotion itself.

In fact, Ryle's own linguistic analyses, and, I suspect, the practice of most Linguistic Analysts, is not and could not be purely divorced from empirical considerations. When Ryle rejects some account of a concept and appeals to what one would say or how we would behave, he is appealing to facts. Consider, for example, Ryle on the concept of pleasure in Lecture IV of *Dilemmas*. Against the Platonic model of pleasure as a sort of upheaval, such as a paroxysm or frenzy, Ryle argues that 'no such con-notations attach to pleasure' for 'if a participant in a discussion or a game greatly enjoys the discussion or game, he is not thereby stopped from having his wits about him.' (P. 65) In short, Ryle is appealing to the *fact* that we can enjoy a game of chess or darts and not thereby be plunged into a state of frenzy or upheaval which would ruin our concentration and aim.

To take another example from Ryle's own work; in his analysis of the intellect in Chapter II of *The Concept of Mind*, Ryle argues against the official doctrine that knowledge is primarily knowledge that or factual knowledge, and that knowledge how is subordinate to knowledge that. The official doctrine describes knowledge how as performing actions efficiently or successfully in the light of certain prescriptions or regulative principles which a person has been told or has worked out for himself or herself. In other words the official doctrine is maintaining that you must first have knowledge of what the principles or prescriptions are before you can apply them and so perform in the light of them. Performing intelligently is then, according to the official Cartesian doctrine, at least two things, the consideration of certain prescriptions or principles, and the action performed in accordance with the prescriptions or principles. For example, the car driver acted intelligently in negotiating that difficult curve because he had learnt the rule 'slow down before a curve and acclerate through it' and then applied it with success. Now one of Ryle's arguments against this doctrine goes as follows:

First, there are many classes of performances in which intelligence is displayed, but the rules or criteria of which are unformulated. The wit, when challenged to cite the maxims, or canons, by which he constructs and appreciates jokes, is unable to answer . . .

[To take another example] Rules of correct reasoning were first extracted by Aristotle, yet men knew how to avoid and detect fallacies before they learned his lessons.

(*The Concept of Mind*—hereafter *CM*—p. 30)

In short, Ryle is arguing that the official account of how we act intelligently cannot be correct because the *facts* contradict it. For there just are cases of people who act intelligently—make jokes or detect fallacies—but do not know, and in some circumstances could not know, any of the relevant rules or principles.

But it should be made clear that genuine conceptual analysis, at least at times, can be purely *a priori*. To take another example from *The Concept of Mind*: when dis-

cussing the concept of imagination in Chapter VIII, Ryle
rejects the official Cartesian version of the concept,
namely that imagination consists in looking at copies in
the mind of real things. He remarks that, while it is easy
and tempting to describe visual imagining as if it were a
case of looking at likenesses, we have no such analogies
for smelling, tasting or feeling. We have no such analogies,
not because there is no factual evidence for the existence
of copies of smells, tastes and feelings within our epidermis, nor because there is positive evidence against
positing their existence, but because the whole notion of a
copy of a smell or taste or feeling is an *a priori* non-starter.
A copy of an acrid smell would have to be an acrid smell,
and so would not be a copy but another case of something
smelling acrid. If the copy theory were true, there would
be no distinction possible between smelling smoke and
'smelling' smoke in one's imagination.

So the Linguistic Analysts themselves, including Ryle,
often appeal to facts when giving or criticising an account
of some concept, and their appeal to what we would
ordinarily say about some concept or what could be said
without oddness in regard to it, is often a covert appeal to
facts. For what we do and can say is hedged in by factual
considerations as well as by considerations of logical
possibility and meaningfulness. If the facts, that Ryle and
other Linguistic Analysts appealed to, are not detailed
scientific data, then this is partly due to their belief that
the facts enshrined in ordinary language, or known more
or less generally, are sufficient for their purposes. So
Ryle's apparent belief that philosophers need not know
about science should be interpreted less as a denial of the
usefulness of scientific knowledge to philosophers than a
conviction that in regard to most of the perennial problems
of philosophy, we have to hand, in this corpus of knowledge of the ordinary man, all the facts we need.

This position, which I think is Ryle's position interpreted in the most generous way, still merits the
criticism that at least some of the perennial problems of
philosophy, including conceptual ones, might not be
solved in ignorance of scientific data. For example, R. J.
Hirst might be correct when he writes in his article

'Perception' in *The Encyclopedia of Philosophy*, Volume 6, that 'the causal and psychological processes essential to perception, as well as its liability to illusion, require abandonment of direct realism for a dualist position', that is, a knowledge of the relevant scientific data on perception —a favourite philosophical topic, and one which Ryle discussed—rules out at least one philosophical position on perception. Generally, it cannot be decided *a priori* that scientific facts are not relevant to a particular philosophical problem, nor, of course, can it be decided *a priori* that they are, though it might be decidable *a priori* that this problem is ultimately an *empirical* one. But Ryle would not have wanted to deny that this could be so, I think, but only that if it is a *philosophical* problem requiring reference to facts, then the facts will not be scientific ones but ordinary, everyday ones. But, this said, it is still true to say that Ryle went too far in cheerfully avowing ignorance of psychology when working in the area of philosophy of mind, but I shall leave a more extended discussion of this important criticism to a later chapter.

Finally, Ryle's account of philosophy also merits the criticism that it is not in keeping with what he, and other Analysts, in fact did. Ryle's ringing manifesto of 1932, telling us what was the task of philosophy, leaves itself open to being interpreted as saying that philosophy is purely *a priori* and divorced from scientific or empirical knowledge. It led us to believe that one could always proceed by discovering *a priori* paradoxes and absurdities in our flawed concepts and the connections and incompatibilities needed for drawing a map of non-flawed concepts. It led us to believe that philosophy was just restating in unmuddled form what we found *a priori* to be muddled. For Ryle had written that

Philosophy must then involve the exercise of systematic restatement . . . For we can ask what is the real form of the fact recorded when this is concealed or disguised and not duly exhibited by the expression in question. And we can often succeed in stating this fact in a new form of words which does exhibit what the other failed to exhibit. And I am for the present inclined to believe that this is what philosophical analysis is and that this is the sole and whole function of philosophy.

('Systematically Misleading Expressions' (1932) *CP*2, p. 61)

For this manifesto is to be read in conjunction with such uncompromising statements as the following: 'Philosophical arguments are not inductions . . . *Nor have* either *facts* or fancies *any evidential force in the resolution of philosophical problems.*' ('Philosophical Arguments' (1945) *CP* 2, p. 196; italics mine) One might want to say, not that Ryle's preaching and practice were at variance, but that his view of philosophy evolved from 'Systematically Misleading Expressions' and the other early papers, through *The Concept of Mind* to *Dilemmas*, at each stage moving further away from the position that philosophy was purely an *a priori* enterprise. But I can imagine someone complaining that such a defence would be a little strained. Since Ryle did not, after those early papers, again address himelf to the question What is Philosophy? there is nothing in his writings to suggest that he had changed his *view* or *doctrine* about what philosophy is. So what we should say is that there is a discrepancy between what he often did in *The Concept of Mind* and *Dilemmas*, and what in his early papers he said he was going to do.

Finally, Ryle's version of Linguistic Analysis must be contrasted with the other main stream of it, that stemming from J. L. Austin. Ryle's approach clearly comes from Russell in his Logical Atomist mood and from Wittgenstein in his therapeutic—untying knots in our thinking and grammar—phase, for Ryle saw ordinary language as something whose frequent mishandlings needed to be corrected and rendered innocuous. Ryle did not believe that ordinary language was a repository of philosophical truths, on the other hand Austin did. His work is best seen as a successor to that of Moore, for he usually referred to ordinary language in order to underline the sophisticated distinctions and ontological subtleties hidden in it, and used it as a weapon to belabour reductionists, such as the Positivists and those influenced by them, for their crudities. As Austin put it in his paper 'A Plea for Excuses',

Our common stock of words embodies all the distinctions men have found worth drawing, and the connexions they have found worth marking, in the lifetimes of many generations: these surely are likely to be more numerous, more sound, since they have stood up to the long test of the survival of the fittest, and more subtle, at least in all ordinary and reasonably practical matters, than any that you or I are likely to think up in our arm-chairs of an afternoon—the most favoured alternative method. (*Philosophical Papers*, eds. J. O. Urmson and G. J. Warnock, Oxford University Press, 1961, p. 130)

Austin said that this view of philosophy might best be called 'linguistic phenomenology'. He did allow, however, that this approach only served to solve problems of an ordinary sort, the ones that the 'inherited experience and acumen of many generations of men' would most likely have solved. But this was definitely not Ryle's approach. For him ordinary language—misused as it frequently was—very often became a rag-bag of philosophical errors and mistaken theories, especially Cartesian ones. Such underlying false assumptions were to be exposed and then reformulated in a non-misleading way or else discarded altogether.

Chapter 3
WIELDING OCCAM'S RAZOR IN THE LOGICAL ARENA

In the 'Introduction' to his *Collected Papers*, Volume 2 Ryle tells us that, 'especially in the earliest papers the Occamizing zeal is manifest', and that this zeal grew out of his views on the nature of philosophy.* His first approach to the task of laying bare the logical form of propositions took the negative path of showing us some of the logical muddles logicians are led into by an uncritical acceptance of the grammatical form of certain ordinary language sentences. But never far behind this attack on the superfluous entities of the logicians was a tendency to carry the attack over into the field of philosophy of mind in order to loosen our hold on some of the entities which we think inhabit our mind, and this Ryle usually does with an unsettling ingenuity. Later, as we shall see when we come to discuss *The Concept of Mind*, it was this battle in the area of philosophy of mind which came to engross him.

The first important paper among the reductionist forays of Ryle's into the area of logic was his 'Are there Propositions?' (1930), which questioned the doctrine that propositions, while not existing physically, are none the less real and so must be said to at least subsist. As Ryle describes this theory about the reality of propositions:

There are (at least) two main sorts of being, namely, actual and ideal being or existing and subsisting. Things in the world are existents, existing at a time and for a time and in many cases also in a place. These are sub-divided into physical things and mental things, both supporting qualities, states and relations. The system of them may be called the World.

But there is another realm of being which our 'prejudice in favour of the actual' causes most of us to ignore or repudiate. This may be called,

---

* The phrase 'Occamizing zeal' refers to Ryle's latterday use of the methodological principle of parsimony or economy in explanation, namely that 'entities are not to be multiplied without necessity', which was reputedly first postulated by William of Occam (or Ockham) *c.* 1285–1349, an English Franciscan philosopher and theologian who taught at Oxford and elsewhere in Europe.

after Frege, the Third Realm, and its members are not physical but are not, for that, any the more mental . . . Entities in the Third Realm do not exist, for they are not anywhere or anywhen, but they *are* in some other way, for they too have qualities and relations. Their mode of being may be called *subsistence*. . .

The proposition theory holds then that propositions are 'objective' or 'genuine entities' in the sense of being *substances* . . . Every sentence that makes sense is, then, a proper name and unambiguously denotes a substance.

(*CP* 2, pp. 21–2)

The arguments put forward for this theory were of the following sort. Firstly, if it is allowed that the contents or 'accusatives' of consciousness, such as the thought you are conscious of or the person in the room you are conscious of, are real, then one must allow that propositions are real. For propositions can be the contents or 'accusatives' of the conscious acts of knowing or believing, and so on. I can believe, for example, that men are mortal, where 'Men are mortal' is a proposition. This proposition, 'Men are mortal', has properties quite different from the conscious act of thinking about the proposition. The conscious act occurs at a definite place, in someone's head, and at a definite time, on such and such a day, and does not exist before or after that space-time slice. The proposition, on the other hand, is not confined to such slices, for it is untrue to say that 'Men are mortal' only in someone's head on a certain day. It has a 'life' which transcends any particular moment and place when it may be thought of. All propositions are true or false timelessly, and are so independently of anyone thinking of them. The proposition 'That Britain will become a republic next year' is either true or false independently of whether anyone is now entertaining or has ever entertained that proposition in his or her mind.

While only the person engaging in the conscious act of entertaining the proposition can have any share in that conscious act, more than one person, or the same person at more than one time, can share the same proposition by having it as the content of their conscious act of thinking. A proposition is open to scrutiny by more than one person, and can be passed from one person to another in an act of communication. A proposition is not a segment of a private cognitive process but the object or target or content of such a cognitive process.

Most philosophers probably hold a correspondence theory of truth, at least in regard to factual propositions, and explain that factual propositions are said to be true in so far as they match up with or correspond with the world. Thus it makes considerable sense to hold that propositions are something real if one holds for a theory of truth which entails matching them with a real world. It seems more sensible to match something real with the real world than to match something unreal with it.

Now Ryle argues against this theory of the reality of propositions by first, typically, employing a *reductio ad absurdum* argument, though not one that would worry, I feel, the proponents of the proposition theory. Such a theory, says Ryle, commits one to holding the rather absurd view that false propositions and nonsensical ones subsist in some Platonic heaven along with true ones. But I can imagine a proposition theorist denying that to assert the reality of false or nonsensical propositions is patently absurd if one has first accepted the reality of true propositions. For the reality of propositions, on this theory, resides in their being independent of thought, and it could be argued that one can give an account of nonsensical propositions which are so independently of their being the accusative in an actual bit of thinking. A nonsensical proposition is not a stupid utterance or a badly formed thought but a set of meanings which are not well formed when put together. If it is the case that, according to the propositional theory, a meaningful proposition is one that has the meanings of the expressions, that express it or would express it, arranged without category mistake or other semantic malformation, and it is not absurd to think of this as subsisting, then it is no more absurd to think of a meaningless proposition as subsisting. For a meaningless proposition, on this view, would be one that has the meanings of the expressions, that express it or would express it, arranged in such a way as to involve a category mistake or other semantic malformation.

Again, if it is allowed that a true proposition is a subsistent reality that happens to correspond with existent reality, and that this is not patently absurd, why should it be absurd to hold that a false proposition is a subsistent reality that happens *not* to correspond with existent reality?

More cogently, and more importantly, Ryle argues that the theory cannot explain how we could have knowledge by grasping a proposition, or indeed why we need a proposition at all in the process of knowledge. For knowledge implies that we have a belief that something is the case which belief has been certified as correct. If it is a factual belief this certification takes the form of observing or gaining evidence that it corresponds in some sense to some aspect of the world, but just to grasp a proposition with one's mind omits this certification step. By just grasping a factual proposition we cannot thereby know whether the proposition corresponds to the world or not. This knowing about the correspondence would have to be another grasp which included grasping the relevant aspect of the world which the proposition is to be compared with. But if we can grasp the world independently of grasping the proposition why do we need the proposition? The proposition, as Ryle puts it, has become a superfluous 'logical changeling' standing between and in the way of our knowledge of the world.

Ryle's alternative to the proposition theory is to say that what one knows is the *meaning of the sentence* expressing what one knows. If the sentence is a factual statement, then its meaning is the *fact* it states. It is the fact itself, not some intervening proposition, which is known.

But Ryle realises that this account creates problems in connection with beliefs true but not yet known to be true, and with false beliefs. For one can know the meaning of such beliefs but one cannot be in possession of any relevant facts, for, if one were, the former belief would not be a belief but knowledge, and the latter belief would now be known to be false and so would no longer even be believed. But if this is so why call the beliefs factual ones?

Ryle's solution of these problems is to say that what one is in possession of when one has only belief and not knowledge, is 'a hypothetical fact', namely what the world would be like if the statement of one's belief were true. As

Ryle puts it: 'We can see what would have to be the case for them [statements of beliefs] to be standard statements of fact, namely, that *if* so and so was the case, *then* this sentence would be the standard statement of it.' (*CP* 2, p. 34).

Now the obvious response to this solution would be to say that Ryle's hypothetical facts seem to be very like propositions, and with all the drawbacks that Ryle drew attention to in regard to propositions. Hypothetical facts seem to be subsistent realities that take the place of facts when the cognitive state is one of belief and not knowledge proper.

Ryle's reply to this sort of criticism would be to explain that the expression 'hypothetical facts' does not refer to subsistent realities or to any other sort of realities, for one is only tempted to think of hypothetical facts as real things grasped when a person believes something, if one has a mistaken view of believing (and, most likely, knowledge as well) as an active conscious state. Ryle then goes on to give an account of the nature of knowing and believing which, in the long run, is perhaps more important than his solution to the problem about the nature of propositions, as this account is the embryonic beginning of his investigations in the area of philosophy of mind which were to form his most lasting achievement in philosophy.

Ryle asks us to reflect on the nature of knowledge and belief. They are not, he says, states of conscious attention but something more like the possession of some 'deposit' which can be dragged up into our attention and so be actively 'thought of' from time to time but otherwise be dormant and unnoticed.

There does seem to be some sense in which one may have *known* or *believed* something for years, and only to have *thought of* it a few times, just as one may have possessed some property for years and only used it a few times. In this sense, knowing something does not involve attending to it in the way in which getting to know it or reflecting upon it does. (*CP* 2, pp. 30–31)

Ryle expands on this point by drawing our attention to the fact that actual conscious activities of thinking of something must be done in terms of images or words (and, if in words, in the words of some particular language) but knowledge and belief do not.

So, to return to the solution of the problem about propositions, when one believes that X is Y, for a start one may not be thinking of anything at all. The belief may lie in our mind or brain as a deposit. Now, if my belief is brought before my attention, what I am doing is not grasping something called a hypothetical fact, but what I am doing is forming a statement of the form 'That X is Y' and realising that if X turns out in fact to be Y, then 'X is Y' would present a fact.

Thus Ryle is telling us that the true logical form underlying a statement of one's belief of the form 'I believe that X is Y' is 'I believe that if X turns out to be Y, then the statement "X is Y" presents a fact.' In short, statements of belief are disguised hypothetical statements. They are not *about* hypothetical facts they are about *statements* which are hypothetical ones. So we do not need propositions or any surrogate for them in connection with beliefs, we only need statements.

To sum up, statements of knowledge present facts, statements of belief tell us what the facts would be like if these statements were true, that is, statements of belief tell us that they are would-be factual statements. So hypothetical facts are not quasi-facts or pretended facts, they are not facts at all. They are simply statements. At the psychological level, when one entertains such statements, one imagines what the world would be like if they were true. So this account of propositions is really to be bolstered by an account of imaginary objects.

Ryle gave us such an account in 'Imaginary Objects' (1933). In this paper Ryle again wielded Occam's razor against one of the entities adopted by philosophers for use in the logical arena. He suggests that sentences such as 'Mr Pickwick wore knee breeches' have led logicians into postulating that Mr Pickwick is an imaginary object because the sentence must be about something, for it attributes the attribute 'wearer of knee breeches' to something, yet it is clearly not about an ordinary object, for Mr Pickwick did not exist.

Ryle argues that we have no need of the item termed 'imaginary object' in our logical inventory of objects, for we are only led into thinking that there must be such objects because we wrongly think that 'Mr Pickwick' in the sentence 'Mr Pickwick wore knee breeches' is a referring expression. In fact it is not a referring expression but a 'concealed predicative expression', and the sentence is not about anything at all.

That this is so, Ryle argues, can be shown quite easily. A sentence is only about something if its alleged referring expression actually does refer to or designate something. Whether it does or not cannot be discovered just by looking at the sentence. Quasi-referring expressions or pseudo-designations look exactly the same as referring expressions or genuine designations. It is all a matter of examining the world to see whether it contains something which bears the name, or corresponds completely to the description which is the would-be referring expression.

Indeed, this enables us to see clearly the difference between a lie and an utterance which is part of fiction. A lie is about something but attributes some quality to that something which it does not in fact possess. A sentence in fiction is not about anything at all but merely pretends to be. Thus, when we say 'Mr Pickwick is an imaginary object', we are not attributing some status to someone called 'Mr Pickwick', but saying that the expression 'Mr Pickwick', whenever it occurs, is a pseudo-designation but deliberately modelled on real designations in a context where this could not deceive. (One would have to add, 'whenever it occurs in connection with Dickens' *Pickwick Papers*, for, of course, there may exist someone named 'Mr Pickwick'.)

The expression 'Mr Pickwick' is really a predicative expression because, when we understand the term, we do not do so by having our attention drawn to some person in the world who bears that name, for there is no such person, but do so because we relate the expression to the description of Mr Pickwick in Dickens' book. The expression 'Mr Pickwick' is just shorthand for those descriptions.

Now there is an interesting spin-off from this reductionist policy towards the logician's imaginary objects in the area of philosophy of mind. When in imagination we depict things in images the images are equivalent to concealed predicative expressions like 'Mr Pickwick'. For example, we might imagine Mr Pickwick by depicting in our mind's eye a portly gentleman in knee breeches. The picture is not a picture of anything, it is simply a picture which has the same status as a description in words. Indeed one could do one's imagining in words. So there is nothing special about the images of imagination, they are just the symbols in a different sort of describing from our describings in words.

That this is the correct way of looking at imagination can be shown by the fact that, as Ryle puts it, as with descriptions in words, the images of imagination can refer or fail to refer to something in the world. I can imagine President Carter sitting in his oval office, and get it right, or I can imagine him sitting there and get the picturing all wrong. I might have imagined him as thin when he is not, and the office to be decorated in red, when it is not, and so on. The images of imagination are just 'look'-predicates which form a description which may or may not designate something or someone.

What is clear, if this account of the propositions of fiction, and the account of the nature of imagination underpinning it, are correct, is that there is no room for anything with the status of imaginary *object*. As Ryle puts it, 'nothing is left as a metaphysical residue to be housed in an ontological no-man's land'. (*CP* 2, p. 76) As Ryle returned to this problem of imaginary objects, when he came to discuss the nature of imagination in Chapter VIII of *The Concept of Mind*, and as the latter account builds on the former, I shall postpone critical discussion of the doctrine on imagination implied here till Chapter 9 where I discuss Ryle's work on imagination.

What I want to examine here is Ryle's alternative account to the propositional theory. Ryle's alternative account is that statements of beliefs present facts if they are true and hypothetical facts if they are false or not yet known to be true. In spelling out what he meant by hypothetical facts, in such a way as to avoid inventing something which does the work of subsistent propositions and has all the difficulties associated with positing such subsistents, Ryle identified them with the statements themselves of those hypothetical facts, which in turn he analysed as descriptions. Such descriptions could be in words, spoken out loud or under one's breath, or could be in other forms such as the 'look'-predicates or 'smell'-predicates or 'taste'-predicates of imagination. He also implied that these descriptions could exist at times in some less obvious way, embedded in our mind or brain, held subconsciously.

Now this theory bears some resemblances to Wittgenstein's picture theory of the meaning of propositions in the *Tractatus*. Wittgenstein held that a proposition, at least certain basic or primitive ones, gained their meaning by being pictures of the world. They did not picture the world in any obvious pictorial sense, in the way that hieroglyphics do, but in a way that was analogous to that obvious sense of picturing. These basic or atomic propositions had the same logical form as the world. This logical form, as displayed in a sentence expressing the proposition, would be revealed by the syntactic or grammatical form of the sentence. Sometimes, of course, a sentence was not expressed in the correct logical form which mirrored the underlying proposition, and it was one of the tasks of a philosopher to correct such sentences and so obviate certain muddles which might otherwise occur. The correct logical form might underlie the expressed logical form and need revealing. But the correct logical form of a basic proposition, if the proposition were true and a factual proposition, matched the logical form of facts in the world. The relations displayed in the basic structures of true propositions and expressed in the sentences expressing those propositions, for example, the relation between a predicate and what the predicate is predicated of, are mirrored in the world. Rather, they are a mirror of the facts and not vice versa. The world is such, for example, that the fact displayed in a proposition such as 'The sun is bright' has the relation mirrored by the logical form of the proposition and the sentence expressing the proposition. Wittgenstein explained that 'A logical picture of facts is a thought.' (*Tractatus* 3) 'In a proposition a thought finds an expression that can be perceived by the senses.' (*Tractatus* 3.1) 'A proposition is a picture of reality.' 'A proposition is a model of reality as we imagine it.' (*Tractatus* 4.01) Again, like Ryle in regard to statements, Wittgenstein linked propositions with imagining and, as Ryle was to do with statements, indicated that propositions should be viewed as projections or depictions of possible situations which, when true, matched up with the actual situations or facts. 'We use the perceptible sign of a proposition (spoken or written, etc.) as a projection of a possible situation.' (*Tractatus* 3.11) Similarly, as Ryle was also to stress in regard to statements, Wittgenstein pointed out that propositions could be expressed in other than linguistic ways. 'The essence of a propositional sign is very clearly seen if we imagine one composed of spatial objects (such as tables, chairs, and books) instead of written signs. Then the spatial arrangement of these things will express the sense of the proposition.' (*Tractatus* 3.1431) Of course, the major difference between Wittgenstein's and Ryle's picture theories is that Wittgenstein's keeps propositions. Indeed, they are central to his account in the *Tractatus*. Ryle's unit of picturing is the statement which is a description, which can be expressed with linguistic predicates and names or with non-linguistic ones. Besides Ryle's uneasiness with propositions themselves Ryle would undoubtedly have been unhappy with Wittgenstein's alliance of propositions with thoughts. As we shall see, for Ryle thoughts are just as *noires* as those other *bêtes noires*, propositions.

Strictly speaking, the view of propositions revealed by Ryle in this early paper 'Are there propositions?' should have led Ryle to describe the task of philosophy as, not the laying bare of the correct logical form of *propositions*, but revealing the correct logical form of *statements*. But it may be that Ryle was never completely at ease with his excision of propositions from the logicians' pantheon, and one can see some reasons why this might be so.

Ryle's view was that what one *knows* is the meaning of a sentence expressing what one knows. This meaning turned out to be the world or facts themselves. Now it would seem to follow from this line of reasoning that what one *believes* is the meaning of a sentence expressing what one believes. Ryle tells us that this meaning is a hypothetical fact. *But* he goes on to cash out a hypothetical fact as a statement. Now the statement which is the meaning of a sentence expressing what one believes is either identical with the sentence or it is not. If it is identical with the sentence then Ryle is landed with the curious view that the meaning of a sentence is itself. If it is not identical with the sentence then Ryle has invented something that stands in relation to a sentence in much the same way as a proposition, in the discredited proposition theory, was related to a sentence. For Ryle's explanation of a belief is that a sentence expressing the belief has as its meaning something which is neither a fact in the world, nor a sentence, namely a statement which is expressed by the sentence. But this position is vulnerable to Ryle's own attack on the proposition theory. If knowledge is gained when such a belief becomes justified or certified as true, then it looks as if this certification must involve checking that the statement matches some fact in the world. But to check whether something matches something else, in this case a statement with the world, implies grasping or contacting both of the items to be checked to see if they match. But if one can grasp the world directly, then, in converting a belief into knowledge, one does not need to go via matching a statement with the facts. The statement can be discarded. It merely clogs one's view of the world and is an unwanted intermediary. It has become a logical changeling like the proposition.

Ryle might reply that to convert beliefs into knowledge one does not need to engage in any matching of a statement to the world, one can go directly to the world. The statement is only needed as a content for beliefs not yet converted into knowledge (or failed to be so converted and discarded as false). But this move is also open to the proposition theorist and, if it is a good move, Ryle's major criticism of that theory collapses. The proposition theorist can say simply that propositions are not needed in the process of certifying beliefs which, as yet, have not truth value, they are posited only as the content of beliefs not yet certified. Knowledge is not the upgrading of a proposition's status but a completely different activity or process. Proposition theorists can claim that they employ propositions to explain just those difficult cases for which Ryle introduces statements, namely as part of the account of the meaning of a sentence expressing beliefs not yet certified as true or false.

But it may be the case that the force of Ryle's account has been missed. For Ryle buttressed his account of the meaning of sentences expressing beliefs in terms of statements with a further account of statements as descriptions, and descriptions as imagining which could be done with or without words. So it may not be nonsensical, on Ryle's view, to identify the meaning of a sentence expressing one's belief with the sentence itself. For Ryle would say that uttering a sentence is a sort of imagining. To say 'The chair is painted black', where this expresses a belief, is akin to imagining a black chair. Now, if it could be said that the meaning of imagining a black chair is the images themselves conjured up, why could it not be said that the meaning of the sentence 'The chair is painted black' is the words conjured up, either vocally or subvocally?

If this account is acceptable, then Ryle can claim that, in holding a belief whose truth value is not yet known, then one is holding a picture about which it is not yet known whether it matches the world or not. But, in spelling out Ryle's view like this, we have again used the word 'match'. Thus Ryle will still be involved, on his account, when certifying the belief as true or false, in matching something to the world. To collapse sentences into images or pictures, or to attach propositions which are pictures (albeit logical ones) to sentences, seems to make little difference. We need a content to sentences expressing our beliefs which are as yet uncertified.

But there may be reasons to prefer the old proposition theory about the meaning of sentences expressing beliefs to Ryle's theory of sentences as picturing in a crude sense. One can see how an image of a chair can be said to picture the world. One might even find little difficulty in holding that 'This is a black chair' is an imaging or picturing of the world. But one's connivance with Ryle's theory is strained when one attempts to make sense of the sentence 'Honesty is the best policy', which expresses someone's belief, in terms of verbally imagining or picturing the world. There are no obvious pictorial qualities in the words 'honesty', 'best' and 'policy', or in any particular concatenation of them. It is not obvious that 'honesty', just the word, or 'Honesty is the best policy', just the sentence, picture honesty.

Ryle would have to fill out his theory by explaining how sentences depict. To do this he would probably have to refer not merely to the logical form of the sentences but also to the meaning of the words in the sentences. But once meanings are mentioned one is back in the world of propositions, for 'proposition' is usually used as the label for the unit of sentence meaning.

It is probably fair to say that the position on meaning which Ryle was searching for was the sort of account proposed by Wittgenstein in the *Philosophical Investigations*: 'You say: the point isn't the word, but its meaning, and you think of the meaning as a thing of the same kind as the word, though also different from the word. Here the word, there the meaning. The money, and the cow that you can buy with it. (But contrast: money, and its use.) (Part I, 120) Indeed, Ryle refers to this passage in one of his last pieces of work, 'On Bouwsma's Wittgenstein' (1972), and he clearly adopts the inherent view in a paper he wrote in the same year, 'Thinking and Saying' (both reprinted in the collection *On Thinking*).

Wittgenstein's point is that meaning is not a thing—or subsistent reality—alongside spoken or written words. It is not something that words or sentences label or refer to. Meaning is the use to which words are put, just as the value of a coin is what can be done by employing the coin, not a particular cow which I might have purchased with the coin. This was the view Ryle was clearly endorsing in these late papers. Meaning was not a thing or reality which sentences referred to or designated, it is the manner in which some thing—a word or sentence—was to be employed according to stateable conventions.

Chapter 4
CATEGORY MISTAKES AND DISPOSITIONS

In *The Concept of Mind* Ryle's Occamizing zeal and the logical tools he was developing to pursue this zealotry were at their highest pitch. The programme which he was developing in the nineteen thirties as being the correct way of philosophising was on full display, presented with a rare wit and with a gift for metaphor and the telling illustration. But more importantly, by means of his engaging style, time and again he makes the telling point that sets us back on our heels and makes us, if not reject some of our most cherished beliefs about the mental, at least hold them less dogmatically.

The target in *The Concept of Mind* was the Cartesian concept of mind. As Ryle himself puts it in the Introduction to *The Concept of Mind*:

... it is part of the thesis of this book that during the three centuries of the epoch of natural science the logical categories in terms of which the concepts of mental powers and operations have been co-ordinated have been wrongly selected. Descartes left as one of his main philosophical legacies a myth which continues to distort the continental geography of the subject. (*CM* p. 8)

In Chapter I of *The Concept of Mind* Ryle goes on to tell us what this myth, or 'the official doctrine' as he also refers to it, is:

The official doctrine, which hails chiefly from Descartes, is something like this. With the doubtful exception of idiots and infants in arms every human being has both a body and a mind. Some would prefer to say that every human being is both a body and a mind. His body and his mind are ordinarily harnessed together, but after the death of the body his mind may continue to exist and function.

Human bodies are in space and are subject to the mechanical laws which govern all other bodies in space. Bodily processes and states can be inspected by external observers. . . .

But minds are not in space, nor are their operations subject to mechanical laws. The workings of one mind are not witnessable by other observers; its career is private. Only I can take direct cognisance of the states and processes of my own mind. A person therefore lives through two collateral histories, one consisting of what happens in and to his body, the other consisting of what happens in and to his mind. (*CM*, p. 11)

While we have no access to the minds of others, our knowledge of our own minds, via introspection, is 'commonly supposed to be immune from illusion, confusion or doubt' (*CM*, p. 14), that is, one has a 'privileged access' to one's own stream of consciousness. And this stream of consciousness is made up of occurrences which are labelled as 'knowing' or 'believing' or 'hoping' or 'dreading' and 'intending' and so on. And, with some of his most memorable phrase-making, Ryle describes this account of our mental life as 'the life of a ghostly Robinson Crusoe' (*CM*, p. 14), and this whole dualist account or the mind plus body view of human persons as 'the dogma of the Ghost in the Machine'. (*CM*, p. 15)

Now, says Ryle, his task in this book is to show that

[the dogma of the ghost in the machine] is not merely an assemblage of particular mistakes. It is one big mistake and a mistake of a special kind. It is, namely, a category-mistake. It represents the facts of mental life as if they belonged to one logical type or category (or range of types or categories), when they actually belong to another. (*CM*, p. 16)

In short, the strategy in *The Concept of Mind* is to demolish the Cartesian dualist dogma of 'the ghost in the machine' by showing that it is one large category mistake. A category mistake is committed when, in seeking to give an account of some concept, one says that it is of one logical type or category when in fact it is of another. 'The logical type or category to which a concept belongs is the set of ways in which it is logically legitimate to operate with it.' (*CM*, p. 8) Thus one makes a category mistake if one says 'My pain was green' for pain is not the sort of thing which can be green. Feelings, such as pains, are not coloured, only visible objects are. Or, to use one of Ryle's famous examples, a foreigner visits Oxford for the first time and is shown round the university. After having seen the colleges, libraries, offices, laboratories and playing fields, he then asks 'But where is the University?' The foreigner had mistakenly thought that 'The University' was the name of one of the buildings he might be shown rather than an umbrella term which applied to the whole collection of buildings which he had already been shown.

Ryle, following on his general view of the way philosophy should be engaged in, tells us that the way to expose category mistakes is to attempt *reductio ad absurdum* arguments, for, if they are successful, one has exposed a concept which has been assigned to a logical type or category to which it does not belong. 'I try to use *reductio ad absurdum* arguments both to disallow operations implicitly recommended by the Cartesian myth and to indicate to what logical types the concepts under investigation ought to be allocated.' (*CM*, p. 8) That is, Ryle is going to show that, by taking the Cartesian dogma of the ghost in the machine at face value, we end up with a string of absurdities which are an indication that the dogma is a category mistake. But he is not just going to stop at this negative stage of presenting evidence that the dogma is absurd and so guilty of a category mistake, he is going to attempt a positive account of the concepts involved, which account assigns them to their rightful categories.

We might add to this account of the outlines of Ryle's method of arguing in *The Concept of Mind* his own gloss to the effect that, while the key arguments employed in the book are the *reductio* ones,

I do not, however, think it improper to use from time to time arguments of a less rigorous sort. . . . Philosophy is the replacement of category-habits by category-disciplines, and if persuasions of conciliatory kinds ease the pains of relinquishing inveterate intellectual habits, they do not indeed reinforce the rigorous arguments, but they do weaken resistances to them. (*CM* p. 8)

While Ryle believed that this may licence the more phenomenological parts of the book, where he, by means of multiplied examples, seeks to display how a concept is used, it may not excuse the fact that in many such passages he does not argue as tightly as he might that the concept is of the type he says it is rather than of the type the dogma proclaims it is. But the force, if any, of this complaint will become clearer when some of Ryle's analyses are discussed in detail later on.

It is time to fill out in some detail the positive aspects of

Ryle's strategy in *The Concept of Mind*. In correcting the category mistakes of the dogma of the ghost in the machine, by and large Ryle is going to argue that what the dogma continually describes as occurrences, episodes or processes are most often dispositions. Indeed, it is fair to say that Ryle's own case for the abolition of mind as a shadowy entity which initiates ghostly actions rests almost entirely on his claim that most putative mental items and activities should be redescribed as dispositions of the physical observable person, indeed, as Ryle adds, 'many of the cardinal concepts in terms of which we describe specifically human behaviour are dispositional concepts.' (*CM*, p. 117)

It is in Chapter V of *The Concept of Mind*, entitled 'Dispositions and Occurrences', that Ryle gives his detailed account of what dispositions are. He tells us that a disposition is an ability, tendency, liability or proneness to act or react, or fail to act or react, in a certain way in certain circumstances. To say, for example, that an animal is a ruminant is to attribute a disposition to it, for it is to make a claim that the animal in question will chew its cud if and when it has any to chew. Thus to attribute a disposition to X is to say that X is prone to do something Y, or a variety of things M, N, O and P which could be said to be of type Y, in circumstances C.

Because saying that a person or thing has a disposition is saying that the person or thing *would* act or react in a certain way if certain circumstances occurred, sentences embodying dispositional claims are, strictly speaking, always hypothetical in form, 'If circumstances C occur then X will do Y.' As Ryle puts it, dispositional attributions which are true are 'inference tickets' which enable us to predict how someone or something will act or react, or fail to, in certain circumstances. A dispositional statement is a statement that sums up that person or thing's past history of behaviour in particular circumstances in a law-like way, such that knowing this quasi-law—this true dispositional claim—one can predict how the person or thing will act or react in just those circumstances.

So, while related to particular past occurrences or episodes of that person or thing in the relevant circumstances, for such occurrences are the inductive evidence for the law-like dispositional claim, the dispositional attribution itself is not a reference to an occurrence or state of affairs. A disposition or proneness is not a state of affairs. One does not have a disposition in the way that one has an arm or leg. Nor is a disposition a piece of behaviour like running or talking. A disposition is a behaviour pattern. One does not possess a behaviour pattern, one displays it through a number of pieces of behaviour. To say that this animal is a ruminant is not to say that this animal possesses some property, like having a tail, or having two stomachs, it is to say that whenever such an animal feeds, from time to time it brings back food from its stomach (its first stomach) into its mouth for a second chewing over. To say it is a ruminant is to talk about, not behaviour that is going on, but behaviour that from time to time goes on in known circumstances.

Ryle now goes on to tell us that there are two basic sorts of disposition: determinate ones, or pronenesses to do things of one unique kind, and determinable ones, or pronenesses to do things of lots of different kinds but of one generic type. Being a cigarette smoker is a determinate disposition as it is a proneness to do one unique thing, smoke cigarettes. So is being a ruminant. Being greedy, on the other hand, is a determinable disposition, for a greedy person will be prone to a fairly wide variety of behaviour describable as greedy. For example, a greedy person might eat more than his share, or covet more money than he needs, or continually complain that he never gets enough to eat. In other words, to attribute a determinate disposition to someone or something is to say precisely what that person or thing is liable to do, but to attribute a determinable disposition is only to draw attention to the sort of thing the person or thing is liable to do.

Further, there are distinctions in dispositions which cut across both determinate and determinable dispositions. For example, there is the capacity-tendency distinction. Some dispositions are capacities or abilities for they are not just tendencies or pronenesses to do certain things but tendencies to do certain things successfully. To say someone is a mathematician is not just to say that such a person does mathematics, it is to say that he or she does mathematical problems and gets them right. But to say that someone is claustrophobic is merely to say that they do something or exhibit certain behaviour, namely become alarmed in small enclosed spaces.

Ryle believes that there are also semi-dispositional claims or, as he puts it, 'mongrel-categorical statements', which explain something as being an occurrence but at the same time a disposition, that is, they explain something in terms of both categories, occurrence and disposition. Such claims are connected to dispositions proper in that they are employed when one refers to an activity which is the actual display or activation of a disposition. This sort of account is important because it seems to make sense of some of our so-called mental concepts, ones, for example, such as heeding and minding. For such concepts seem always to include an element of the actual or here and now. To say Jones drove his car carefully or with his mind on the job is not to say that Jones drove the car and at the same time a ghostly part of Jones, his mind, watched over his driving, checking all the time what he was doing, engaged, as Ryle puts it, in higher level 'executive' monitoring. To say Jones drove his car carefully is to say that he drove it in such a way that he could be said to have driven it according to the canons of correct driving. To say this is not to claim that Jones was driving the car and his ghostly self was checking his driving against the canons, but it is merely to say that, having coached himself in driving carefully, his present driving is an activation of his ability to drive carefully. Thus, while Jones is now merely engaged in driving, this behaviour can be viewed as the result of having coached himself to drive in just such a manner which is termed 'careful'. Thus, the full description of Jones's present driving refers both to an occurrence and to a disposition.

But, of course, it is the straight dispositional accounts which Ryle is going to appeal to most of the time to help him demolish the Cartesian dogma. And it is not too difficult to see how he is going to proceed. He is going to say that the basic mental items and processes beloved of the Cartesian dogma, items such as the intellect and processes such as knowledge, are neither items nor processes but dispositions, which in turn are chartable behaviour patterns.

So Ryle's account of dispositions is central to his philosophy, for he liberally substituted behavioural dispositions for Cartesian mental substances and activities. Since dispositions are the most important weapon in his Occamist armoury, and it was the enthusiastic adoption of dispositions that led Ryle to his peculiar brand of behaviourism, it is especially important to look carefully at his account of them.

Ryle explained that to attribute dispositions to someone or something is to make some law-like generalisations or hypotheses about that person or thing. To attribute dispositions is to make projections or inferences about what people or animals or things are likely to do or how they are likely to react if certain circumstances occur in the future. To attribute dispositions is to form hypotheses about likely behaviour or reactions in the future based on observing and noting in what circumstances and with what constancy such behaviour or reactions occurred in the past.

An initial difficulty with Ryle's account of dispositions is that it is ambiguous as to what sort of account it is. If Ryle were merely giving us a semantic account of dispositions, that is, telling us what the term 'disposition' means or how it is used linguistically, then his account is adequate. It is a reasonable account of the meaning of 'X has a disposition Y' to explain that this means 'whenever circumstances C occur, X will do Y or a variety of things M, N, O and P which could be said to be of type Y.' But if, as Ryle seems to believe, his account is also or chiefly meant to be what I shall call a genetic account of dispositions, that is, an explanation of what they are ontologically and how they arise, then his account is inadequate. I suspect Ryle believed that his account was not merely an account of how we use the term 'disposition' or of what we mean to say when we attribute a disposition to someone or something, because he argued from his account of dispositions to ontological conclusions, not to mere semantic conclusions. He did not claim to be merely pointing out what we mean by the term 'dispositions', he claimed to be telling us what they were and how they arose and how they worked. He was accusing the Cartesian dualists of thinking mind was one sort of ontological category, substance, when in fact it was another, a disposition. Ryle analysed what the Cartesians held to be substances and their activities into pronenesses to activities of a certain type in certain circumstances. He was accusing the Cartesians of elevating pronenesses or potentialities into actualities. This initial ambiguity in Ryle's account becomes a major flaw when his account is used as a genetic account of dispositions. It is important now to see why Ryle's account of dispositions will not do as a genetic account and so will not do the Occamist dirty work he asks of it.

If someone wanted to know why that piece of glass broke when dropped or why that man vomited as soon as the boat left the pier, it would not do as an explanation to say simply that the glass was brittle and that the man was prone to seasickness, and then to give a Rylean account of these dispositions. For to do this would be merely to explain that the glass broke because that is the sort of glass that breaks when dropped, and that the man vomited because he is the sort of person who vomits in just those circumstances. The explanation is a pseudo-explanation. It just explains that X had reaction Y in circumstances C because X is the sort of thing that has reaction Y in such circumstances. To say such a thing is certainly true, and while it will help us predict when this sort of glass will break and this person will again be seasick, it would not help us to work out why the glass is brittle and so help us to make unbreakable glass nor help us to cure seasickness. It does not do this because the Rylean account of dispositions does not really explain how they arise. It neglects the causal processes which lead up to the glass shattering and the person vomiting.

Thus, the account of dispositions which is the chief rival to Ryle's as a genetic account is that which says that 'If circumstances C occur then X will do Y, if, and only if, a certain causal factor F, which causes Y by interacting with C, is still present in X.' So this rival account is a much more complicated story, and that it is a fuller, more explanatory account will become clearer by seeing how it works in connection with some examples. You can be said quite definitely to be prone to seasickness, even though you are now on dry land, if it has been discovered that there is in you now something which in the past was found to react with the motion of ships at sea so as to cause you to heave up the contents of your stomach. In more detail, the correct causal story about your bouts of sea-sickness might be that, say, you have an imbalance in the fluids in your inner ear such that, when this is affected causally by the motion of ships at sea, then this interaction in turn unsettles your stomach and causes you to jettison its contents. Often, of course, the causal factor which is operative when dispositions are activated is not easy to isolate, and so, in such a case, when we assert that someone has a disposition, we only presume that the causal factor, whatever it is, is still present. But our presumption might be wrong and our resulting attribu-tion of a disposition mistaken. The important point is that a proper account of what dispositions are and how they work will alert you to the fact that there must be some categorical causal factor at work here. The true genetic account of dispositions makes it clear that dispositions are not just potentialities. They are potentialities based on the existence of real factors. Thus, this causal factor, which lies dormant or is presumed to be lying dormant in the person or thing to which a disposition has been attributed, is often called the structural or categorical basis of the disposition, because it will often turn out to be a structural property of the thing to which the disposition is attributed, and because to refer to an actual property is to refer categorically rather than hypothetically.

The advantage of this more complex account of dis-positions as a genetic account is that it is methodologically more sound. It draws attention to the fact that, if one can discover in some person the presence of the causal factor which interacts with the motion of ships at sea to cause the host to this factor to be seasick, then one can attribute the disposition to be seasick even to some person who may never have been seasick before. Moreover, it enables one to say with much more certainty whether the person who has previously been sick whenever he went to sea will or will not continue to be so.

Now if this rival, more complex genetic account of dispositions is correct, it will radically affect Ryle's use of dispositions. As we shall see later on in detail, Ryle will often throw out the Cartesian account of some inner mental item by saying that we do not need to refer to it when explaining behaviour, so its *raison d'être* has been removed. We need only say that this person is disposed to behave in this way in certain circumstances. We need only refer, apart from the person concerned, to two other things, behaviour and circumstances. But if the more complex account of dispositions is correct, then to explain a disposition one will have to refer, at least implicitly, to three other things, behaviour, the circumstances *and* the structural basis. As regards explaining dispositions attributed to humans, this will usually entail referring to something inner. Ryle and Ryleans can of course reply that to refer to something inner is not to be committed to referring to the mental. And this is surely correct. But it is a separate debate whether this inner basis should be termed mental or not, and to describe the behaviour which it gives rise to in dispositional terms is not to eradicate this inner something.

So the upshot is that Ryle explained dispositions as if they were completely divorced from the person or thing to which the disposition was attributed, that is, as if there was no causal connection between the person to whom the disposition was attributed and the behaviour or reaction which that person was said to be disposed to or prone. Ryle argued that dispositions were just observed behaviour patterns and that to explain and justify the attribution of such a pattern to a person or thing does not entail attributing anything to that person or thing other than the behaviour or reaction which it is forecast will reoccur in suitable circumstances in the future and which has occurred in just such circumstances in the past. And he believed that he had argued convincingly that, what Cartesians took to be mental happenings or factors or other occurrences (that is, something actually present and real) were, just dispositions to behave. For Ryle, dispositions do not involve 'any hidden internal causes' and a disposition is 'neither a witnessable nor an unwitnessable act' for 'it is not a happening at all. It is a disposition, or complex of dispositions, and a disposition is a factor of the wrong logical type to be seen or unseen, recorded or unrecorded.' (*CM*, p. 33)

As we have seen the criticism of Ryle's account of dispositions, when it is taken to be a genetic account as well as a semantic account, has been that dispositions do involve causes, hidden or otherwise, and that such causal factors are witnessable, at least in principle. To make this criticism will not, of course, be to reinstate Cartesian dualism, for the structural or categorical basis of human dispositions may not turn out to be mental occurrences.

But Ryle is not the only one to confuse the semantic and genetic accounts of dispositions. For example, David Armstrong criticises Ryle's account of dispositions in Chapter 6, Section VI, of his book *A Materialist Theory of the Mind*. Armstrong calls Ryle's account of dispositions the Phenomenalist or Operationalist account and opposes this with what he calls a Realist account.

According to the Realist view, to speak of an object's having a dispositional property entails that the object is in some non-dispositional state or that it has some property (there exists a 'categorical basis') which is responsible for the object manifesting certain behaviour in certain circumstances, manifestations whose nature makes the dispositional property the particular dispositional property it is. It is true that we may not know anything of the nature of the non-dispositional state. But, the Realist view asserts, in asserting that a certain piece of glass is brittle, for instance, we are *ipso facto* asserting that it is in a certain non-dispositional state which disposes it to shatter and fly apart in a wide variety of circumstances. (P. 86)

It is not correct to say that 'in asserting that a certain piece of glass is brittle, for instance, we are *ipso facto* asserting that it is in a certain non-dispositional state.' To say that is to confuse the semantic and genetic accounts of dispositions. In asserting that a piece of glass is brittle we are merely asserting that if let fall it would break. We are not asserting anything about a categorical base. But to give an adequate explanation of why this glass is brittle one would have to refer to some categorical basis for the brittleness.

Armstrong has been taken to task for identifying dispositions with their categorical basis, and this criticism is correct. It has been argued with some cogency by, for example, Squires and Stevenson in the journal *Analysis*, 1968–9, that dispositions are not to be identified with their bases and so are not causes as such though they point to where an underlying cause may be found. But this discussion did not bring out that, a great deal of the time, the Phenomenalists or Operationalists and the Realists are speaking with crossed purposes. The Realist account is viable as a genetic account of dispositions but not as a semantic account. The Phenomenalist or Operationalist account is only adequate as an explanation of how we use the word 'disposition' or of what we are saying when we use some dispositional term such as 'brittle'. Ryle and Armstrong both err by fudging the two accounts. Indeed the whole debate on dispositions has been bedevilled by this unfortunate confusion.

Alston is one who does not fall into this confusion but I am inclined to think that he does not identify correctly the nature of the two accounts which are confused. Alston suggests that Ryle's account of dispositions may well be the result of confusing meaning and reference. It is probably correct to say that the *meaning* of a dispositional term, such as 'brittleness', can be explicated in terms of typical reactions in typical circumstances, but the *reference* of the dispositional term will be some internal occurrence, its categorical base. As Alston puts it,

It should be a familiar story by now, thanks to the labors of Frege, Strawson, and others, that reference is a very different matter from meaning. What I refer to by use of some linguistic expression is by no means a unique function of the meaning of that expression, though it is undoubtedly limited in ways by that meaning. When I use a definite description like 'the banker who lives next door,' the meaning of that expression leaves many questions unresolved as to the nature of the entity to which I am referring. First it leaves open the possibility that I fail to refer to anything, in case there is no banker living next door to me. Second, if there is such a person, he may be fat or thin, young or old, intelligent or stupid, married or unmarried, etc., etc. However penetrating an understanding I have of the meaning of the phrase 'the banker next door', that will not in itself suffice to resolve these issues. In other words the entity referred to by a linguistic expression may have many properties not reflected in the meaning of that expression, and such that an account of the meaning of that expression will afford no basis for anticipating them.

('Dispositions and Occurrences', *Canadian Journal of Philosophy*, Vol. 1, 1971, p. 151)

I think that Alston is correct in saying that Ryle's account may do as an account of the meaning of the word 'disposition' but that Ryle thought that he was giving an account of more than just the meaning of the word, for Ryle clearly argued to ontological conclusions from his account of dispositions. Ryle argued from his account to the conclusion that dispositions are not occurrences— whether states, processes or activities—nor even partly occurrent. For Ryle dispositions were just hypothetical law-like generalisations. But I do not think that Alston is correct in saying that the distinction to be made here is between the meaning of the term 'disposition' and its reference. An occurrent categorical basis is not the reference of the term 'disposition' or of dispositional terms in the way that the man over there is the reference of the phrase 'the banker next door'.

'Brittle' means 'liable to break easily when let fall or when struck even lightly' or 'breaks whenever it is struck even lightly or let fall from even a modest height.' As the description is hypothetical, its reference will be the hypothetical event of its falling from even a modest height and breaking or being struck lightly and breaking. Just as the definite description 'the banker next door' picks out someone—if there is anyone—by means of the given description, so 'brittle', in so far as it is a description, describes an event of breaking in certain circumstances, and so must be said to pick out this (albeit hypothetical) event. When I use the word 'brittle' of something, what I am referring to is the fact that, if let fall, it would break. So the meaning/reference distinction does not capture the two competing accounts of dispositions. While Ryle and the Phenomenalists may be said to be giving an adequate account of the meaning of the term 'disposition' or 'brittle', the Realists cannot be said to be giving the reference of these terms. The Realists are at pains to explain that an adequate explanation of why someone or something has a certain disposition or proneness must make reference to a categorical basis, but the dispositional term is not a reference to that basis.

Ryle, as we have seen, gave a more or less adequate account of what the term 'disposition' may be taken to mean but he certainly did not give an adequate account of what dispositions are and how they give rise to behaviour. It is for that reason that Ryle's account of dispositions is unlikely to be of much use to psychologists. When a psychologist asks about dispositions he is asking about the *nature* of dispositions and the *causal processes that give rise to them*, not about how the word 'disposition' is used. A psychologist will want a causal explanation, for example, of this person's disposition to be extrovert and that person's disposition to be introverted. The psychologist wants to know what is it that is *in* an extrovert which makes him or her behave in a way that is the opposite of the introvert, and vice versa of course. So the psychologist, rightly, looks for internal factors to explain the workings of dispositions and, with a laudable liking for the most tangible factors available, looks first for clearly isolatable physiological factors to explain dispositional behaviour patterns.

Chapter 5
KNOWING HOW AND KNOWING THAT

Having looked at Ryle's basic strategy in *The Concept of Mind* we are now in a position to see it in action. One of the more famous parts of the book is his exposing of the alleged category mistakes in the Cartesian account of the intellect. Indeed, says Ryle, this is the most fundamental category mistake in the official doctrine: [for] 'both philosophers and laymen tend to treat intellectual operations as the core of mental conduct; that is to say, they tend to define all other mental-conduct concepts in terms of concepts of cognition. They suppose that the primary exercise of minds consists in finding the answers to questions.' (*CM* p. 26) That is, the fundamental category mistake is to take knowledge of facts, and especially theorising about facts to form scientific generalisations, as the core of intelligence and so as the core of the mental life. Thus, the official doctrine places the core of intelligent operating in the private world of 'internal monologue or silent soliloquy'.

The combination of the two assumptions that theorising is the primary activity of minds and that theorising is intrinsically a private, silent or internal operation remains one of the main supports of the dogma of the ghost in the machine. People tend to identify their minds with the 'place' where they conduct their secret thoughts. They even come to suppose that there is a special mystery about how we publish our thoughts instead of realising that we employ a special artifice to keep them to ourselves. (*CM*, p. 27)

But, says Ryle, knowledge of facts and theorising about them is not even the core of intelligence, much less the most fundamental form of mental life. The official doctrine does not even get that right. We can begin to see this if we reflect that, when we apply to someone intelligence-epithets such as 'shrewd' or 'silly', 'prudent' or 'imprudent', 'the description imputes to him not knowledge, or ignorance, of this or that truth, but the ability, or inability, to do certain sorts of things.' It is an assessment

57

of 'people's competences' and not their 'cognitive repertoires'. (*CM*, pp. 27–8) The shrewd punter is the one who bets *and* wins, not the one who knows the Timeform chart off by heart. The prudent farmer is the one who farms his land in such a way that he survives and prospers in seasons which bankrupt others, not the one who has read and can recite the facts contained in various manuals on farming. Intelligence is a *knowing how*, a knowing how to do various things, and the analysis of knowing how is logically prior to *knowing that* or knowledge that such and such is the case, that is, factual knowledge.

So what is this knowledge how? Ryle tells us that it is basically a way of behaving or performing. First of all it is performing correctly or efficiently or successfully. You would not say that someone knew how to drive a car if he invariably crashed whenever he attempted a right turn. Secondly, it is performing in such·a way that one is clearly applying regulative and corrective principles when performing. A car driver shows his intelligence if, having crashed his car when he free-wheeled round a tight curve, he takes to watching Grand Prix and other experienced drivers and attempts to copy their technique for coping with curves. So next time he slows down before the curve, accelerates gently through it and thus negotiates the tight curve successfully. 'A person's performance is described as careful or skilful, if in his operations he is ready to detect and correct lapses, to repeat and improve upon successes, to profit from the examples of others and so forth. He applies criteria in performing critically, that is, in trying to get things right.' (*CM*, pp. 28–9)

The adherents of the official doctrine will object that this account of knowledge how shows that, contrary to Ryle's view, knowledge how is logically subordinate to knowledge that, for it describes knowledge how as performing actions efficiently or successfully in the light of certain prescriptions or regulative principles which a person has been told or has worked out for himself or herself. In other words, goes the objection, you must first have knowledge of what the principles or prescriptions are before you can apply them and so perform in the light of them. Performing intelligently is then at least two things, the consideration of certain prescriptions or principles, and the action performed in accordance with the prescriptions or principles. The car driver acted intelligently because he learnt the rule 'slow down before a curve and accelerate through it' and then applied it with success.

Ryle replies that this objection misfires on two important accounts:

First, there are many classes of performances in which intelligence is displayed, but the rules or criteria of which are unformulated. The wit, when challenged to cite the maxims, or canons, by which he constructs and appreciates jokes, is unable to answer. . . .

[To take another example] Rules of correct reasoning were first extracted by Aristotle, yet men knew how to avoid and detect fallacies before they learned his lessons. (*CM*, p. 30)

In short, says Ryle, 'efficient practice precedes the theory of it.' Unless Aristotle realised that he himself or others could detect fallacies, he would never have decided to try and systematise this ability.

[But] the crucial objection to the intellectualist legend is this. The consideration of propositions is itself an operation the execution of which can be more or less intelligent, less or more stupid. But if, for any operation to be intelligently executed, a prior theoretical operation had first to be performed and performed intelligently, it would be a logical impossibility for anyone ever to break into the circle. (*CM*, p. 30)

In other words, Ryle is saying that the crucial objection is that the official doctrine about acting intelligently, with its two parts, referring to a rule about how to act and then acting in accordance with the rule, is involved in an infinite regress or, if differently emphasised, in a vicious circle, and so is absurd. For example, if one refers to a book of rules about how to play chess in order to play chess well, this enterprise will be unsuccessful unless one reads the book intelligently. But to read intelligently is itself to act intelligently which, on the official doctrine, must again have two episodes to it, referring to rules about how to read intelligently and applying these rules. But, again, these rules about how to read intelligently also need to be read intelligently, and so on for ever. Or, to put this official doctrine in terms of a vicious circle, acting intelligently must be preceded by knowledge of rules, which, to be useful, must be preceded by an act of reading or listening to them intelligently, which being an intelligent act must be preceded by knowledge of rules, and so on round and round from acting in accordance with rules backwards to being intelligently acquainted with rules, to acting in accordance with rules to being intelligently acquainted with rules.

On Ryle's view the solution of the official dogma's troubles is in realising that 'when I do something intelligently, i.e. thinking what I am doing, I am doing one thing and not two. My performance has a special procedure or manner, not special antecedents.' (*CM*, p. 32) Driving or writing or reading or betting or farming intelligently is not two things, driving or writing or reading or betting or farming preceded by an internal glance at a ghostly book of rules, it is an action seen in the light of a disposition. That is, it is an action seen as part of a particular sort of behaviour pattern. Thus, to say he drives a car intelligently is just to attribute to him one performance, driving, but it is also to realise that the driving is part of a pattern which includes such other performances from time to time as negotiating tricky weather conditions, poor road surfaces, mistakes on the part of other drivers, dangerous hairpin bends, and remembering to turn on lights on grey days and to park in only the permitted and safe places, and so on. One could not say a person drives intelligently just by seeing him or her drive a hundred yards when there are not difficult road conditions and no traffic about. To say someone drives intelligently, one must know that the person concerned can negotiate difficult situations of various sorts. Thus to say X drives intelligently is to attribute a disposition to X to do various things which are examples of driving carefully, efficiently, safely, skilfully and the like. Driving intelligently, or doing anything intelligently, and so being intelligent, is a determinable disposition. Not a single-track disposition or disposition to do a single thing, like smoke cigarettes, but a disposition to do a variety of things which can be summed up as ϕ-ing intelligently.

To sum up then, the official doctrine is that intellectual operations are the primary activities of minds and that intellectual operations are primarily acts of cognition or knowing that. Ryle, on the other hand, criticised the doctrine by arguing that intellectual operations were chiefly cases of knowing how. Indeed they must be for as regards the display of intelligence, knowing how is logically prior to knowing that, for we only learn facts about driving or farming if we ourselves or someone else has first driven or farmed, and at some time done so successfully. For performing successfully or efficiently after less successful performances and after modifying the less successful ones so that they become successful is the display of knowing how. Knowing how is doing something until one gets it right. This is not two performances, learning criteria or rules or principles which enable us to get it right and then performing an act correctly in the light of these criteria, rules or principles, but it is the one successful performance seen in the light of the whole history or pattern of actions or performances through which one learned to get it right. Knowing how is the disposition to do something successfully and efficiently, which disposition has been inculcated over some time, that is, it is a capacity or ability. Thus, the exercise of intelligence is a public performance not a private monologue. 'Overt intelligent performances are not clues to the workings of minds; they are those workings.' (*CM*, p. 58) And since intellectual operations are thought of as the principal activity of minds, this analysis will tell us a great deal about the nature of mind. 'To find that most people have minds (though idiots and infants in arms do not) is simply to find that they are able and prone to do certain sorts of things, and this we do by witnessing the sorts of things they do.' (*CM*, p. 61)

What are we to make of all this? It might be best to start with a careful look at Ryle's claim that, contrary to the Cartesian doctrine, knowledge how is prior to knowledge that, and, in general, at his distinction between knowing how and knowing that. Ryle, it will be recalled, answered the objection, that knowing how to do something is not prior to knowledge that because knowledge how presupposes knowledge of the principles telling one how, by pointing out that 'there are many classes of performances in which intelligence is displayed, but the rules or criteria of which are unformulated.' His examples were the wit who makes jokes but could not enunciate rules or maxims for making them, and the pre-Aristotelian philosophers who could detect fallacies in arguments before any models for correct syllogistic reasoning were formed.

One worry about that reply of Ryle's is that it does not show that the wit or comedian, and the pre-Aristotelian philosophers, are not in fact acting in accordance with principles which they know, unless one proposes that one can only be said to know something if one can not merely enunciate it but formulate it as well. But this would be a very austere demand on knowledge. For instance, it has long been a contention of clinical psychology that we can have unconscious and subconscious beliefs and knowledge. Given the correctness of this contention, it might be the case that the comedian or primitive logician does not act in accordance with rules or principles he is conscious of but in accordance with ones that he or she holds beneath the threshold of consciousness and therefore is unable to enunciate.

But there are other alternatives to the Rylean view than to posit unconscious and subconscious beliefs and knowledge. More plausibly in these examples of the comedian and the philosopher, it might be the case that they have grasped the relevant reasons and concepts which enable them to make jokes and detect fallacies respectively, but that they have never sat down to formulate these reasons and concepts into enunciable rules or principles. The philosopher may have grasped that it is not a good argument to say that what Mary said must be untrue because she is living in sin, and know that it is a bad argument for the same reason to say that Marx's social theories must be wrong because he had an illegitimate child by his servant and refused to acknowledge the child, yet not be able to explicitly enunciate the reason. He may not even be able to explain the difficult concept of relevance (though he may grasp it) let alone formulate rules for arguing relevantly. But it would be wrong to argue from this that, in detecting *ad hominem* fallacies, the philosopher cannot be acting in accordance with knowledge about what counts as relevant. The pre-Aristotelian philosopher may well be acting on ,quite definite knowledge when he performs correctly the task of detecting logical fallacies, namely the quite definite though unformulated grounds for rejecting certain arguments as irrelevant.

Ryle's reply to this defence of the Cartesian position is, presumably, contained in his 'crucial objection', namely that, even if he were to allow that the wit or comedian and the pre-Aristotelian philosopher, in making jokes and detecting fallacies were acting in accordance with knowledge gained previously, still this would not entail that knowledge that precedes knowledge how. For to be in possession of facts or knowledge that, one must first grasp them, and grasping is an operation or performance. This being so, such grasping can be done well or badly, or foolishly or intelligently. To do it well, one must know how to do it. Therefore knowledge how—how to grasp correctly the relevant fact—precedes the actual grasp or possession (the knowledge) of that fact, that is, the knowledge that. Further, if one slots in the Cartesian version of knowing how into this account, then to grasp a fact involves one in following rules about how to correctly grasp or understand a fact, and then to follow these new set of rules involves one in a further level of grasping rules for following rules, and so on *ad infinitum*.

But while some Cartesians may have viewed understanding facts, or rules or anything else, as an operation of grasping or as some other sort of performance, they certainly need not have done so. For an alternative way of looking at understanding would be to view it as much more instinctive than a performance. Cartesians could suggest that the mind instinctively knows how to grasp, and that it does not have to learn to do so as one would with a performance. The mind, they might put it, is defined as something whose function is to grasp or understand facts or truths. Indeed, they might go further and suggest that understanding is not an active operation at all, even an instinctive one, but a passive process that is automatic. Just as a sponge does not have to learn to soak up water, or even strive to do so, so a mind does not have to learn to soak up facts or even strive to do so. Given that the senses are functioning normally the mind just passively receives primitive facts; it just does it. Thus the Cartesian can stop Ryle applying his infinite regress to his account of knowledge by positing that basic facts are not acquired as the result of some performance, operation or activity, but passively. Thus, there can be no question of there being rules for grasping these facts, for there is no grasping going on. There is, rather, a soaking up.

But Ryle might reply that the sort of knowledge, even if intuitive, which the comedian or philosopher might be said to have, and which enables him or her to make original jokes and detect fallacies in arguments not previously confronted, could not be explained away as a passive soaking up of facts. One might 'soak up' the fact that it is now raining! But one could not 'soak up' whatever it is that makes *ad hominem* arguments fallacious. One must work out that *ad hominem* arguments are fallacious. Some people never do. Yet few, if any, fail to register when it is raining. Becoming aware of the fallacy of *ad hominem* arguments, unlike becoming aware that it is raining, is more than just registering what is going on. Certainly, to work out that *ad hominem* arguments are fallacious, one must listen to and note at least one *ad hominem* argument. But one must do a lot more, one must think about it, and puzzle over whether such an argument does overturn what it claims to overturn. In short, such knowledge is only gained after quite difficult intellectual activity.

This putative reply of Ryle's certainly makes things more complicated for the Cartesian. He cannot simply say that the comedian can make original jokes of his own because he has passively registered and stored up, though he has not formulated, knowledge of what is needed to make a good joke. As Ryle says, one must work out what makes a good joke, and working out is finding out (or knowledge of) *how* it works. This, I think, is correct. But this should not trouble the Cartesian overmuch. He could agree that the knowledge which enables the comedian to make original jokes is knowledge how (at least initially, a process of working out how to make jokes), but also maintain that this process of working out how to make jokes is intrinsically a private, silent and internal operation. And that does not commit him, as Ryle originally suggested, to holding that the comedian ought therefore to be able to formulate this knowledge of how to make jokes into propositions or rules. The comedian may have worked out how to write his own material but not be able to formulate rules for writing jokes.

Ryle is right in suggesting that the knowledge which the comedian utilises is knowledge how rather than simple factual knowledge. But it would not follow from this that knowledge how is always prior to knowledge that. Simple factual knowledge, such as that it is now raining, does not seem to be the result of any working out in the way that one might work out how to make jokes. But Ryle would reply most probably that such simple factual knowledge has nothing to do with intelligence, which is what he was concerned about.

But a very important point does arise out of all this. It might be claimed that the distinction between knowledge how and knowledge that cannot always be made cleanly and clearly. For when the would-be comedian listens to Morecambe and Wise, Bob Hope, and other professional comedians, and consciously or unconsciously works out how they make jokes, and begins to write his own material, he is not only learning how to make jokes, he is learning what is a good joke and what is a bad joke, and so learning, even if intuitively, what is the formula or pattern for good jokes. If he were able to formulate the results of his self-teaching, he might put it in the form of a proposition or series of propositions beginning 'A good joke has. . . .' Learning is a process but its results are often knowledge of facts, sometimes formulable as factual propositions. Not simple facts like 'It is now raining' but complex ones like 'If you do x then y' or 'If you begin with an m, then the middle must be an n, and the end of the joke a p.' So even the knowledge required to perform some complex operations, such as making jokes, while it is knowledge about *how* to make good jokes, it also seems to involve knowledge *that* good jokes are ones that are so and so. Of course those who hold this view would grant that there are some cases of knowledge how, such as how to ride a bike or how to eat with a spoon, which probably do not yield much if any knowledge that. But they might want to maintain that, among the cases of knowledge which are a hybrid of knowledge how and knowledge that, there are cases of intellectual operations. So some intellectual operations are to be given an account involving knowledge that.

But Ryle's view cannot be so easily brushed aside, though it may require some fairly radical changes to be made in it. John Hartland-Swann, in an article entitled 'The Logical Status of "Knowing That"' (*Analysis*, 1955–6), has suggested that, on Ryle's own account of knowledge, there should not be any distinction at all between knowing how and knowing that, because all cases of knowing are really cases of knowing how, for all knowledge is to be analysed as the exercise of a capacity. For example, it might be claimed that knowing French is a mixture of knowing *how* to translate and read French, and knowing *that* certain French words, such as 'garçon' and 'couteau', have the same meaning as certain English words, in this case 'boy' and 'knife'. But, since for Ryle knowledge, in all its forms, is a disposition (in this case a capacity) to do something, then knowing that 'garçon' means the same as 'boy' should be analysed as being able to answer 'boy' when asked the question 'What does the French word "garçon" mean?' or some similar question, actual or implied. But Hartland-Swann also points out that intuitively we do feel that there is a distinction to be made between knowing how and knowing that, for we do see as distinct the process of learning an ability, and so how to do something, and the state of being in possession of information. However, to maintain this distinction, one must clearly posit something which Ryle would be most uneasy about, namely an actual occurrent possession (in some internal storeroom?) of facts. As Hartland-Swann suggests:

Moreover—and ironically enough—in order to restore the distinction and thus find a proper logical niche for knowing *that*, it looks as if we must return to that scandalous past when knowing *that* was taken to mean possessing an actual piece of knowledge, privately stored in my ghostly memory-chamber like a document in a pigeon-hole. (P. 113)

Hartland-Swann, being at heart convinced by Ryle's account of knowledge as dispositional, believes that Ryle should insist that all knowledge is knowledge how, no matter what our intuitions are, and to forego the knowing how and knowing that distinction, though Hartland-Swann admits that 'many people will find it difficult to believe that "knowing that the earth is round" is ultimately on a par with "knowing how to swim".' (P. 114)

Jane Roland, in her article 'On "Knowing How" and "Knowing That"' (*Philosophical Review*, 1958) suggests that Ryle, and Hartland-Swann, can both reduce 'knowing that' to 'knowing how' on all occasions and at the same time assuage our intuitions. For, she argues, we can show that 'knowing how' is ambiguous, where the ambiguity cloaks two quite different sorts of knowing how. So the real distinction to be made is between two sorts of knowing how. The first sort is akin to the old 'knowing that', as it is 'knowing how to answer certain questions'. The second sort is the old 'knowing how', that is 'knowing how to perform certain tasks'. The latter, she says, implies an ability or capacity gained through practice, the former does not.

Roland also adds a third sort of 'knowing how'. An example of this sort is someone's knowing that he should be quiet when others are speaking, where the knowing implies not just that he has heard of a rule to that effect but that he has sincerely adopted the rule. This sort of knowledge is not really a capacity at all but the adoption of a mode of behaviour. But the difficulty with this suggestion is that, leaving aside that we may express this linguistically as 'he *knows* that he should . . .', it does not really seem to be a case of knowledge. It is a commitment to something, not the possession of something, but knowledge in the ordinary sense is possessing some fact or skill or ability. But perhaps Roland could say that, in making this behaviour his own, he now possesses it as a would-be habit, and so it is a form of possession and therefore a candidate for being a type of knowledge. But if such a move is made it would seem that such commitments of manners or morals are reducible to the acquiring of capacities.

But there are other difficulties with Ryle's assimilation of all knowledge to knowledge how. If one assimilates, as Ryle does, all 'knowing how' to the general model of 'knowing how to perform a task', then, in turn, this seems to entail that one must have learnt how to perform the task. But the following case seems to be a counter-example to this model. An intelligent person might solve a practical difficulty, such as, say, how to ford a river, which he has never previously confronted. One would have reason to say that he solved this problem of how to cross over the river, rather than happened by sheer chance to cross over successfully, by seeing the methodical and thoughtful way he went about it. But there may have been no attempted fordings such that he could be said to be learning how to ford rivers. He may have succeeded first shot. That he is intelligent is revealed by the fact that he has solved other sorts of problems as well, but this would not be evidence for saying that he knew how to ford rivers. Yet in a sense he clearly did, and in circumstances such that it would not seem appropriate to give this knowledge a dispositional analysis. He was not disposed to ford rivers intelligently or otherwise, for he was not given to fording rivers at all.

What I am getting at here is a very fundamental difficulty with any analysis of intellectual activities in terms of dispositions, namely that it cannot make sense of the pre-dispositional intellectual activity which eventually becomes dispositional. It cannot make sense of learning to play chess, but only of playing chess intelligently because one has a disposition or proneness to do so. The learning, which was part of the process of inculcating the disposition, cannot itself be a disposition.

The difficulty of explaining original or creative intellectual work—stepping where no one has stepped before—is just a variation of this fundamental difficulty, for it amounts to a demand as to how a dispositional explanation can be given of a new intellectual move which no one has ever made before and which, at least on Ryle's account of dispositions, no one could have a disposition to do.

Ryle might be able to solve these difficulties by saying that, when someone proposes a new theory or, in general, a new intellectual move, then he is activating a second-order disposition, namely to make new intellectual moves. The inventor is just that sort of person who has a disposition to speculate, experiment, and so on.

But what if one has not such a disposition, but, once only, makes a new intellectual move? The person of one idea. The circumstances were such that, just this one time, the person invented something.

Another very fundamental problem with Ryle's ability (dispositional) account of intellectual activity is that he has committed himself to a *behavioural* dispositional account. Now how can such an account cope with silent, internal, intellectual activity; activity such as silent reading, mental arithmetic, and composing in one's head? How can an account in terms of behavioural dispositions make sense of intellectual activities where no behaviour is going on?

These are very formidable difficulties for an anti-Cartesian, and Ryle realised that they were. It was these sort of difficulties which made him state quite unequivocally that he was dissatisfied with the account of the intellect which he gave in *The Concept of Mind*, and which led to his writing a long series of articles on thinking in the last twenty-five years of his life. In Chapter 13, then, we shall see how Ryle attempted to circumvent these difficulties and how this manoeuvre led him to formulate an uncharacteristically non-dispositional account of speculative, theoretical thinking.

Chapter 6
THE MYTH OF VOLITIONS

Ryle begins his demolition of the concepts of the will and its acts, volitions, by reminding us that philosophers are to blame entirely for these pieces of foolery. He goes on to make it clear that his target is not the voluntary/involuntary distinction but the picture of us as inhabited, in our ghostly private world, by an entity called the Will which, through its activities called Volitions, helps us to translate our ideas into facts. As we shall see, Ryle's own positive account of the involuntary/voluntary distinction does connect up with the previous chapter in that Ryle's account of 'voluntary' is in terms of knowledge how.

Ryle's demolition of the concepts of will and volitions is devastating. His first objection to the theory of will and volitions is its own very awkwardness and artificiality, which is underlined when we try to speak of these mental activities, volitions, as we would of other activities.

No one, save to endorse the theory, ever describes his own conduct, or that of his acquaintances, in the recommended idioms. No one ever says such things as that at 10 a.m. he was occupied in willing this or that, or that he performed five quick and easy volitions and two slow and difficult volitions between midday and lunch-time. (CM, p. 64)

Indeed, Ryle continues, 'By what sorts of predicates should they [volitions] be described? Can they be sudden or gradual, strong or weak, difficult or easy, enjoyable or disagreeable? Can they be accelerated, decelerated, interrupted, or suspended? Can people be efficient or inefficient at them?' (CM, p. 64) In short, Ryle is saying, no ordinary person ever reports the existence of acts of volition and no one, not even the adherents of the official doctrine, seems able to settle any of these simple questions about what volitions are like. Indeed, any attempted answers appear ridiculous. This difficulty of making sense of the doctrine, plus the fact that no one actually gives reports of volitions having taken place, should suggest that something rather odd is going on.

Ryle's second objection suggests that the oddness lies in the fact that no evidence can ever be adduced for this theory.

He [an adherent of the official doctrine of volitions] can only infer from an observed overt action to the volition from which it resulted, and then only if he has any good reason to believe that the overt action was a voluntary action, and not a reflex or habitual action, or one resulting from some external cause. It follows that no judge, schoolmaster, or parent ever knows that the actions which he judges merit praise or blame; for he cannot do better than guess that the action was willed. Even a confession by the agent, if such confessions were ever made, that he had executed a volition before his hand did the deed would not settle the question. The pronouncement of the confession is only another overt muscular action. . . .
Nor could it be maintained that the agent himself can know . . . either from the alleged direct deliverances of consciousness, or from the alleged direct findings of introspection, that he had executed an act of will. . . . The connection between volitions and movements is allowed to be mysterious, so for all he knows . . . the pulling of the trigger may have had some other event for its cause. (*CM*, pp. 65–6)

What Ryle is arguing here is that the only possible evidence for the presence of an act of will could be either indirect evidence whereby an observed overt action somehow revealed that it was caused by an act of will or direct evidence whereby the will revealed its presence to someone in consciousness or when he or she introspected.

As regards the indirect evidence, the best one can do is guess that this action is a willed one, for the will does not leave its stamp upon actions. According to the official doctrine itself, the same muscular activities occur in doing X as a result of an act of will, and doing X as a result of something else. Further, one cannot infer from the fact that this action is voluntary to the fact that it is willed, for, on the official doctrine, a voluntary act is defined as one which is caused by an act of will. Therefore, to call something 'voluntary' presupposes that one can already identify it as caused by an act of will.

As regards direct evidence, consciousness or introspection cannot reveal the moment when the alleged volition causes the muscles to move, for even the most doctrinaire advocate of the official doctrine admits that the connection between volitions and bodily movements is mysterious. More importantly, according to the official doctrine, the connection is necessarily unknowable, as it can be revealed as neither part of one's mental life nor as part of one's public behaviour, it is in an unknown and unknowable limbo. As Ryle puts it:

> The problem how a person's mind and body influence one another is notoriously charged with theoretical difficulties. What the mind wills, the legs, arms and the tongue execute. . . . But the actual transactions between the episodes of the private history and those of the public history remain mysterious, since by definition they can belong to neither series. They could not be reported among the happenings described in a person's autobiography of his inner life, but nor could they be reported among those described in someone else's biography of that person's overt career. They can be inspected neither by introspection nor by laboratory experiment. (*CM*, p. 12)

So the upshot is that, according to the very terms in which the official doctrine is presented, no evidence, direct or indirect, is possible for the presence of an act of will as the cause of some piece of public behaviour. Not merely is the theory very bizarre, it cannot be founded on evidence of any sort.

A third argument, says Ryle, would be that, the putative causal interaction between alleged volitions and bodies is not merely unknowable, but that, according to the official theory itself, this interaction is impossible anyway. 'Minds, as the legend describes them, live on a floor of existence defined as being outside the causal system to which bodies belong.' (*CM*, p. 66) That is, minds and the inhabitants of minds, such as the will and its volitions, cannot cause bodily movements because the mental is so defined that it could not causally interact with the physical.

Fourthly, says Ryle, one can generate a dilemma for the official doctrine by asking the following question: 'So what of volitions themselves? Are they voluntary or involuntary acts of mind? Clearly either answer leads to absurdities.' (*CM*, p. 67) Ryle is arguing here that, since volitions are acts—acts of will—then it is legitimate to ask of them whether they themselves are voluntary or involuntary acts. But by definition prior acts of will are what, in terms of the official doctrine, make acts voluntary, so that if acts of the will themselves are said to be voluntary, then they must be preceded by prior acts of will, *ad infinitum*. If acts of the will are not said to be voluntary but are pronounced involuntary, then we would have the curious situation of involuntary acts issuing from the will, and being the cause and explanation of public behaviour being termed 'voluntary'.

At this point Ryle anticipates a fairly obvious objection, namely that the evidence for the existence of the will and its acts is the evidence of choice; indeed it might be said that volitions are choosings. Ryle's reply is, first of all, that choice could not be the evidence for the existence of volitions on all occasions, for putatively voluntary acts are alleged to occur in non-choice situations. One can do something, like go to the pictures, voluntarily, even if it was the only thing one thought of doing. Besides, writes Ryle, if volitions are choices, we are involved once again in an infinite regress, for one can always ask the question 'Was the choice voluntary or not?'

Finally, Ryle gives us his own analysis of the concepts voluntary and involuntary, which analysis, of course, makes no reference to the will or volitions. Ryle declares that a great deal of the mystery goes out of this notion of 'voluntary', when we reflect that, ordinarily, the term is only used when things go wrong, that is when there is a question of blaming someone for his or her action. We ask whether the boy broke the window voluntarily or on purpose but not whether he got his homework right voluntarily or on purpose. This sense of 'voluntary' means merely that the person did it, rather than it was done to him or her, and that he or she committed the wrong or error when he or she was quite competent to do otherwise. That the boy broke the window voluntarily or on purpose means that he broke it, that is, was the cause of its breaking, and that he was quite able to have avoided breaking it. So the account of voluntarily is mapped on to our account of competence or knowing how.

Unfortunately, says Ryle, philosophers cloud the issue by extending the notion of voluntary to cover actions which do not go wrong and do not merit blame of any sort. Philosophers say that the boy can be said to have voluntarily got his homework right, as well as wrong. This extension of the usage is just superfluous and so wrong, says Ryle. Indeed the unnaturalness of using the word 'voluntary' in this stretched sense is borne out if we attempt to transfer our analysis of the ordinary usage to this stretched usage.

When we say that someone could have avoided committing a lapse or error, or that it was his fault that he committed it, we mean that he knew how to do the right thing, or was competent to do so, but did not exercise his knowledge or competence. He was not trying, or not trying hard enough. But when a person has done the right thing, we cannot then say that he knew how to do the wrong thing, or that he was competent to make mistakes. For making mistakes is not an exercise of competence, nor is the commission of slips an exercise of knowledge *how*; it is a failure to exercise knowledge *how*. (*CM*, p. 70)

In short, Ryle's account is that the use of the term 'voluntarily' is a reference to knowing how, and one is only interested in this question if there is some doubt, that is if someone has not done what he ought, was expected or predicted to do, but it is suspected that he was capable of doing what he ought, was expected or predicted to do. We are not interested in whether someone knows how to get his sums right or not, if he has just got them right. The query is superfluous.

Finally, Ryle suggests that 'the tangle of largely spurious problems, known as the problem of the Freedom of the Will, partly derives from this unconsciously stretched use of "voluntary".' (*CM*, p. 71)

As is evident from the posthumously published *Philosophical Investigations* which brings together the ideas he was wrestling with and discussing in his classes at Cambridge in the nineteen thirties, Wittgenstein held doubts similar to those of Ryle about the viability of the Cartesian account of volitions. Wittgenstein pointed out that if one looked upon volitions as *acts* of willing which *cause* bodily movements, then one is confronted with the absurd possibility that one could will willing.

I can't will willing; that is, it makes no sense to speak of willing willing. 'Willing' is not the name of an action; and so not the name of any voluntary action either.

(*Philosophical Investigations* I, 613)

When I raise my arm 'voluntarily' I do not use any instrument to bring

the movement about. My wish is not such an instrument either.
(*Philosophical Investigations* I, 614)

Wittgenstein's alternative to the volition theory is by no means clear. It seems to be a suggestion that we should consider willing as part of voluntary actions, as somehow not merely parasitic on the bodily movement which is voluntary but symbiotic with it. 'Willing, if it is not to be a sort of wishing, must be the action itself. It cannot be allowed to stop anywhere short of the action.' (*Philosophical Investigations* I, 615) But the difficulty is in isolating exactly what it is which constitutes the voluntariness of actions. As Wittgenstein put it, 'And the problem arises: what is left over if I subtract the fact that my arm goes up from the fact that I raise my arm?' (*Philosophical Investigations* I, 621) G. N. A. Vesey in his paper 'Volition' (*Philosophy*, 1961) suggested that, since we can say that 'So far as he, but not necessarily his arm, was concerned, he moved his arm' (p. 363), that is, since he can fail to move his arm (it is, say, anaesthetised and held down), but has willed it to move, and believed his willing to have been successful when it was not so, then the voluntariness of a voluntary action is separate from the physical action. Like Wittgenstein, however, he does not want to say that the voluntariness consists in some special inner mental act but, like Wittgenstein, he does not tell us in what exactly this voluntariness consists. Ryle's account, on the other hand, does not locate voluntariness in the act itself but in its circumstances. A voluntary action is a bodily movement where the person could have done otherwise, where it was within the competence or know-how of the person to do otherwise in the circumstances.

Since Ryle's attack on volitions in *The Concept of Mind* there have been a number of attempts to reinstate them by replying to his major objection to the theory of volitions, namely his dilemma argument which suggested that, if volitions were thought of as mental acts, then one must answer the question 'Are volitions themselves voluntary or involuntary?' If one replied that they were voluntary, then one was involved in an infinite regress for the definition of voluntary act was 'one caused by a volition'. If one replied that they were involuntary, then the resulting view seemed absurd, for one would have to hold that at the heart of a voluntary action was an involuntary mental act.

The most popular reply to this dilemma has been to say that Ryle's question is misplaced, for while my arm rising is voluntary only if it is the result of a volition, it makes no sense to ask whether a volition itself is the result of a volition or not. Why this is so is to be explained in the following way. Volition is an action which is at a more basic level than the action of which it is asked 'Is it voluntary or involuntary?' This question can only be asked of non-basic actions which are made up of a basic action and its result, for it is really asking whether a certain result is caused by a particular sort of basic action, a volition, or not. For example, raising one's arm is a non-basic action, for it involves a basic action, willing the arm to rise, plus a result, the bodily movement of the arm rising. As Ryle's question 'Is it voluntary or involuntary?' is really the question 'Is this movement or change the result of a volition or not?', and since volitions are not themselves a resulting movement or change, then it is a category mistake to ask of volitions themselves whether they are the result of a volition or not.

Hugh McCann, for example, argues for a view along these lines in 'Volition and Basic Action' (*Philosophical Review*, 1974). He writes: 'The purpose of this paper is to defend the view that the bodily actions of men typically involve a mental action of volition or willing, and that such mental acts are, in at least one important sense, the *basic* actions we perform when we do things like raise an arm, move a finger, or flex a muscle.' (p. 451) In another paper, 'Trying, Paralysis, and Volition' (*Review of Metaphysics*, 1975), McCann argues that we have inductive evidence in support of this theory of volitions in medical data about paralysed people. 'Even a cursory look at the medical literature on testing for deficiencies in the power of movement indicates that a paralytic *can* try to make what appears to be normal movements.' (P. 428) McCann suggests that it is more accurate to substitute 'will' for 'try' in such cases for, if the person was not paralysed, whatever it is that he does would succeed. The mental part of moving a limb is completed, paralysed or not, and 'will' has the more correct connotations of completed mental act. 'Volition is intentional: it counts as the basic move on the agent's part to execute what he plans to do.' (*Ibid.* p. 437) 'The modality of volition has therefore to be fundamentally executive, an exercise of the agent's general power consciously to cause, and aimed at causing what is willed.' (*Ibid.* p. 439) But the more McCann sheds light on his version of this move to avoid Ryle's dilemma, the less viable it seems. For if volitions are basic actions—'an exercise of the agent's general power consciously to cause' —why should Ryle be refused permission to ask whether this exercise of power was voluntary or not, that is, to ask whether it was caused by a prior exercise of this sort of power or not? For exercises of power would seem to be genuine changes. The person, the agent, has changed from the non-exercise of some power to its exercise.

McCann might reply that we can allow Ryle to ask the question and that the answer is no. An exercise of a person's power is caused but yet not the result of another exercise of this particular sort of power. So a volition is caused but not by another volition. But to say this implies that volitions are involuntary exercises of power.

If McCann tried the other horn of the dilemma then Ryle's infinite regress comes into play: volitions must be caused by volitions which must be caused by volitions. . . .

But the reply McCann would probably favour would be one that says you cannot ask of volitions what caused them. On one interpretation this is to say that volitions are uncaused causes; notoriously mysterious items upon which to found theories. On another interpretation this is to say that volitions are not the things of which it can be sensibly asked if they are caused or not. But if, as McCann has done, volitions are explained as exercises of power, such a veto on the question seems to be *ad hoc* and amount only to a refusal to answer this awkward question.

In the earlier of these two papers, McCann did write that

We must, then, think of volition as under the agent's control. And doing so need not in the least be taken as committing us to some further act by which the control is exerted. To suppose that if volition provides the element of control in actions like raising one's arm, volition can itself exhibit control only through something like a further volition, is rather like supposing that if we explain the wetness of a wet street by saying there is water on it, we must explain the wetness of water by postulating further water. Volition can be voluntary in the way water is wet—that is, essentially, in a way that does not require some means as explanation.

('Volition and Basic Action', *Philosophical Review*, 1974, p. 472)

That is, McCann is arguing that, just as water causes things to be wet while it itself is wet though not by being caused to be so by water, so a volition causes movements and changes to be voluntary but its own voluntariness is not the result of being caused by another volition.

Unfortunately this analogy does not work. Streets become wet by being smeared with water, but bodily movements do not become voluntary by being smeared with voluntariness. According to the theory of volitions, bodily movements become voluntary by being *caused* by items called 'volitions'. Streets do not become wet by being brought into existence by water or caused by water. So while it is redundant to ask whether water is watery or smeared by water, it is not redundant to ask whether a volition (a particular form of exercising power) is caused by another volition (a similar exercise of power) or not.

Lawrence Davis in his recent book *Theory of Action* follows a line of argument similar to but significantly different from that adopted by McCann. He tells us that 'A volition, then, is an event which is normally a cause of the agent's belief that he is acting in a certain way, *and* which normally causes such doing-related events as make it true that he *is* acting in that way.' (P. 16) Davis cautions us against thinking that this entails that volitions must be short, sharp, discrete events. They might be longish monitoring processes. Like McCann, Davis holds that volitions are actions, indeed the only real actions that ever occur. And again like McCann, Davis suggests that there is inductive evidence to support the existence of volitions.

Consider a kind of experiment described by William James. 'Close the patient's eyes, hold his anaesthetic arm still, and tell him to raise his hand to his head; and when he opens his eyes he will be astonished to find that the movement has not taken place.' Here the agent thought he had complied with the request. Why? The most natural explanation is that he had all the 'awareness' he ever has when performing actions of this kind, except for whatever his eyes and the arm itself normally contribute. In other words, feature X was present and caused him to believe he was moving his arm as requested . . . [and] feature X [is] what we are now calling a volition. (P. 16)

But Davis's way of avoiding Ryle's dilemma is to say that raising one's arm is to be analysed, *not* as an arm movement *caused* by a volition, *but* as an arm movement *generated* by a volition.

Now volitions are attempts, and attempts are doings. They can generate other doings, then—and in particular, it seems that *every doing which is an action is generated by a volition.* . . . Precisely what it means to say that a particular doing was an action, according to the volitional theory, is that it was generated by a volition. But if generated by a volition, then neither preceded nor caused by a volition. (P. 40)

By means of his distinction between causing and generating, Davis believes that his version of the volition theory escapes Ryle's question 'Are volitions voluntary or involuntary?' How exactly this escape is engineered is not clear, but a further clue to what Davis means by 'generation' might be gleaned from the following passage:

Additional support [for the belief in the existence of a non-causal process called 'generation'] comes when it is appreciated that generation is not exclusively a relation of actions and act-types. 'Sam became president by being elected unanimously' and 'Sam got himself excused from jury duty by catching pneumonia' seem to be perfectly acceptable examples of non-causal and causal generation, respectively, though presumably none of the doings involved were actions. (Pp. 39–40)

The claimed example of non-causal generation is that of a unanimous election making Sam president. Leaving aside that electing may involve volitions—and so be doings which are Davis actions—why should we not consider the electoral process as causal? Why should we not say that the voting caused Sam's being declared president?

What Davis probably has in mind is that 'We elect Sam', if unanimous, could be construed like 'I thee wed', as a performative, such that to do such and such, cast votes or say certain words, is to bring about a certain further state of affairs, though it is not a causal 'bringing about'. When we have cast our votes, and the votes are counted, and Sam is announced as the victor in the poll, then automatically it is the case that Sam is also president. To put it another way, there was only one doing (or set of doings), the election, but it generated several layers of true descriptions of the doing, such as 'An election took place' and 'Sam became president'.

Now, by parallel argument, Davis seems to be suggesting that volitions are akin to performatives, at least at times.* I might hold a pistol in my hand and will to shoot Sam. Nothing might be brought about; no true description other than 'I willed to shoot Sam' is generated. But something might be brought about by my volition. The gun might go off. Sam might fall down dead. My volition might generate new layers of true description, such as 'The pistol was fired' and 'Sam was shot' and 'Sam was killed'.

From here on, it might be suggested, Davis can easily avoid Ryle's dilemma, for in asking whether this action, shooting Sam, was voluntary or not, we are not asking whether some event was caused by a volition but whether it was generated by one, which in turn amounts to asking whether this true event-description is a description of a volition. So this question becomes tautologously true if asked of volitions themselves, and so the dilemma is dissolved. One can only answer 'Yes' to the question 'Is this true volition-description a description of a volition?' For, of course, true descriptions describing that volitions have occurred are generated by the occurrence of volitions.

But the plausibility of this account seems to hang on the plausibility of Davis's unspoken but underlying analogy between performatives and volitions. This analogy seems to be his argument in support of the claim that volitions generate but do not cause voluntary bodily movements. One point at which this analogy does not hold is that, while a performative, if sincerely uttered, always generates some new state of affairs, a volition, if sincerely done (performed?), does not thereby necessarily succeed in generating what it set out to generate. To put this in terms

---

* J. L. Austin, who coined the term, described performative utterances as those speech acts where 'the uttering of the sentence is, or is part of, the doing of an action'. (*How To Do Things With Words*) Thus to say 'I thee wed' or 'I do' in the appropriate circumstances is a performative utterance, for the very utterance itself is the action of marrying oneself to someone else. Performatives were to be constrasted with constatives which merely describe, thus 'I got married today' is a constative.

of examples: 'I apologise', if uttered sincerely, cannot fail to generate an apology, but the willing 'I will shoot Sam', if sincere, does not thereby generate the shooting of Sam. This is not just a quibble but a very important difficulty with Davis's account. A volition does not succeed just, so to speak, by being 'uttered' internally, something else is needed. It is a contingent matter whether volitions have upshots or not. Davis's opponents, of course, will suggest that this contingency is the conditions allowing *causal* interaction to take place.

To put this point another way. Sam's being president, when the result of the voting is officially announced, is not the production of physico-chemical changes in Sam by some utterance, it is the conferring on him of a role with future duties, obligations, and rights by the uttering of certain conventional words. No change can be discerned in Sam, at the moment of the electoral announcement, which is identifiable as his presidency. On the other hand, if my willing to shoot Sam generates the true description 'Sam is shot', it has to be the case that some physico-chemical change occurred in Sam. A bullet must have entered Sam. Willing is a theoretical doing postulated, not to explain the generation of roles or commitments, or of descriptions, but of real changes. If it does not do so it is not a volition theory, that is, a theory to *explain* why some real bodily movements are produced in a particular way, that is, voluntarily. If we do not allow Davis his account of volitions as only generating but not causing anything, then Ryle's dilemma remains. 'Are volitions themselves voluntary or not?' is just the old question 'Are they caused by volitions or not?'

Another recent attempt to derail the progress of Ryle's dilemma is Arthur Danto's in his book *Analytical Philosophy of Action*. He asks, 'Why, in order for an action to be an event caused by a volition, need volitions themselves be actions?' (P. 53) He suggests that if volitions are not actions, then Ryle's dilemma is derailed, for Ryle can no longer ask whether volitions are voluntary (that is, involve events caused by volitions) or not, for this question only applies to putative actions.

The difficulty with such a reply is that again the

resulting position seems just as untenable as the one it is designed to avoid. Danto's account of volitions means that they cannot be events or involve events for, if they were or did, then one could ask whether such events were caused by volitions or not. But if volitions are not mental acts or events, what are they? Danto's only enlightenment here is that 'Volitions are amongst the things we *are*: we are not something to one side, which then has to make the volition happen.' (P. 53) But this hardly sheds light on the status of volitions. All we know about them, ontologically, is that they are not actions or events. But Danto's only grounds for saying this is the desire to avoid Ryle's dilemma. No additional grounds are adduced.

Danto does refer to volitions as 'occurrences' and this admission may be sufficient for Ryle to introduce his dilemma again by asking whether the occurrence was the result of a volition or some other cause. For why should we allow just one species of occurrence to be immune from being caused? Danto's reply to this might be to say that because volitions do not cause events such as bodily movements with transeunt or Humean causality, but in an immanent way, to ask whether volitions themselves are voluntary is not to ask whether they are caused by further volitions, at least in the normal transeunt meaning of 'caused'. So volitions are not occurrences which are threatened by causality if it is asked of them whether they are voluntary or not.

But clearly everything hangs, in Danto's account, on the notion of immanent causality (just as everything hung, in Davis's account, on the notion of generation). But Danto explains immanent causality only to the extent of telling us that it is not causality *between* events in the way that transeunt causality is, but causality *within* one event.

The Immanentist denies this analysis. For him, the doing of *b* [a bodily movement or other event] by *m* [a person], for example, is an event and it contains a component event, namely *b*, with which it is not identical. But when we subtract *b* from the doing of it by *m*, something is left over which is not an event in its own right: for there is no *mere* doing: doing is always *of* something. (*Ibid*. p. 57)

Indeed Danto admits that 'the Immanentist has no real *argument* in favor of the irreducibility of complex events

[events caused immanently by non-eventival occurrences such as volitions] to compound ones [events caused transeuntly by events] except the suggestion that *doing* is not something which can occur on its own: there is no doing which is not the doing *of* something.' (*Ibid.* p. 57) That is, Danto's position amounts to just postulating that volitions are occurrences called 'doings' which—it now turns out—*cannot* themselves be caused as they are not events. But all this seems *ad hoc*, derived in the face of the Rylean dilemma.

So, after the dust has settled, and after acknowledging the subtlety of the manoeuvres designed to avoid Ryle's dilemma, I confess that I at least remain unconvinced that his dilemma has been avoided by any of these reconstituted theories of volitions. In consequence, I also find Davis's comments, that Ryle's dilemma 'has been answered in many different ways and is now of historical interest only', quite gratuitous. What is not gratuitous is that Ryle's attack on the theory of volitions has been very important, at least to the extent that it has generated a large number of attempts to make the theory of volitions plausible. Indeed the great variety, and complexity, of such theories of volitions is an indication that no single one has seemed compelling.

Chapter 7
THE BOGEY OF CONSCIOUSNESS

It had been the dream of the psychologists around the turn of the century to do away with that exceedingly trouble-some part of the subject matter of psychology, namely consciousness. For this would make the programme of doing away with introspection as a source of knowledge of the psychological, and of making psychology into a hard, experimental science, more plausible. In a paper entitled 'Does Consciousness exist?', published posthumously in 1921, William James wrote,

I believe that 'consciousness', when once it has evaporated to this estate of pure diaphaneity [as it does in the writings of neo-Kantians], is on the point of disappearing altogether. It is the name of a nonentity, and has no right to a place among first principles. Those who still cling to it are clinging to a mere echo, the faint rumor left behind by the disappearing 'soul' upon the air of philosophy. During the past year, I have read a number of articles whose authors seemed just on the point of abandoning the notion of consciousness, and substituting for it that of an absolute experience not due to two factors. But they were not quite radical enough, not quite daring enough in their negations. For twenty years past I have mistrusted 'consciousness' as an entity; for seven or eight years past I have suggested its non-existence to my students, and tried to give them its pragmatic equivalent in realities of experience. It seems to me that the hour is ripe for it to be openly and universally discarded. (*Essays in Radical Empiricism*, Harvard University Press, 1976, pp. 3–4)

This suggestion was startling enough at the time, though James's sketch of how this programme might be carried out was less than convincing, for James explained that

Breath moving outwards, between the glottis and the nostrils, is, I am persuaded, the essence out of which philosophers have constructed the entity known to them as consciousness. *That entity is fictitious, while thoughts in the concrete are fully real. But thoughts in the concrete are made of the same stuff as things are.* (P. 19)

That last claim was 'explained' in the following way. Chaotic 'pure experiences' are the basic stuff of the universe. They become differentiated into an inner world, the psychological, and an outer one, the physical. There

84

is, as James puts it, an '"evolution" of the psychical from the bosom of the physical, in which the esthetic, moral and otherwise emotional experiences would represent a halfway state.' (P. 19) So, while the details remained obscure, the general double-aspect framework was clear enough. Dualism of a sort was still being advocated.

John B. Watson, as even his strongest opponents would admit, never indulged in obfuscation, and it was his work which really put muscle behind the urge to do away with consciousness and dualism altogether. In his Behaviourist manifesto, 'Psychology as the Behaviorist views it', Watson wrote that 'the time seems to have come when psychology must discard all reference to consciousness.' (*Psychological Review*, Vol. 20, 1913, p. 163) He did not, at that time, deny that consciousness existed, he merely stated that scientific psychology, the 'science of behavior', need take no notice of it, indeed it could not as it was unsuited to scientific treatment. For consciousness had no part in the causal connections on which a scientific psychology could and should concentrate. But his disciples soon felt the need to do away with consciousness altogether, and Watson himself was later to endorse this view as well. In the year following Watson's manifesto, E. P. Frost, in his curious, royal *oratio obliqua*, exclaimed that, 'For him [Frost], the term "consciousness" with its psychic implicates, has long seemed to be a misnomer. Within his so-called "world of experience", he can find no psychic attachment.' (*Psychological Review*, Vol. 21, 1914, p. 208) But Frost's reductionist account, like most of those at this time, was barely sketched in. He suggested that what is commonly called 'consciousness' could be explained as a second-level physiological process, a beta-arc, which has as its stimulus-object an alpha-arc, which in turn is just a neural, physiological adjustment to some external stimulus-object. But he did not say much more than that.

By now this general approach to consciousness has become the orthodox view in psychology. Psychology is defined in the textbooks, more or less unanimously, as the science of behaviour, and this is usually accompanied by no mention at all of consciousness in the books. It is very rare for the term 'consciousness' to appear in the index of modern textbooks of psychology. The bogey has been successfully exorcised or, at least, ignored.

But, because consciousness was ignored as a topic in psychology rather than explained away or given a detailed reductionist account, it is and has for a long time been rare to find among psychologists any account at all of what non-psychologists still refer to as consciousness. I think it is fair to say that the classical source of solid and sustained argument for discarding the Cartesian concept of consciousness, and replacing it with a Behaviourist substitute, is to be found in the work of Ryle.

In Chapter VI of *The Concept of Mind* Ryle turns his attack upon the very heart of the Cartesian dogma of the ghost in the machine, namely, the belief that we have direct evidence for the existence of the ghost via self-consciousness and introspection. Just as we have direct evidence of the world about us via the perception of it through our senses, so we have direct evidence of the inner mental world of consciousness via introspection or inward perception. Further, via a sort of fluorescence given off by mental activities whenever they take place, we are conscious of these activities as they take place and without any need for direct attention to them. As Ryle puts it:

It is often held therefore (1) that a mind cannot help being constantly aware of all the supposed occupants of its private stage, and (2) that it can also deliberately scrutinise by a species of non-sensuous perception at least some of its own states and operations. Moreover both this constant awareness (generally called 'consciousness'), and this non-sensuous inner perception (generally called 'introspection') have been supposed to be exempt from error. A mind has a twofold Privileged Access to its own doings. (*CM*, p. 154)

And Ryle goes on to tell us that he proposes to show that 'the official theories of consciousness and introspection are logical muddles' and then to give his own de-mythologised account of self-knowledge which shows that 'the sorts of things that I can find out about myself are the same as the sorts of things that I can find out about other people, and the methods of finding them out are much the same.' (*CM*, p. 155)

Ryle's first attack is launched against the idea of self-consciousness as a sort of fluorescence given off in our internal theatre by mental activities and thereby noticed by us, such that it follows that we are necessarily aware of our own conscious states:

The things that a mind does or experiences are self-intimating, and this is supposed to be a feature which characterises these acts and feelings not just sometimes but always. . . . Or, to use another simile, mental processes are 'overheard' by the mind whose processes they are, somewhat as a speaker overhears the words he is himself uttering. (*CM*, pp. 158–9)

Ryle argues that this whole way of thinking about consciousness as the fluorescence given off by mental activities is 'a piece of para-optics'. '"Consciousness" was imported to play in the mental world the part played by light in the mechanical world. In this metaphorical sense, the contents of the mental world were thought of as being self-luminous or refulgent. . . .' (*CM*, p. 159) So, in being conscious of one's present mental states and activities, a person is said to know these mental states and activities, not in a dispositional sense, but in an occurrent sense. According to the official theory a person is 'actively cognisant' of his mental states. However, this activity is not a deliberate monitoring of these mental states by another second-level mental state, but is something akin to a light given off by mental states and activities, which light one cannot help but notice even though one's attention is not directly on it.

This then is the official doctrine of self-consciousness, and Ryle proceeds to argue that it is a logical muddle. First, to soften us up, he gives a 'persuasive argument' rather than a knock-down one. Ordinarily, people never report happenings to one another with the words 'a direct deliverance of consciousness' or saying that it was 'from immediate awareness'. (*CM* p. 161) Only philosophers, and Cartesian ones at that, ever propose that we have something called 'self-consciousness' which performs in such a way.

Secondly, says Ryle, the fluorescent account of how self-consciousness reveals to us what mental activities are taking place as they are taking place is not even adequate as an account. That mental activities provide us with 'light' to 'see' them by is not sufficient ground for saying that mental activities provide us with the grounds for being able to recognise these mental activities for what they are. To put it another way, one might own a private road along which travelled a variety of vehicles. Now if it was the case that, as dusk approached, lights along the roadside automatically turned themselves on and illuminated the vehicles, while this would mean that I could see the vehicles, it would not imply that I *would* see the vehicles or that I must be able to recognise what sort of vehicles they are, and *a fortiori* it would not imply that I could infallibly know what sort of vehicles they are.

Following on from this point, Ryle reminds us that, in fact, we often do make mistakes about our mental activities. People 'mistakenly suppose themselves to know things which are actually false; they deceive themselves about their own motives; they are surprised to notice the clock stopping ticking, without their having, as they think, been aware that it had been ticking.' (*CM*, p. 162) This being so, it follows that we do not have infallible knowledge of the nature of such states, and, secondly, since we are sometimes not even aware of such states, it cannot even be the case that we are constantly apprised of their presence.

Finally, says Ryle, the consciousness of a mental activity is different from the consciousness which is the mental activity. If I am working on a problem in geometry, my working will involve being conscious that this or that conclusion can be inferred from the premisses, and over and above this consciousness there will be the consciousness that I am working on a problem in geometry. But this implies that there are two sorts of awareness or consciousness going on, the awareness of the connection between premisses and conclusion, and the awareness of this awareness. But if the first level of awareness breeds a second layer of awareness, does the second layer in turn breed a third layer? If it does, then 'there would have to be an infinite number of onion-skins of consciousness embedding any mental state', if not, it would mean that there are some layers of consciousness that are mental processes of which we are not conscious, and 'then "consciousness" could no longer be retained as part of the definition of "mental".' (*CM*, p. 163)

To put this another way, if this fluorescent and so automatically noticed aspect, or self-illuminating aspect, of mental processes is itself a mental process, then it should be fluorescent and self-illuminating as well, and so on *ad infinitum*. If not, it is a mental process of which we are not aware, which is a contradiction.

Ryle believed that, with this series of arguments, the view that we are invariably conscious of our mental states has been shown to be muddled. So he now turned his attack on to the notion of introspection. This, he says, is said by the official doctrine to be a non-sensual process of attending to and introspecting our inner mental states and activities, and, unlike our perception of the outer world, it is immune from anything equivalent to optical illusions. Introspection differs from self-consciousness or the automatic deliverances of mental activities into consciousness in that it is an operation which does not go on automatically or all the time. It is something we have to attend to and engage in.

Ryle's first argument against this official picture of the nature of introspection is that this account of introspection entails that we must be able to divide our attention. Namely, we must be able to attend, say, to a geometrical problem and then deliberately, at the exact same time, attend to this attending. But, allowing that such problematic splittings of one's attention are possible, such a thesis implies either that the number of the splittings of one's attention at any one time is either finite or it is infinite. If it is finite, then it must be the case that, when the maximum number is achieved, if we then introspect this maximum bundle, this introspection itself cannot be introspected for this would split our attention beyond the maximum possible. This means that there are some mental acts which are themselves unintrospectible, which seems to be contrary to the official doctrine. On the other hand, if the number of splittings possible is infinite, it is hard to conceive how any mere mortal could attend to an infinite number of acts at the same time, or over a period of time.

A second argument to the effect that the official doctrine of introspection is muddled is that it is notorious that no two reports based on introspection ever seem to agree. Further, it seems odd that while possessed of this marvellous inward-looking telescope, which is immune from illusions or errors of focus, we still argue about its findings. If introspection was just like inspection, then the existence of such putatively inner activities as volitions would be as unproblematic as the existence of tomatoes or 'a smell of onions in the larder'.

Finally, there is Hume's objection to introspection, namely, that some states of mind are such that, when we are involved in them, they seem so to take up all of our attention, and so to arouse us, that we cannot concentrate so as to reflect on or introspect such states. For example, Ryle claims, such turbulent states of mind as pain and fury, and such engrossing ones as amusement and puzzlement, can only be examined in retrospect. Indeed, this observation becomes the bridge to Ryle's own positive reductionist account of consciousness. This important concept, retrospection, is, he says, the key to the solution or, rather, dissolution, of this myth of introspection and self-consciousness.

States of mind such as these more or less violent agitations can be examined only in retrospect. Yet nothing disastrous follows from this restriction. We are not shorter of information about panic or amusement than about other states of mind. If retrospection can give us the data we need for our knowledge of some states of mind, there is no reason why it should not do so for all. And this is just what seems to be suggested by the popular phrase 'to catch oneself doing so and so'. We catch, as we pursue and overtake, what is already running away from us. (*CM*, p. 166)

Thus, wielding Occam's Razor with verve, Ryle asks why— if it is the case that whatever information we do have about our own so-called mental states is explainable in terms of the unmysterious operation of retrospection or looking back at—we need to posit the existence of such mysterious processes as introspection and self-consciousness?

Retrospection is simply the process of recalling our own public or silent behaviour and talking dispositionally about it, that is, finding patterns in it. It is more or less the same process as discerning such patterns in the behaviour of others.

I learn that a certain pupil of mine is lazy, ambitious and witty by following his work, noticing his excuses, listening to his conversation and comparing his performances with those of others. Nor does it make any important difference if I happen myself to be that pupil. I can indeed then listen to more of his conversations, as I am the addressee of his unspoken soliloquies; I notice more of his excuses, as I am never absent, when they are made. (*CM*, p. 169)

In other words, discovering that you are lazy or ambitious or witty is just a matter of seeing a certain pattern in your own public behaviour emerge over a period of time. To say someone is, say, ambitious, is just to impute to that person a disposition to behave in a certain patterned way in suitable circumstances because one has observed him or her behaving in this patterned way in the past. Discovering that I myself am lazy or ambitious or witty is to do the same in regard to my own behaviour. The only advantages in the latter case are that I also have access to my covert behaviour, my sub-vocal talk, my imagining, and so on, and that I am constantly in my own presence. These advantages could be said to be counterbalanced by the fact that we miss out on the view of our facial expressions and gestures (at least most of the time) and have a tendency to be biased in our own favour when we come to sum up the behaviour in question in order to impute to it some pattern or other. I may believe that my behaviour shows a becoming frankness while others may see in it the unmistakable signs of coarseness.

So it must be said that we learn about our hopes, yearnings, wants and ideas in much the same way as we learn about the hopes, yearnings, wants and ideas of others. We inspect their behaviour intermittently and objectively, we retrospect our own constantly but less objectively. All we need to refer to is behaviour, and ordinary observation is the means to do it. We have no need either to invent mysterious processes such as introspection or self-consciousness, or to invent mental entities and activities to be discovered by them in their own special inner field of activity.

A *prima facie* objection to the Rylean account might

take the form of saying that this dispositional account seems to cover our knowledge of our own personality traits, characteristics and motives well enough, but it could hardly fit, say, our knowledge of our own present thoughts, for this looks very much like an occurrence not a proneness to do something.

Ryle's reply is to say that knowledge of my own thoughts is not intrinsically different from knowledge of your thoughts expressed in words. The test of whether I followed your argument is whether I am able to paraphrase it, discuss it critically and so on. The test of whether I can recall my own reasoning is the same. To claim knowledge of my present thoughts is nothing other than to make a claim to be able to run back over my imaginings or sub-vocal reasonings, or to comment on them if required. So knowledge of my own present thoughts is just a case of retrospecting, not retrospecting in order to discover and attribute some pattern or disposition to myself, but just retrospecting. It is retrospecting over a short period.

But it is time to look more critically at Ryle's arguments. His first 'persuasive' argument against the Cartesian doctrine of self-consciousness, namely, that only phil-osophers and not ordinary people use phrases like 'the direct deliverances of consciousness', is neither here nor there. The Cartesian philosopher can easily reply that his theory of consciousness, which entails self-consciousness, is a technical theory and so one could not expect its technical phraseology to be used by ordinary people. On the other hand, it would be disturbing for the Cartesian theorist if ordinary people had no *equivalent* phrases, for this would incline one to the view that they did not advert to their own mental acts in the way that the Cartesian doctrine says that they could and, at times, must do. But, the Cartesian could reply, ordinary people do say such things as 'I felt so and so' and 'I'm thinking of such and such' or 'I'm imagining a castle', all of which could be taken as at least compatible with a belief that one is conscious of mental states, at least at times.

Let us now examine Ryle's assertion that the Cartesian account of self-consciousness amounts to a claim that mental activities give off a fluorescence or refulgence but that this alone is not grounds for the Cartesian claim that we cannot fail to notice our mental activities, for 'x is fluorescing' does not imply that 'x is noticed' but only that it is noticeable. *A fortiori*, Ryle continued, if the fluorescence account of mental acts does not imply that they are invariably noticed, it cannot imply that they are infallibly noticed or, even if infallibly noticed, then infallibly recognised for what they are.

There may have been, or still are, doctrinaire Cartesians who hold that we are *always in fact* aware of our mental activities, and infallibly so, and infallibly aware of their true nature, but it is certainly the case that a Cartesian need not hold such immoderate views. A moderate Cartesian could maintain that, in principle, though not necessarily in practice, mental events are noticeable, meaning that we can be conscious of them, at least at times, and yet hold that not only are we not conscious of them some times but that, even when we are, we can be mistaken about them. A Cartesian could quite easily hold, without contradiction, that we can in principle be aware of most mental states—and this is what he means when he speaks of consciousness as a mark of the mental—but be mistaken about them from time to time in at least two different ways. We can notice them but generate false beliefs about them, and we can notice them, and generate true beliefs about them, but make errors when reporting on them.

This moderate Cartesian will also be untroubled by Ryle's regress argument whereby it was suggested that if a mental event fluoresces and is automatically noticed then this noticing must itself be a second-order mental event which in turn must automatically ensure that it is noticed, and so on. For the moderate Cartesian, as we have seen, denies that mental events are automatically, that is, invariably noticed.

This in turn leads to more fundamental worries about Ryle's account of the Cartesian position. Firstly, there is Ryle's tendency at one time to imply that the fluorescence given off by the mental event is consciousness, at another time that noticing the fluorescence is consciousness, and at still other times that consciousness is the combination of the two, that is, consciousness is the process by which the fluorescence given off by mental events is invariably noticed because of the very qualities of this *sui generis* fluorescence. Yet Ryle's arguments presuppose that this latter position is the one, true Cartesian position. I, on the other hand, have suggested that a moderate Cartesian could hold that the link between the fluorescing and the noticing is not instantaneous, automatic or invariable.

But there is a deeper worry about Ryle's account of the Cartesian position. I can imagine another sort of Cartesian quite plausibly claiming that this whole way of depicting the Cartesian view—as consisting of two levels, the fluorescing and the noticing—is mistaken. This sort of Cartesian might claim that there is only one level and that the true analogy is not that of seeing things bathed in self-fluorescing light but of something, like a radio, being turned on or off. Consciousness is turned-on-ness. It is a phenomenal life-stream. The events, the only events, in this stream are conscious or phenomenal ones, such as pains, seeings, noticings, and wonderings. They only exist as conscious moments; they cannot then exist subconsciously waiting to be noticed. We might also subject these phenomenal moments to second-order scrutiny but that is another matter; that would not be the essence of consciousness but merely a reflex, monitoring look at it. Further, such a Cartesian could hold also that there were other inner events which are not part of this stream of consciousness. Now, if this picture of Cartesian consciousness is accepted, Ryle's counter-arguments by and large evaporate, because they all hang on pointing out the implausibility of invariably noticing first-level fluorescing.

As regards Ryle's arguments against introspection, they also are not as devastating to the Cartesian position as he believes. Ryle argues that the Cartesian account of introspection must be wrong because, while entailing that every mental event is introspectible, it also entails that a person's mental capacity to introspect is either finite or infinite, yet either answer is untenable. If finite, then the Cartesian must admit that beyond the limit or finish of his introspective powers there are non-introspectible mental happenings. If infinite, the Cartesian is forced to hold that humans have at least one infinite capacity.

To this argument a Cartesian could reply quite simply that his position is not that there are no particular mental events which cannot be introspected but that no type of conscious state as such is immune from introspection. Of course a Cartesian must admit that a human's mental capacities are finite and that therefore a human's capacity to introspect, or direct his attention inwards, is confined to a finite number of such events on any one occasion. After all, a Cartesian should admit that we can attend only to a very limited number of external happenings or events, and that much escapes our externally-directed attention. Why then should it disturb a Cartesian to concede also that, just as our external attention is limited and fallible, so is our internal one, that is, our introspection? Likewise, the Cartesian ought, quite simply, to grant Hume his point about certain states, such as panic, making introspection impossible.

Ryle's arguments against the Cartesian model of consciousness and introspection would not force a Cartesian to abandon his model though they would force him to hold a very undoctrinaire version of it. To get round Ryle's objections, a Cartesian would have to give up the claims—though it may be that few, if any, Cartesians ever held them—that consciousness is a type of automatic noticing of inner events of a certain sort, that we are aware of all mental states, that all mental states are, in any circumstances, open to introspection, and in consequence that we have infallible knowledge of all our mental states. The Cartesian must retreat to the view that only some inner states are conscious, that only in certain circumstances are some inner states open to introspection or inwardly directed attention, and that, even when they are, we can be mistaken about them. To be able to make this retreat does not mean that the Cartesian model is saved. It is merely safe for another day. As will become clearer later on, perhaps the strongest grounds for abandoning the Cartesian model are the positive attractions of rival models, and of these attractions the most alluring may be the confluence between some of these models and new facts about our brains.

These remarks about alternative models lead us naturally to a consideration of Ryle's own alternative analysis of consciousness, whereby he reinterprets all cases of self-consciousness or introspection as retrospection. This account is enticing. It clearly copes well enough with dispositional states. To realise one is vain may well be a process of retrospecting, or more precisely of recalling and analysing one's own behaviour in order to conclude that one is prone to boasting whenever possible. But such an account seems to get into grave difficulties when confronted with what even Ryle is hard put to deny are occurrent happenings. For example, whatever is occurring immediately after one says 'I am now going to think of the concept of justice', would it not be the case that if one adverts to this occurrence, then one must be adverting directly to some internal occurrence rather than retrospecting some external behaviour? For it may be that no external behaviour is being performed by the person thinking. Ryle might suggest that what the person thinking is adverting to is his or her imaginings or, more likely, he or she is recalling sub-vocal reasonings. Imaginings do not seem to fit the case of thinking of a concept like justice, for such a concept does not seem to have any imaginable qualities (besides, as we shall see, Ryle is going to say that imagining is really a mode of thinking). So what of the other alternative, sub-vocal reasoning?

What is sub-vocal reasoning if not mental reasoning, one might ask? One might be able to make some sense of this notion, without referring to anything mental, by recalling the fact that, at least in some American hospitals, patients who have had throat operations are forbidden to read because reading—even under one's breath or in one's head—can entail the use of certain throat muscles. But it is not plausible to claim that what is going on, when one is retrospecting one's present thoughts, is retrospecting certain movements of the throat muscles. For it happens to be a fact that we are *not* aware of such movements. It needs a trained physiologist to discover them.

Ryle might reply, correctly, that we do not need to advert to these muscular movements to be able to report on them. Thinking might be nothing more than these movements (which we are unaware of as movements) which we can report because we are hooked up in a neurophysiological way which causes us so to report.

But such an account would be getting a long way from the claim that knowledge about our own thoughts is nothing more than retrospecting our own behaviour. For retrospecting, like 'specting' or ordinary looking, is a process the subject controls and directs to a great extent. But being hooked up to report automatically on inner muscular throat movements is not. Besides, if gaining knowledge of our own thoughts was not an operation that we can control, but an automatic print-out via a landline to these muscular movements, then we should expect the print-out to be infallible if the hookup is neurophysiologically healthy. But knowledge of our thoughts, as Ryle himself informed us, is not infallible. Self-deception does occur, so do plain errors.

Ryle realised that an anti-Cartesian was in difficulties if he granted that thinking was occurrent. For the plausible possibilities open to the anti-Cartesian seem to be to reduce thinking to a brain state or to some subtle muscular activity, neither of which we can easily inspect and report on, and neither of which bear any ready connection to the content of our reports on our thoughts. Besides, there are empirical data which suggest that there is definitely not a one to one correlation between the favourite Behaviourist muscular substitute for Cartesian thoughts, namely, muscular movements in the throat, and silent reading or thinking in one's head. In his later theories of thinking, Ryle gradually adopted the view that thinking is not an occurrence in the sense of a happening at all but a modality of some real happening. But this account has its own difficulties which I will go into in a later chapter.

There has been a recent interesting revival of Ryle's retrospecting account of consciousness. Daniel Dennett, in his paper 'Toward a Cognitive Theory of Consciousness' (in his collection, *Brainstorms*), suggests that 'at least to a first approximation—that of which we are conscious is that of which we can tell, introspectively or retrospectively.' (P. 152) Dennett is not being inconsistent in giving an anti-Cartesian account of consciousness in terms of introspection, for he explains introspection in terms of short-term or buffer memory—plus a hankering to explain this access in terms of 'perceiving' these mental processes with our 'inner eye'. But, for Dennett, consciousness is not just retrospecting for, since what is retrospected are inner happenings, such an account could still be given a Cartesian interpretation. The kernel of his account is that 'that of which we are conscious is that of which we can *tell*.' Consciousness—and Dennett has a predilection for computer terminology—is not just having retrospective access to the data of inner processes, it is utilising that access. It is primarily the print-out of these results in utterance, gesture or some other form. Conscious experiences are the input of sensory data or the results of inner computations which *both* reach our buffer memory *and* are of the right sort and last long enough to be published. Subconscious experiences are just those which, for one reason or another, fail to get published.

It is an ingenious account, but I fear it does not keep pace with our more strongly held convictions about consciousness. Such an account should match all the cases which intuitively we hold are definite cases of consciousness because it purports to be a true explanation of what is going on in all the cases which naïvely we explain in terms of Cartesian consciousness. The central cases which such an account does not fit are clearly those where we would claim that an organism is conscious yet *cannot publish* the content of its conscious experiences, for Dennett must hold that where there is no publication there is no consciousness. His account is a functionalist one. Something qualifies as conscious only if it performs or is capable of performing the function of publishing or printing out inner data in propositional form.

Dennett is aware of the sort of counter-examples that spring to mind, or at least of some of them. For he does consider whether animals can be said to be conscious, though his consideration seems to amount merely to dismissing as implausible the suggestion that they are

conscious, while disarmingly denying that he has thereby
cast himself in the role of the Village Verificationist.

Nonhuman, nonverbal creatures have no print-out faculties, or at best
very rudimentary and unexpressive print-out faculties, yet some philosophers—notably Nagel—insist that full-blown, phenomenological
consciousness is as much their blessing as ours. I think one can be
skeptical of this claim without thereby becoming the Village Verificationist, but the issue deserves an unhurried treatment of its own.
(*Ibid.* p. 152)

Dennett has yet to provide that unhurried treatment. But
let us for the sake of argument allow Dennett his promis-
sory note. There are, nonetheless, a number of large
obstacles still remaining. For example, what about children
before they can talk? What about deaf and dumb people
who have been unable to learn or understand any language
because of their disabilities? What about people who are
paralysed and unable to speak or write or signal in any way
whatsoever? On Dennett's view, since they cannot publish
the input of their senses or other data from their inner life,
they must be said to lack consciousness. Yet to come to
that conclusion seems to show that his account of consciousness cannot cope with many of the obvious cases of
consciousness. To employ a Rylean move, to come to that
conclusion seems to be a *reductio ad absurdum* of the
theory.

However, I am inclined to think that, with some tinker-
ing in the light of some recent work in physiology, the
Ryle-Dennett view can be made more plausible. The work
I have in mind is the split-brain experiments first performed by Myers and Sperry at the University of Chicago
in the early nineteen fifties, then later by Gazzaniga and
Sperry at the California Institute of Technology in the late
nineteen fifties and nineteen sixties. Michael Gazzaniga
describes these first experiments of Myers and Sperry in
his article 'The split brain in man':

The brain of the higher animals, including man, is a double organ,
consisting of right and left hemispheres connected by an isthmus of
nerve tissue called the corpus callosum. . . . When this connection
between the two halves of the cerebrum was cut, each hemisphere
functioned independently as if it were a complete brain. The phenomenon was first investigated in a cat in which not only the brain but
also the optic chiasm, the crossover of the optic nerves, was divided, so

that visual information from the left eye was dispatched only to the left brain and information from the right eye only to the right brain. Working on a problem with one eye, the animal could respond normally and learn to perform a task; when that eye was covered and the same problem was presented to the other eye, the animal evinced no recognition of the problem, and had to learn it again from the beginning with the other half of the brain. (*Scientific American*, Vol. 217, 1967, p. 24)

Now when this experiment (minus the severing of the optic chiasm) was repeated by Sperry and Gazzaniga on humans the results were extremely interesting, not least as regards their implications about the nature of consciousness, or so I will suggest. In fact, it was not a case of just transferring these experiments to humans. The operation of cutting the cerebral commissures of the human brain arose in connection with seeking a cure for epilepsy, and, as Gazzaniga reports, such operations proved to be remarkably successful.

Now to understand the other findings, and their implications, from these experiments on humans, it should be remembered that the left side of the body is controlled by the right hemisphere of the brain and the right side of the body by the left hemisphere, but a unity of operation and experience is maintained by means of the commissural tracts, especially the corpus callosum. Input into one hemisphere is often communicated to the other hemisphere; in cats, for example, the sharing is almost universal. But one result of these experiments was that it is quite definite that, in humans, one hemisphere, the left, is dominant. While most of the basic perceptual information received by the right hemisphere is communicated to the left hemisphere, and vice versa, the left seems to have to itself higher level operations and activities, such as reasoning, discrimination, evaluation, and control, and the higher level data from these operations and activities are not communicated to the more lowly right hemisphere, though there is some reason to believe that if the left hemisphere were severely damaged, the right one could take over some of its functions. But most remarkably, the left hemisphere receives and controls everything, or almost everything, connected with speech and, presumably, other operations involving symbols, codes or calculi. The right hemisphere is not in all respects inferior to the left. It has a few specialised functions of its own; for example, it is superior at non-verbal visual discrimination. But, on the whole, it is the left hemisphere which engages in higher operations and activities, especially ones involving language and other forms of communication. Thus J. C. Eccles gives us the general picture that results from these experiments in the following terms:

The most remarkable findings stem from the almost invariable uni-lateral representation of language in the dominant cortical hemisphere, which is the left in all these cases. For example, they are unable to read with the left half of the visual field, which feeds exclusively into the right hemisphere (the minor hemisphere), and commands conveyed verbally are carried out with the right side only. They react to stimuli applied to the left visual field, sometimes appropriately, but without being able to give an account of what they are doing. Similarly, they have no detailed knowledge of touch or movements on the left side, and if blindfolded they do not know what the left side is doing. Evidently, the dominant hemisphere of the brain neither 'knows' nor 'remembers' the experiences and activities of the other hemisphere. . . .

All the evidence produced by the nine cases is explicable by the postulate that, when bereft of commissural linkages with the dominant hemisphere, the minor hemisphere behaves as a computer with inbuilt skills of movement, with recognition of the form and function of objects, and with the ability to learn; nevertheless, the dominant hemisphere with its ability of linguistic expression remains oblivious of all this performance. . . . We can summarize this by stating that the goings-on in the minor hemisphere, which we may refer to as the computer, never come into the conscious experience of the subject. (*Facing Reality: Philosophical Adventures by a Brain Scientist*, Longman, 1970, pp. 76–8)

I should mention that Eccles' account includes a certain amount of interpretation of his own. Gazzaniga, for example, maintained that one result of these experiments was that 'separation of the hemisphere creates two in-dependent spheres of consciousness within a single cranium, that is to say, within a single organism.' (*Op. cit.* p. 29) Gazzaniga presumes, apparently, that whenever we have a hemisphere registering perceptual input and organising, even if only in a fairly rudimentary way, some sort of reaction to that input, there we have consciousness.

I side with Eccles in maintaining that when the hemispheres are split, consciousness goes with the left hemisphere, for I am going to propose for consideration that certain findings from these experiments suggest that consciousness is tied to the ability to report on input and on one's reactions to such input.

In the first place, Gazzaniga himself reports that, when subjects were asked what they saw when flashing lights were presented to their left visual field only, they replied that they had seen nothing, even though the data was registering in the inferior right hemisphere of the brain. They again claimed to have seen nothing even though, when asked, they were able correctly to point with their left hand at the lights whenever they were switched on. The important point is that they did not just report that something had happened and then add that they did not know what it was. They were not even aware that anything had happened. Awareness, consciousness, seems to go hand in hand with the ability to give a verbal report, or some sort of report on input.

There are other experiments which also lend some support to this account.

New experiments, in the United States, England and France, show that such people [with scotoma or a blind patch in their visual field owing to brain damage] can actually see without knowing it. The patients in question have indubitable injuries of the visual cortex; they never see a flashing light inside the resulting scotoma; in fact they deny seeing anything there at all. Yet if such a light is briefly flashed and they are asked to *guess* where it is by *pointing* to it, they do so with remarkable skill. They can even guess reliably whether a line flashed within the scotoma is horizontal or vertical, even though they claim that they see no line at all, and find the whole exercise rather foolish. . . .

The phenomenon of 'blindsight', as it has been called, establishes that the cortex is the home of *conscious* perception, but some kind of sensory function can continue without it.

Then why, one might ask, have the cerebral cortex at all? What is it that the intact brain does that the man with 'blindsight' cannot do? It constructs a *description* of outside reality, a *model* in which it has confidence and sufficient faith to speak. (Colin Blakemore, *Mechanics of the Mind*, Cambridge University Press, 1977, p. 65)

That is, to see consciously the visual input must be put in an acceptable form. It must be encoded in the right way, and this encoding seems to amount to a form in which the input could be reported and described.

These experiments certainly do not prove that consciousness is just the ability to give a verbal report or input or even that it must be coupled with that ability. For, in the split-brain experiments it could be that the right hemisphere is conscious but, having no access to the speech areas, its consciousness cannot form part of any verbal reports. To put this another way, the right hemisphere might not be an automaton but a conscious unit which happens to be unable to communicate either that it is so or of what it is conscious, unless it is hooked up to the left hemisphere. This would be so even if one could anaesthetise or freeze the functions of the left hemisphere, rather than cut through the corpus callosum, then let the anaesthetic wear off and see what happens. If, after the anaesthetic had worn off, it turned out that the person was still unaware of any input to the right hemisphere during the period when the left had been anaesthetised, then this might only mean that, while the right hemisphere had been conscious during that period, its conscious episodes could not be stored in the speech memory in the left hemisphere and so these episodes were 'lost' as data for the left hemisphere's speech centre when the anaesthetic wore off.

In the scotoma cases, those of a Cartesian persuasion could say that here we have merely a case either of subconscious mental goings-on or else just brain functions with no mental correlate.

But both sets of experiments do lend some support to the view that at least some claims about conscious episodes may amount to nothing other than a claim to be able to produce reports about input, for while these experiments do not rule out the Cartesian model, they do not falsify the ability-to-report model as they might have done. It could have turned out that split-brain humans did claim to be conscious of input to their right hemispheres without being able to say anything about it. But they did not even claim to be conscious.

However, now it is time to test and refine, or discard, this hypothesis by looking again at the very obvious but fundamental objections that I posed to Dennett's account, namely, would it not follow, from reducing consciousness to the ability to report on visual and other input, that those who are unable to speak, write or signal in any way whatsoever must be said to have no consciousness? And would it not follow from such a view, therefore, that paraplegics, children, deaf and dumb people who have yet to learn any language, and animals, are all to be denied consciousness? William James, for example, in *The Principles of Psychology*, relates the reminiscences of a Mr Ballard who was born a deaf-mute:

I have a vivid recollection of the delight I felt in watching the different scenes we passed through, observing the various phases of nature, both animate and inanimate; though we did not, owing to my infirmity, engage in conversation. It was during those delightful rides, some two or three years before my initiation into the rudiments of written language, that I began to ask myself the question: *How came the world into being?* When this question occurred to my mind, I set myself to thinking it over a long time. My curiosity was awakened as to what was the origin of human life in its first appearance upon the earth, and of vegetable life as well, and also the cause of the existence of the earth, sun, moon, and stars. (*The Principles of Psychology*, Macmillan, 1890, Vol. 1, Ch. IX, 'The Stream of Thought', p. 267)

So clearly here we have a case of a child, before he could speak, being not merely aware of his surroundings but also consciously posing for himself metaphysical questions of the order 'How came the world into being?' Surely, it might be objected, the view of consciousness I have suggested would have to claim that the pre-language Mr Ballard had no consciousness.

I think that such an objection can be answered by holders of the view under discussion. It can accommodate cases where a person is conscious but unable, even in principle, to put the contents of consciousness into language. For I think that a clue to a solution in terms of this account can be gained from those same reminiscences of Mr Ballard. On the previous page of those reminiscences, as transmitted by James, Ballard admitted that, while he had no language, 'I could convey my thoughts and feelings to my parents and brothers by natural signs or pantomime.' In other words, Ballard had begun to encode in some way his perceptual data, and to engage in higher order shuffling and ordering and categorising of that data, such that it could be put in propositional form. Even if Ballard were then unable to signal or mime his thoughts to others, on the view of consciousness under consideration, Ballard would be conscious in so far as his sensory input or higher order activities upon that input could be put in such a form as to be stored in memory, either long or short term. So in a modified version of the Dennett view, a person is conscious whenever there is sensory input and higher order processing of that input, encoding it in a form which, in principle, can be reported if and when that person acquires a suitable language, code or other vehicle for reporting it.

This formula for consciousness saves our intuitions about children, deaf-mutes, paraplegics, and animals. In so far as all these receive input and engage in activity upon it, *and* can store it in such a form as that it could be reported, then at such times they can be said to be conscious. In principle, even the earliest of a child's experiences could be dredged back from memory, say, under hypnosis or analysis or by chance, in later life if and when speech or some other vehicle for reporting it is formed. So we must grant consciousness even to the earliest of childhood experiences. Whether the child was deaf and dumb or not is irrelevant. Similarly, with animals. In so far as, in principle, their experiences—their sensory input and what is then done to it and with it in their brain—are encoded in some form of memory in a reportable form, then they are conscious. In the evolutionary higher animals, reporting will be in some form of language, in lower ones it might only be in terms of expression or behaviour. Animals can and do signal and even mime to one another. In the mating season, a male toad seeks females to mate with in the following way: he simply jumps on top of the nearest toad in sight; if it croaks, it is male—for females have no call—and so he realises he must try again.

To put all this as plainly as I can, this account of consciousness, which I have traced from Ryle but have modified extensively, amounts, not to any form of occurrent introspecting or noticing of some internal fluorescence, nor even to retrospection of any behaviour, but to reportable cerebral activities.

Though this account may coincide with the *attribution* of our ordinary language term 'consciousness', it clearly gives a very different *meaning* to the term. The account I have given clashes with our intuitions about the nature of consciousness. It is not a description of the logical geography of our term 'consciousness' but a rational reconstruction of its meaning. For example, when we see someone engaging in silent reading, or doing mental arithmetic, we do not think of him or her as silent microchips encoding and shuffling data in such a way that, in principle, it could be reported at some time. We think of the person as actively attending and actively aware. In short, you might grumble, this account misses out on the phenomenal nature of consciousness. This account, you will point out, is also partly dispositional, for it makes something to be conscious now in so far as what is going on now lays down a dispositional base which may be activated in suitable circumstances in the future. The ordinary language or traditional account makes consciousness wholly occurrent; that is, I am deemed conscious when I am doing mental arithmetic, say, solely because of the phenomenal accompaniment, which is a wholly occurrent accompaniment, to my occurrent cerebrations. In the traditional account everything that is packed into the notion of consciousness is happening now.

The tempting short reply to this sort of grumble is that the traditional account, and its accompanying hold on our intuitions, are illusory. There is no inner theatre where we talk to ourselves and listen to ourselves. We only believe there is. But I admit that this would be dogmatism. Some account of the dogged nature of our intuitions must be given by an account which claims that they are illusory. One suggestion is that, in such cases as silent reading, and mental arithmetic, our memory is such that it can deliver immediately, not only a propositional report of some conclusion but a highly complex report of the stages, or at least some of them—there are presumably stages which are never encoded in memorable form—by which that conclusion was arrived at. More importantly, such work-in-progress reports can be given at literally a moment's notice. If interrupted, the silent reader, for example, can probably tell you about the last few sentences. It may be that it is our knowledge of this remarkable ability, and its being underlined by frequent display in ourselves and others, which leads us to be convinced that we are apprised of the goings-on *as* they are going on, and so that the goings-on have a sort of refulgence which shines in our mind's eye and forces its attentions on us, or else that they are items in a stream of consciousness. This, coupled with the fact that the time-span from cerebral event to report, in some cases, can be more or less instantaneous, may be the source of our intuitions about the nature of consciousness.

But even this would not do. For there are intuitively conscious moments which cannot be explained away as instantaneous reporting. Indeed, the strongest case for a Cartesian account of consciousness is such seemingly undeniable phenomenal moments as feeling pain. The normal expression of feelings is not propositional talk but physiological reactions and non-verbal cries. Of course a Ryle-Dennett type of account may be able to make out a convincing case that the physiological reactions and non-verbal cries associated with pain are body-language or non-verbal signals, and are thus still reports of a sort. But even if such an account were made plausible, it would still miss the point of the present objection, namely, that all this would be in addition to the actual phenomenal moment of feeling pain. It is the awfulness of the pain itself, the actual rebarbative sensation which results from a jangling of certain nerve endings that is the Cartesian candidate for consciousness. It does not seem convincing to claim that there are only the physiological reactions and cries verbal or non-verbal. That is, it has never seemed to be a very convincing philosophical ploy to reduce pain to pain behaviour, for this seems to give us no grounds for the fact that we invariably think of pain as awful and wish that it were removed. Why would we continually report verbally or signal non-verbally that we were undergoing phenomenal episodes, which we found unbearable or at least awful, if there were no such episodes? It seems incredible that we could erroneously or would deliberately have invented a model of ourselves in which we pictured ourselves as undergoing feelings—phenomenal moments of consciousness of our bodies—when in fact we never do undergo them. Why should we invent or deceive ourselves or be deceived into inventing such a model? Why would such a picture or model be preferable to the 'true' model in which we do not feel pain but, when our nerve endings are disturbed in certain ways, we behave, act and report as if we did? In short, there seems to be an insuperable difficulty for an account which claims that all cases of alleged Cartesian consciousness can be explained as reportable cerebral activities. This difficulty is the seemingly incontrovertible fact of feelings, such as those of pain, which are mere conscious moments.

Bernard Williams has voiced a doubt that consciousness, such as in moments of pain, is an incontrovertible fact, indeed that it is a fact properly so called.

It may seem a platitude that the contents of consciousness can be conceived only from the point of view of that consciousness, but if it is, it is not one that we think through consistently in trying to conceive what is in the world when there are conscious states. Rather, we are subject to an illusion on that score, an illusion generated by our capacity for reflexive consciousness of our own conscious states, and our ability to project ourselves imaginatively into another's point of view— capacities which are necessary to our raising any of these problems at all, and also essentially connected with each other.

The illusion involved here harmonizes with a mistaken model of self-knowledge. It is widely agreed that the privacy of pains (for instance) is necessary. . . . Yet there remains something incurably mysterious about this privacy so long as an objective, third personal, conception of the content of mental states is thought possible, since that conception must be of an object or state which is 'there', but somehow can announce itself only to the subject. (*Descartes: The Project of Pure Enquiry*, Penguin, 1978, pp. 295–6)

But Williams offers us no solution to the mystery, other than to suggest that, while we may be forced to admit that some version of physicalism is true, as yet we have no account which is rich enough to explain away this mystery.

While this mystery or paradox, of facts which are apparently there but private to a particular subject, persists, Cartesianism of a sort will still have a strong toe-hold, even though we might feel in our bones that the Cartesian model is a 'con' of some sort.

All I can make at this point is a very tentative suggestion which I own I cannot develop very satisfactorily. It is well known that our perceptions are more akin to hypotheses or models than to direct grasps of facts. For example, we concoct the notion of a solid macroscopic object from incoming data from subatomic happenings. Might it not be the case that we also concoct a model of the self from incoming data from microscopic events in our brain and other parts of the body? This model, like any model or map, might be useful, but yet not correspond to the brute facts. Indeed, it might be that the model each of us makes of our own self is much farther away from the brute facts than the model which we have of the external world. Our self-model is private to ourselves, unless we reveal it, because only *our* brains are hooked up to the facts from which it is built, and because it is mainly for our own use. Without it, it might be the case that we would not be a unified higher organism but disintegrate into a lower one. Our model of the external world, on the other hand, is more transactional. We share it with others and use it when we are dealing with or likely to interact with others.

Now it could be the case that, over the centuries, or, more likely, millenia, we have built up a model of our self which depicts it as having phenomenal moments, such as of pain or pleasure. They may not exist as brute facts but it may be very useful to believe, very strongly and indeed more or less immovably, that they do. It may be easier to concoct a model which can be useful for guiding and, in general, looking after ourselves if this model depicts us as having an inner private life of feelings, intentions, hopes, yearnings, thoughts, and so on. It may be that calculations and computations, which are to be used in guiding action, are simpler and more immediate if made with a Cartesian model 'in mind'. But all this is highly speculative and philosophically loose, and I do not know how, if at all, it could be tightened up.

In this chapter I have ranged much farther from Ryle's original account than I have in others, mainly because I believe, as did Ryle, that consciousness is the final sticking point of Cartesianism. If the Cartesian model is to be deposed, a convincing alternative account of consciousness will have to be given. I have also spent more time on this topic because it seems to me that, while Ryle's account may not have taken us very far, it was in the right direction. I suspect that his work on this topic will emerge as among his most stimulating and important work.

Chapter 8
SENSATION AND PERCEPTION

Ryle tells us that another major pylon that props up the official doctrine of the ghost in the machine is the belief that our sensations clearly occur within our epidermis yet equally clearly they would not be revealed by even the subtlest probings of the surgeon's knife. The possessor of sensations alone has access to them. 'Only the wearer knows where the shoe pinches.' Thus we are forced to posit the ghostly arena of mind as the place wherein we should locate sensations. Moreover, since sensations are things of which the owner must be conscious, then sensations reaffirm our belief that there is a stream of consciousness, private to the possessor of it.

But before presenting the details of the official doctrine about sensations, Ryle tells us in Chapter VII of *The Concept of Mind* that we must remember that the official doctrine uses the term 'sensation' in a very different way from the ordinary, unsophisticated use of the term. The ordinary use of the term 'sensations' is more or less coextensive with 'tactual and kinaesthetic perceptions and perceptions of temperatures, as well as for localised pains and discomforts'. (*CM*, p. 200) In short, 'sensation' is ordinarily used as roughly synonymous with 'feeling', as for example in references to feeling hot or cold, or feeling an itch. Now the sophisticated official-doctrine use of the term 'sensation' is very different. For a start it is a much wider term than the ordinary one, being associated not just with feeling-perceptions but with all types of perceptions, whether they be via the sense organs or other sensitive parts of the body. Thus, on the official doctrine, seeing a tomato involves the sensation of a red patch, and hearing Beethoven's Fifth Symphony involves having sensations of different sorts of loud and soft, and high and low sounds, and smelling things involves sensations of different sorts of smells. In short, sensation is made out to be an observational ingredient, the basic observational ingredient, of all perceptions. To see a tomato is to observe a red patch of a certain shape, where the observing of a red patch of a certain shape is the having of a visual sensation. So to perceive something is, basically, to have a sensation, which in turn is to observe the contents of the sensation.

Thus the official doctrine about sensations endorses the sense datum theory. For,

According to the theory, then, having a visual sensation can be described as getting a momentary look, or visual appearance, of something, and having an olfactory sensation as getting a momentary whiff of something. (*CM*, pp. 210–11)

In some statements of the theory, he [a recipient of sense data] is said to perceive or observe them, in a sense of 'perceive' and 'observe' which makes it proper to say that he sees colour patches, hears sounds, smells whiffs, tastes flavours and feels tickles. Indeed it is often thought not only allowable, but illuminating, to say that people do not really see horse-races or taste wines; they really only see colour patches and taste flavours . . . (*CM*, pp. 211–12)

Thus, the official or Cartesian doctrine of sensation agrees with the sense datum theory at least to the extent that sensations involve the observing or perceiving of their primitive contents called 'sense data', which occur in the possessor of the sensations by causal processes from without. In fact, says Ryle, the clearest model of the official doctrine as a whole is the following. The having of sensations should be depicted in much the same way as one might depict a solitary man in a tent who can see a patch of light on the inside surface of the canvas, which patch he infers might be caused by someone outside shining a torch on the surface of the tent, and who can feel an indentation in the canvas of the tent which he surmises might be caused by someone putting his boot into the side of the tent. The patch of light he sees and the indentation he feels are sense data, and his seeing the patch of light and feeling the indentation are the having of sensations. The inference or intuitive leap from patch of light to torch outside and from indentation to boot are what we call the perceptions of the lighted torch and of the boot.

Ryle remarks that the strongest argument in favour of the sense datum view of sensation, and of the sensation view of perception, is the argument which refers to the verbal paradoxes that occur in the description of perceptual illusions. The official doctrine maintains that it can take the paradox out of such paradoxical accounts as 'I saw a snake which wasn't there' and 'I saw the round plate as elliptical', for it says that, in the snake case what the person saw was a sense datum of colours of such a shape that he or she inferred wrongly that there was a snake in the room, whereas there was no snake only a sense datum. Similarly, in the plate case, what one sees is an elliptical sense datum of a plate in one's head, albeit caused by a round plate in the world.

Having depicted the official doctrine of sensation and perception, and given the strongest argument in its favour, Ryle sets about demolishing this official doctrine. His chief attack is going to be that 'this whole theory rests upon a logical howler, the howler, namely, of assimilating the concept of sensation to the concept of observation.' (*CM*, p. 213) This assimilation, he will argue, has led the Cartesians into a basic category error, for they place sensation in the same logical category as observation, namely in the category of activities, when in fact it should be placed in a very different sort of category.

But, as so often he does, Ryle starts with a sort of linguistic softener. He tells us that even to talk about sensation in the way the official doctrine does, namely as if it were a sort of observation, leads to a very strained and extraordinary way of talking, and this should alert us to the fact that something very odd is going on in the official account of sensation. If we ask an ordinary layman to describe his sensations, he does not launch into an account of what colour patches he saw or what flavours he tasted. He describes his sensations in terms of the ordinary objects we associate such sensations with. He would not say 'I saw a red colour patch of thin oblong shape' but 'I saw what looked like a red stick' or 'I saw something shaped like a stick and of roughly the colour of a tomato.' Ordinarily, language doesn't deal in the undiluted and supposedly neutral language of colour patches, whiffs and flavours, but primarily in the language of objects. When colours, tastes and smells are mentioned, it is usually by association with the common objects which usually give rise to them, not *in vacuo*. Besides, when we mention sensation, we normally do so in markedly impersonal terms, with the object perceived as the subject of the sentence as often as not. We say 'It looked like a tomato but smelled like a dead dog', we don't say 'I had a sensation of a red patch and of a sweet nauseous smell.'

Finally, Ryle suggests that, to take the official doctrine seriously, one is involved in talking about seeing the looks of things for, in observing one's sense datum which, say, is a patch of red caused by a tomato, one is seeing the look of the tomato. But, counters Ryle in typically trenchant vein,

A person without a theory . . . does not ordinarily talk of seeing or of scanning the looks of things . . . He would feel that, if he mixed his ingredients in these fashions, he would be talking the same sort of nonsense as . . . talking of eating nibbles of biscuits. And he would be quite right. He cannot significantly speak of 'eating nibbles', since 'nibble' is already a noun of eating, and he cannot talk of 'seeing looks', since 'look' is already a noun of seeing. (*CM*, pp. 216–17)

Next Ryle, again typically, wheels in his big guns, his *reductio* arguments. The first of these are again fairly linguistic in the sense that he argues that sensations cannot be basically the observation of sense data, as the official doctrine would have it, because, when we apply the language of observation to sensations, we end up in an absurdity of one sort or another. And, as he has stressed so often, absurdity is the symptom of a category mistake.

For example, we ordinarily speak of observations as careless and cursory or as sustained and careful, but it makes no sense to speak of sensation in this way. Yet it ought to make sense if sensations were indeed observations. One can listen carefully, but not be said to carefully have a sensation in one's ears. One can observe something but in fact fail to see it, yet, according to the theory, one cannot have a sensation but fail to be apprised of its contents. Indeed, even if we allowed that it was sensible to speak of observing our sense data, as one might observe a robin, the official doctrine does not allow that one can observe sense data but fail to see them, so the official doctrine's use of the term 'observation' is at least very special, unusual and altogether extraordinary.

We should not, says Ryle, confuse the fact that we can pay heed to what we see or hear with the claim that sensations are themselves a form of observation of sense data. Of course we can notice or reflect on or pay heed to our twinges, tickles and throbs. This is not in dispute by either side. But to notice or pay heed or mind something is not evidence that this something is itself an observation or includes it, and, as we have seen in an earlier chapter, heeding, noticing and minding are not forms of observation and so do not imply that sensation includes something observable in its make-up.

Now Ryle wields another favourite weapon against the official doctrine, the infinite regress. Ryle argues that the official doctrine can be reduced to absurdity by showing that it involves an unacceptable infinite regress. For, if we accept the official picture of perception as involving sensation, and the official picture of sensation as involving the observation of our internal sense data in our internal mental arena, then, in effect, the official doctrine is explaining perception by reference to a special fundamental inner private sort of perception, namely sensation. To put it another way, ordinary observation or perception of the external world is explained in terms of a private version of this going on in the inner mental world. But, says Ryle, if this inner, more fundamental observation of sense data is to be genuine observation, surely it must be explained in terms of another sensation-observation still more inner and fundamental. As he puts it:

We are asked to declare that I, though nobody else, can observe the glimpses and the whiffs that I get, and observe them in the same sense of 'observe' as that in which anyone can observe the robin or the cheese. But to grant this would be to grant that if, when I catch a glimpse of a robin, I can observe that glimpse, then, in doing so, I must get something like a glimpse or a whiff of that glimpse of the robin. (*CM*, p. 207)

Finally, says Ryle, there is no need to employ the absurdities of the sense datum theory in order to give an account of seeing snakes where there are none or seeing tilted round plates as elliptical. When someone sees a tilted round plate and says that it looks elliptical, he means simply that 'it looks as an elliptical but untilted plate would look.' (*CM*, p. 217) And he is not referring to an extra object, 'a look', as being elliptical, but to the plate as looking elliptical. The phrase 'looks elliptical' is not to be cashed out as 'causes in the perceiver a sense datum or look which is elliptical' but as 'is seen from this angle to resemble an elliptical plate', or, philosophically more accurately, 'looks as if it were an untilted elliptical plate'. In other words, to speak about the looks of something is to make a mongrel-categorical statement or mixed hypo-thetical-categorical statement about it. The categorical part is the statement that I am seeing a round plate from a certain angle. The hypothetical bit is that, from the angle I am seeing it, I am seeing it as if I were seeing an elliptical plate. After all, says Ryle, this is how we always ordinarily talk about our perceptions. We say it tastes like sugar mixed with dust, and are saying that this tastes as if it were sugar mixed with dust. When we say that tomatoes are red, we are saying that if your sight is normal and if the light is sufficient and if the tomato is ripe, what you will see is what is termed 'red'. All perceptual talk is really mongrel-categorical and round plates looking el-liptical and eider-downs looking like snakes are no excep-tions.

The official theory was right to define perception in terms of seeing, hearing, tasting and touching but wrong to define it in terms of sensation or a special type of observation of sense data. The observation aspect of per-ception comes in on top of or after the looking at or listening or tasting aspect, for the sense of the term 'observation' that we might employ when we perceive is that of an achievement or success. When we perceive something we have got something right. What we have got right is an identification. To perceive with one's ears or eyes or nose is to see things or hear things or smell things and then to identify these things.

All this, perhaps, is made clearer if we consider the case of recognising a tune. Already it is implied that the person concerned has not merely heard something but has identified the noise as a tune which he or she knows.

Recognising what he hears entails hearing. It also entails heeding. . . .
But more than this, he must have met this tune before; and he must not
only have met it, but also have learned it and not forgotten it. If he
did not in this sense already know the tune, he could not be said to
recognise it on listening to it now. (*CM*, p. 226)

Ryle goes on to tell us that recognising a tune is 'hearing
it in a special frame of mind, the frame of mind of being
ready to hear both what he is now hearing and what he will
hear' but this does not imply that recognising a tune is two
operations hearing and then identifying, or hearing and
having thoughts about what one is hearing. There is only
one occurrence, the hearing, but it is also the fulfilment of
an expectation. To have an expectation concerning a tune
is 'to have acquired a set of auditory expectation propensities', and to recognise the tune is 'to be hearing
expected note after expected note'. Thus, to recognise a
tune is to be hearing noises which fulfil auditory expectation propensities. This is to be categorised as a mongrel-
categorical statement because it mentions both an occurrence and a propensity. The propensity is described in
hypothetical terms, while the occurrence, the hearing, is
described in categorical terms.

So Ryle believes that he has shown that there is a quite
simple explanation of perceptual illusions and veridical
perception which does not need to make reference to
sensation, sense data or their cognates. This, coupled with
the inherent absurdities of the official Cartesian doctrine
of perception in terms of sensation, and of sensation in
terms of observation of sense data, ought to convince us
that 'we have no employment for such expressions as
"object of sense", "sensible object", "sensum", "sense-
datum", "sense-content", "sense field" and "sensibilia";
the epistemologist's transitive verb "to sense" and his
intimidating "direct awareness" and "acquaintance" can
be returned to store.' (*CM*, p. 221)

It is not uncommon when one is reeling from Ryle's
attacks on the official doctrine that one slowly begins to
feel that perhaps he is not being quite fair to the official
view, and on this topic one gets this feeling quite strongly.
Ryle, of course, always left himself vulnerable to this sort
of comment, not the least because he never clearly iden-

tifies any particular thinker in connection with his attacks. After all, he never even attributes the doctrines he is attacking directly to Descartes. The holder of these doctrines is the referent of the vague term 'Cartesian'. Thus I sympathise with Anthony Quinton when he writes with some pique in his essay 'Ryle on Perception' (in *Ryle*, eds. Wood and Pitcher): 'Other philosophers are seldom mentioned by name and even less often quoted. The positions criticised are not precisely and historically identified.' (P. 105) I would go further and suggest that not merely does Ryle not precisely identify his targets, he often leaves himself open to being accused of misidentifying them. I believe that this has happened to some extent in his discussion of sensation.

In the first instance I agree with Quinton that the sense datum theorist 'has no commitment to the view that sense-impressions are strictly *observable*'. (*Ibid*. p. 114) All the sense datum theorist need commit himself to is the claim that they are knowable. For it could be the case, for example, that our brain is so constructed that when our eyes are focused on a tomato, we are moved to believe, and are able to assert, that one is seeing a red patch. There need be no question of any internal process of observation of sense data going on; the theory needs only to commit itself to the claim that one be able to report about sense data.

Ryle, of course, does realise this objection and replies that it is not easy to see why, on the above account, sense data should be called *sense* data. If the data are not the object of a sensing through some sort of sensory apparatus, why should we refer to the data as sense data?

We might reply to Ryle that, if sense data are not the object of any act of sensing, but merely the product of it, then there is still reason to call the data sense data. At least some versions of the sense datum theory might construe the data in question, not as the object of some internal sensation or observation, but as the product of the causal chain which forms the perceptual process. One could argue that Ryle has confused the beginning of the causal chain, which is called the object when the beginning is some external thing activating a sense organ, with its final effect. On the sense datum theory, sense data are the final effect not the beginning of the causal chain, or even an intermediary stage.

Quinton also casts doubt on Ryle's use of the infinite regress argument in connection with his version of the official doctrine of perception. Quinton suggests that Ryle's version of the official doctrine could concede that perception is to be explained in terms of sensation which in turn is to be cashed out as an internal observation of internal data without being committed to a further postulating of a still more fundamental and internal observing. I think that what Quinton is suggesting is that this Rylean version of the official doctrine—even if it is a caricature—is not committed to cashing out the observation which is perception in terms of an observation which is sensation, which in turn must be cashed out still further in terms of a more fundamental and inner observation, for it is claiming only that sensation is the observation element in perception. Perception includes sensation as its observational element. Perception is observation plus other elements such as identification and so on. Thus, even in this caricature version, there is no regress from observation to inner observation to still more basic observation. The movement is from whole to part; to explaining the whole, perception, in terms of its parts which include an observational element. If I explain a table by mentioning among other things that it has legs, I am not thereby committed to explaining legs in terms of little inner more fundamental legs.

Ryle's own account of perception as a mongrel-categorical is also less than satisfactory. Quinton rightly points out that the categorical part of the mongrel-categorical account is largely unexplained. If seeing a tomato is undergoing some occurrence which is also to be acknowledged as the fulfilment of some propensity or disposition, what exactly is the nature of this occurrence? After all, the official doctrine at least has the merit of putting all its cards on the table. For it declares that the occurrence, or the final important one, is a sensation. If Ryle's occurrence is not a sensation—that is the producing of sense data—which he seems inclined to say, what is it?

Just to leave it at the stage of describing it as an occurrence is hardly satisfactory. If one looks back at Ryle's account, we will see that, while he declares that we must not refer to the possession of 'looks' of the tomato or plate (for this would commit us to acknowledging the existence of sense data), he does allow that we can speak of the tomato or plate 'looking to us' like so and so. What can this occurrence of 'looking to us' be if not the reception by us of *something* via our sense organs? For surely the concept of perception must be, as Quinton observes, 'intrinsically causal'.

Without the causal implication there would be no distinction between perception and lucky guessing about the contents of one's physical environment. . . . If sensations are taken to be stimulations of the senses by the external world their necessary involvement with perception is simply the factor that is needed to distinguish perceptual beliefs from . . . guesswork. (*Op. cit.* p. 130)

So if, as it seems, Ryle is committed to the view that perception includes the claim that, when Q is asserted to look like P to me, then Q has caused something to happen in me, then it would seem that he is committed to giving some explanation of what this something is. This he conspicuously has not done.

Incidentally, this brings to mind another point about Ryle's account of the official doctrine. Since the official doctrine of perception is basically a causal account, it is not in fact committed to the doctrine that the reception of sense data is automatically and incorrigibly known by the receiver, as Ryle claims it is. The official doctrine ought to and usually does accommodate such things as subliminal perception. The official doctrine would not even be committed to the 'automatically and incorrigibly known' doctrine if it construed sensations as little observations— which we have seen it need not—for observations, no matter how large or small, or outer or inner, can be subconscious.

In *Dilemmas*, the printed version of his Tarner Lectures at Trinity college Cambridge in 1953, Ryle again discusses the nature of perception, but this time against the background of his overall aim in these lectures of discussing category confusions which arise when answers to different questions are mistakenly taken to be answers to one and the same question. Ryle argues that the theory of perception put forward by the neurophysiologist after his studies on the mechanism of perception is not in competition with the ordinary man's view of perception, though it is generally taken to be so. The theory of perception arrived at by the neurophysiologist 'seems constitutionally to entail that there is an unbridgeable crevasse between what people, including himself, see or hear and what is really there—a crevasse so wide that he has apparently and can have no laboratory evidence that there exists even any correlation between what we perceive and what is really there.' (*Dilemmas*—hereafter *D*—p. 2) On the other hand the layman, and the neurophysiologist himself in his ordinary everyday life, is convinced that we do have immediate direct knowledge of the world when we perceive things. But the neurophysiologist is answering the question 'How do we perceive?' or 'What are the mechanisms of perception?' while the layman is answering the question 'What did you perceive?'

The philosopher's question 'What is perception?' is a different question altogether, and leads to philosophical error if assimilated to either of the former questions. Those who study the mechanisms of perception have often thought that they would find the answer to the philosopher's question 'What is perception?', if not among the mechanisms that they study, at least at the end-point or as the product of those mechanisms. If their experiments have not revealed perception itself under the microscope this, they thought, must be because perception is a state or process belonging to the unobservable, conscious world of the mental. But they have been misled into proposing this solution, says Ryle, because they have failed to realise that verbs of perception like 'seeing' and 'hearing' are achievement verbs like 'win' or 'score' and are not the labels of any locatable states or processes.

We may imagine an athletics coach with a scientific training researching into the physiology and the psychology of runners. . . . But then he laments that he can find no physiological phenomenon answering to his subject's winning a race, or losing it. Between his terminal output of energy and his victory or defeat there is a mysterious crevasse.

Physiology is baffled. Then for a moment our experimentally minded coach cheers up. Perhaps winning and losing are not physiological states or processes . . . [but] mental states or processes, experiences which the athlete himself can unearth by careful introspection. . . . But then, alas, it turns out that this hypothesis will not do either. . . . (*D*, p. 105)

What Ryle is arguing here is that 'perceiving is the scoring of an investigational success' for 'we find things out and come to know them by seeing and hearing.' (*D*, pp. 108–9)

In his essay 'Sensation' in *Contemporary British Philosophy*, Third Series, Ryle fills out a little what he means by saying that perceiving is not an extra, final, mental link in the causal chain from stimulus to perception. He tells us that 'finding out something by seeing or hearing is, so to speak, a success or victory in the game of exploring the world.' (P. 442) Perceiving is the exercising of an acquired skill or propensity *successfully*. It is the successful exercise of 'the *crafts* or *arts* of finding things out by seeing and hearing'. (*Ibid*. p. 441)

Here in *Dilemmas* and in his article 'Sensation', Ryle is not concerned with the central problem of what perception is but with what sort of analysis or investigation will supply the answer to the question 'What is perception?' He is concerned to point out that no scientific investigation of the causal processes that lead up to perception will reveal what perception itself is, because it is not a process or part of a process but the achievement aspect of processes. Just as winning is the accolade given to moving one's legs along a running track in certain circumstances, so perceiving is the accolade given to the activation of one's sense organs in certain circumstances. 'Winning' is the value term bestowed upon running faster than others in a race. 'Perceiving' is the value term bestowed upon having your senses activated by an external object and then being able to describe correctly that external object. The substance of such terms is not, says Ryle, revealed by scientific investigation but by philosophical analysis.

But is this correct? Taking Ryle's own analogy, does not the camera play a large part in deciding the winner of some sorts of races, especially when it is a close thing? That is, does not careful, instrument-aided observation often decide winners? If so, perhaps it is the case that careful, instrument-aided observation can at times be needed to decide perceivers? If this is the case, then the scientist does have something important to say about the nature of perception.

Indeed, if what has been said in criticism of Ryle's account of perception in *The Concept of Mind* is correct, then an investigation of the causal processes of perception will tell us a great deal about the nature of perception. For a start, it can tell us whether, say, Ferguson is in fact seeing a tomato or not. For if the activation of the sensory part of the brain, which is occurring when Ferguson says he is seeing a tomato, is to be traced back through various causal links to a tomato, then we have reason to award the accolade 'seeing a tomato' to Ferguson. If, on the other hand, the activation is traced back to, say, a wire inserted into his brain or a wound in his scalp which has penetrated to the sensory part of his brain, then we would not award the accolade 'seeing a tomato' to Ferguson. So, even if we accept Ryle's account of the term 'perception' as an achievement word, it is the case that the investigation of the causal links is germane to its correct use, and so to a correct understanding of the concept underlying its use. After all, it is Ryle himself who has so often stressed that the correct understanding of a concept implies a knowledge of its entailments. So, if the concept of perception entails the proposition that certain causal connections and not others be present, then understanding the concept of perception implies the consideration of causal connections.

Of course, we do usually use the word 'perceive' without undertaking scientific investigations of ourselves or others, but Ryle is wrong to conclude from this that causal considerations are not relevant. When we use the term 'perceive' we *assume* that what we claim to be perceiving has causally affected one of our sense organs. Even the most naïve perceiver is probably aware of the part, the causal role, played by sense organs in perception. We do not check that the sense organs or other physiological parts are in fact playing their causal role because, besides being incapable of such a check ourselves, we assume that, by and large, our sense organs achieve veridical perceptions. If we did not we would be plunged into radical scepticism. Of course, if our claims about the presence of tomatoes started to disagree radically with everyone else's claims, then we might consult an occulist or a neurophysiologist. And that we would do so implies that we do know, at least in a vague way, *that* causal connections are relevant to perception, though we may never know in any detail *what* these connections are.

I have been quite critical of Ryle on the topics of perception and sensation, for I fear that this is the weakest part of his attack on the official Cartesian doctrine of the ghost in the machine. Part of the reason for this is, I suspect, that the sense datum theory of sensation is much less Cartesian than Ryle has tried to make out. There is no official line in the sense datum theory, or need not be, about any internal faculty engaging in internal episodes of a proprietary type, as there is, for instance, in the Cartesian doctrines of the intellect and will. All that a sense datum theory needs is a physico-chemical causal chain plus, at times, the epiphenomenon of awareness. Perhaps Ryle's attack on perception and sensation would have been more successful if he had concentrated on the part played by awareness — which is usually described in terms of colour patches, whiffs and smells — and attempted to give some sort of reductive account of these in terms of dispositions, or else made out some sort of case that, in explaining colour patches, whiffs and smells, we need not appeal to the category of the mental in any way.

Chapter 9
IMAGINATION

As early as 1933 Ryle was puzzling over the nature of imagination in his paper 'Imaginary Objects', which I have already discussed in Chapter 3. In that paper Ryle was mainly concerned with showing that certain names, such as those of fictional persons, for example 'Mr Pickwick', were not really names but 'concealed predicative expressions', so that their use did not commit one to positing imaginary objects as referents for those names. The term 'Mr Pickwick' is really shorthand for the fictional description of Mr Pickwick in Dickens' *Pickwick Papers*. In fact, Ryle suggested in that paper, imaginary 'objects' in the sense of imaged or pictured-in-the-mind 'objects' are just descriptions using 'look'-predicates instead of word-predicates. In Chapter VIII of *The Concept of Mind* Ryle returns to the problem of imagination and ends up giving an account which builds on this view expressed in the paper 'Imaginary Objects'.

As usual, Ryle first discusses and then seeks to demolish the official Cartesian dogma about imagination. The dogma states, he says, that imagining consists in looking at special simulacra of real things with a special faculty in a special theatre, the mind.

If a person says that he is picturing his nursery, we are tempted to construe his remark to mean that he is somehow contemplating, not his nursery, but another visible object, namely a picture of his nursery, only not a photograph or an oil painting, but some counterpart to a photograph, one made of a different sort of stuff. Moreover, this paperless picture, . . . [is] in a gallery which only he can visit. And then we are inclined to say that the picture . . . must be in his mind, and that the 'eyes' with which he contemplates it are . . . his mind's eyes. (*CM*, p. 247)

So the set-up is familiar by now. The Cartesian account of imagination is depicted as that of a special faculty engaged in a special activity in a special arena, namely of 'seeing' or 'smelling' etc. in some special mental way some special mental pictures or models which are either copies of something we have seen in the world or concocted from copies of parts which we have seen in the world. Thus, to fancy one sees one's aunt is to see a real copy of one's aunt, and to fancy one sees a dragon is 'to see a real dragon-phantasm'. (*CM*, p. 251)

Ryle now sets about the official dogma in the usual way. He first points out some linguistic oddities that result from accepting the official story:

When a person says that he 'sees' something which he is not seeing [as occurs in the official account of imagination], he knows that what he is doing is something which is totally different in kind from seeing, just because the verb is inside inverted commas and the vision can be described as more or less faithful, or vivid. (*CM*, p. 246)

For, Ryle is implying, we do not say that our ordinary seeing of external objects is vivid or faithful. That would not make sense, for the external object is the original and so, of course, is faithful to itself. So 'seeing', whatever it is, cannot be just an internal form of seeing. Further, using the adjectives 'vivid' and 'faithful' in connection with imagining suggests that what is going on is not seeing but something akin to narrating or describing.

The official doctrine might reply that the adjectives 'vivid' and 'faithful' are in order in connection with imagination, not because imagination is like narrating but because it is like seeing, not internal originals, but internal copies of them. For copies can be faithful to what they are copies of and vividly portray them. Thus, one's image of the nursery is vivid and faithful if it is a good clear copy of how in fact one's nursery was laid out.

Ryle would reply that this cannot be the reason why 'vivid' and 'faithful' fit the 'seeing' of imagination but not real seeing, because if it were, we would also be able to say of the object of some episode of imagination that it was dim or faint, for our sight of a copy of an original could be dim or faint. But in fact we do not say this of imagined 'objects'.

But a stronger linguistic argument against the copy theory of imagination is that it is a total linguistic non-starter in regard to senses other than sight and one's imagination in regard to them.

So it is easy and tempting to describe visual imaging as if it were a case of looking at a likeness. . . . But we have no such analogies for smelling, tasting or feeling. So when I say that I 'smell' the singed hoof [when I am imagining the blacksmith's shop I knew in my childhood] I have no way of paraphrasing my statement into a form of words which says instead 'I smell a copy of a singed hoof'. The language of originals and copies does not apply to smells. (*CM*, p. 252)

And so the implication is, if the copy theory clearly does not work for the senses other than sight, why should we adhere to it in connection with sight? Besides, while we have seen that the language of copies does not even get going in connection with imagined smells, one is yet able to speak of imagined smells as vivid or faithful. This should be a clear indication that these terms 'vivid' and 'faithful' are not being applied on such an occasion to copies in one's mind. This in turn is further confirmation that a more likely account is that the use of 'vivid' and 'faithful' in connection with imagination is to be cashed out as adjectives being applied to some form of description.

More basically, says Ryle, the whole notion of a 'copy of a smell' is odd. What could such a copy be but the smell itself? We can make sense of visual copies of things, that is, the reduction of three-dimensional views to, say, two-dimensional representations of those views, but how could one have a copy of a real smell in different dimensions or whatever category is appropriate to smells? One just could not distinguish between smelling smoke and 'smelling' smoke in imagination if the copy theory were true. The same is true of 'a taste and a likeness of a taste, a tickle and a dummy-tickle.' (*CM*, p. 253)

Ryle suggests that, if we think through a detailed example, the copy theory is not even very convincing as regards visual imagination. For a visual copy of, say, a doll's smile, ought to be a two-dimensional version of the smile. But the visual copy of imagination cannot be in dimensions, for it is a non-physical copy. It is not a copy in space but in the mind. But what could a non-dimensional yet visualised smile amount to?

Part of the reason why the official Cartesian doctrine of imagination amounts to a copy theory is that 'as visual observation has pre-eminence over observation by the other senses, so with most people visual imagination is stronger than auditory, tactual, kinaesthetic, olfactory and gustatory imagination, and consequently the language in which we discuss these matters is largely drawn from the language of seeing.' (*CM*, p. 247) But part of the reason is that there is something common to both imagination properly construed and seeing copies which has misled Cartesians into saying that the former is an instance of the latter. This common factor is that both seeing copies and imagining are connected with retelling or narrating. Seeing copies of originals can help us recall the originals while imagining originals is the process of recollecting in the sense of describing them.

So we have come to Ryle's own account of imagination, an account which is one of the most arresting and interesting parts of *The Concept of Mind*, though, I shall suggest, ultimately unsatisfactory. First, says Ryle, imagination is something like make-believe. For a child is being imaginative when he imagines, for example, that he is a bear. The only episodes on account of which the child is said by an observer to be imagining he is a bear are such as the child's putting the rug around his shoulders, his stooping walk and his growling. In short, here we have a case of an observer pronouncing the child to be imagining without reference to anything in the child's mind. Indeed, given the official doctrine, the observer could not make reference to anything in the child's mind such as 'seeing' visual but mental copies.

The more positive point to take from the child's imitation of a bear as an example of imagination is that imagination is a sort of narration or description. In imitating the bear by putting the rug around his shoulders, walking with a stoop and growling, the child is describing or recalling in actions what a bear looks like and how it acts.

It is no objection to say that imagination cannot be like make-believe, imitation or pretence because we can imagine something but think it real yet we cannot make-believe, imitate or pretend to something and then mistake the performance for the real thing. For, says Ryle, a child could pretend, say, that he is in the jungle when he is playing in the garden and then at least half believe it is real and fear that a bear may be waiting to pounce on him from behind the compost heap. 'The fact that people can fancy that they see things, are pursued by bears . . . without realising that it is nothing but fancy, is simply a part of the unsurprising general fact that not all people are, all the time, at all ages and in all conditions, as judicious or critical as could be wished.' (*CM*, pp. 258–9)

Further argument that make-believe and pretend performances are forms of narration can be tied in with the examples of shadow-boxing or sparring. Here a boxer either throws punches at nobody or pulls his punches at somebody, either way he is merely imitating what he would do if he were really fighting. The point of this is usually instruction. His coach teaches him how to box by getting him to describe in mock form what he should do if he were in a real fight. A pulled-punch is a description of a real punch rather than a truncated or failed real punch. In shadow-boxing and sparring boxers are 'both plying their fists and also plying propositions'. (*CM*, p. 261)

But by means of both the case of the child imitating the bear and the boxer being instructed via sparring and shadow-boxing, one can now grasp a further important point. Narrations or descriptions do not have to be couched in words. Both the child and the boxer are narrating by performing non-linguistically. Indeed, a person may not be able to describe something linguistically but may be able to do so only non-linguistically. The child may not be articulate enough to describe a bear in words, but he may be able to tell us by his performance what he saw at the zoo.

Now, says Ryle, is it such a big step to think of imagining as describing or narrating non-linguistically? Just as one can relate to others by means of an external performance, so one can relate or recall something to oneself by means of a private—though not a mental—non-linguistic performance. The immediately obvious objection to this, says Ryle, is that there seems to be no non-linguistic medium of narrating for internal imagination as there is for playing bears or sparring. The child tells us what a bear is like in his observable behaviour, the boxer describes to himself what he should do in the fight tomorrow in the combinations he runs through during today's sparring and shadow-boxing. But in terms of what can the internal imaginer imagine?

To answer this objection Ryle refers us to his account of sensation and perception which I discussed in Chapter 8. He reminds us that recognising a tune consisted in hearing the tune in a certain frame of mind, such that the noises heard are recognised as fulfilling certain expectations. A similar account is to be given of imagining a tune or running over a tune in one's head: 'A person with a tune running in his head is using his knowledge of how the tune goes; he is in a certain way realising what he would be hearing, if he were listening to the tune being played.' (*CM*, p. 266) But Ryle realises that this account still has a large hole in it. When one is recognising a tune one is listening as well, that is, some occurrence, namely hearing the notes of the tune being played, is taking place which can be referred to as the fulfilment of the expectation-propensity aspect of recognising a tune. But in the case of running over a tune in one's head, that is, imagining a tune, it is not clear what, if anything, is the occurrence which fulfils his expectations of how the tune goes. That is the gap or hole in the account. But Ryle's 'filling' of the hole is somewhat surprising:

A person listening to a moderately familiar tune may on some occasions describe himself as having got the tune wrong, meaning by this that . . . all he 'did' was to be listening for what was not due to come, in place of what was due to come, and this listening for notes is not a deed done, or a series of deeds done.

This very point brings us to the case of a person following an imagined tune. To expect a tune to take one course, when it is actually taking another, is already to suppose, fancy or imagine. (*CM*, p. 268)

So Ryle's answer to the question 'What, in the case of imagining a tune, is the occurrence which fulfils our expectations of how the tune should go?' is that there is no occurrence. The hole is left unfilled. Imagining a tune or running over a tune in one's head is just expecting certain notes to follow certain other notes if someone should play it. Imagination is not a mongrel-categorical like perception, not something to be described both in terms of a categorical account of the details of some occurrence and in terms of a hypothetical statement of the role of this occurrence in fulfilling some propensity or disposition. Imagination is just the propensity or disposition.

Going through a tune in one's head is like following a heard tune and is, indeed, a sort of rehearsal of it. But what makes the imaginative operation similar to the other is not, as is often supposed, that it incorporates the hearing of ghosts of notes similar in all but loudness to the heard notes of the real tune, but the fact that both are utilisations of knowledge of how the tune goes. This knowledge is exercised in recognising and following the tune . . . it is also exercised in fancying oneself humming or playing it and in fancying oneself merely listening to it. . . . Fancying one is listening to a known tune involves 'listening for' the notes which would be due to be heard, were the tune being really performed. It is to listen for those notes in a hypothetical manner. Similarly, fancying one is humming a known tune involves 'making ready' for the notes which would be due to be hummed, were the tune actually being hummed. It is to make ready for those notes in a hypothetical manner. It is not humming very, very quietly, but rather it is deliberately not doing those pieces of humming which would be due, if one were not trying to keep the peace. We might say that imagining oneself talking or humming is a series of abstentions from producing the noises which would be the due words or notes to produce, if one were talking or humming aloud. (*CM*, p. 269)

It is interesting to note that a psychologist, Ulric Neisser, has suggested an account of imagining similar to Ryle's account of imagining as anticipating. Peter Sheehan has summarised his view in 'Mental Imagery' (*Psychological Survey*, No. 1, ed., B. M. Foss, George Allen & Unwin, 1978).

One such theory is that proposed by Neisser, who in his most recent statement [*Cognition and Reality*, Freeman, 1976] argues that mental images should be viewed as perceptual anticipations. According to this account, a description of a visual image is a description of what a person is ready or set to see, and images are conceptualized as plans for 'obtaining information from potential environments'. (p. 65)

What, then, are we to think of all this? In the first place, what are we to think of Ryle's attack on the official doctrine of imagination?

Ryle's attack on the Cartesian or official doctrine of imagination is mainly directed against the copy theory version of it. Ryle's major objection is that it makes no sense to explain visualising or imagining, say a smell, in terms of 'smelling' a copy of it. A copy of a smell would have to be a real smell and so 'smelling' would be just ordinary smelling.

Gareth Matthews, in his paper 'Mental Copies' (*Philosophical Review*, Vol. 78, 1969), has suggested that what a copy theorist might mean by imagining a smell is really the having of a smell which more or less reproduces the original one. And, one might add, the copy theorist could say that this having of a reproduction is to be called 'imagining a smell' because the person having the smell knows that the external physical conditions required for having a normal sensation of that smell do not obtain. One is, say, smelling violets though there are no violets about nor anything else which smells like them, and one knows this. One realises that the causes of the smell of violets must be internal.

Matthews also refers to some early psychological work on imagination which seems to support the copy theory of imagination.

A rather striking bit of evidence is due to C. W. Perky [see his 'An Experimental Study of Imagination', *American Journal of Psychology*, Vol. 21, 1910]. Perky conducted a series of psychological experiments in which he placed his subjects before a ground-glass wall, asked them to fix their attention at a point on the wall and to visualize various objects there (for example, a tomato, a book, a leaf). Each time he asked a subject to visualize something, he had an appropriate image projected faintly on the ground-glass wall. He did not tell his subjects about the image projections and (except when the projector was jogged inadvertently) they did not realize they were there. But when the subjects were questioned about what they had visualized, they described objects corresponding to the faintly projected images. For example, if a subject had been asked to visualize a book and the image of a book with a blue cover had been projected, the subject, upon being questioned, would report that the book he had visualized was blue. Thus the subjects apparently saw the faint projections, but took them for their own visualizations. (*Ibid.* p. 58)

Besides suggesting that the images of imagination are like real images or, at least, that they can be readily confused with the latter, these experiments also suggest that the visual images of imagination are less vivid than those of sensation. This does not, as some critics have suggested, create problems of plausibility for the copy theorist in regard to how he distinguishes between an image of a blurred X and a blurred image of an X. The copy theorist is not at a loss to distinguish between, say, whether he is imagining a tree in a fog or is having difficulty in imagining a tree in any clearcut way, because most forms of imagination (though certainly not all) differ from sensation in being much more under the control of the subject. If I am imagining something which, if a neutral observer could observe it, looks like a blurred tree, I can state categorically that I am imagining a tree in a fog because that is what I set out to imagine. This will not be true of some trance-like hallucinations, for example, the hypnagogic images occurring when one is still drowsy after sleep. Here the subject of imagination is much more like a neutral observer at a film show; much less involved than in fancying or imagining something for oneself. Such a person in a state of drowsiness, on waking could indeed have difficulty in deciding whether what he was visualising was a tree which he saw only in a blurred way or a tree in a fog. There is a difficulty in deciding what account one is to give of what was visualised, but this does not cast doubt on the possibility of such visualising. After all, one can have similar difficulties with sight. Are the branches moving or am I seeing the tree through a heat haze?

But a copy theory construed in this way is probably more akin to a trace theory than the sort of copy theory Ryle had it in mind to attack, and it may be significant that Ryle's objection to the trace theory is rather innocuous. The trace or reactivation theory of imagination is an offshoot of the sense datum theory and it may be that, since Ryle had already subjected that theory to sustained attack (see the previous chapter), he did not see any need to renew it. The trace theory describes, say, imagining one's aunt as a reactivation of the sensum which was the end-point of perceiving one's aunt, which reactivation is brought about, presumably, via some activation of the correlated sensory part or sense traces in the brain. So, in imagining one's aunt, one is not 'seeing' a copy of one's aunt, one is recalling or reactivating the original sight—without inverted commas—of one's aunt. Where a pure copy theory had difficulty making sense of the notions of copies of smells, tastes and feels, a reactivation theory (or re-activation version of a copy theory) has no such difficulty. If smells, tastes and feels can occur in the first place, and if it is true that they are physiologically based and so leave physiological traces—real traces—which can be reacti-vated, then the original smells, tastes and feels can be reproduced. The causal sequence in reproducing smells in imagination will be different from that which precedes smelling something external, but so what? Imagination differs from sensation partly in that very respect the trace theorist will say. As Peter Haynes has put it in his paper 'Mental Imagery' (*Canadian Journal of Philosophy*, Vol. 6, 1976):

Of course, seeing is not imaging and imaging is not seeing, although they both involve visual experience. What distinguishes the one from the other are the circumstances in which the visual experience occurs. If we think of perception as the standard case, then we can say that when someone has a visual mental image he has a visual experience under abnormal circumstances. (P. 709)

The psychologist Alan Richardson made a similar claim in his book *Mental Imagery* (Routledge & Kegan Paul, 1969):

Mental imagery refers to (1) all those quasi-sensory or quasi-perceptual experiences of which (2) we are self-consciously aware, and which (3) exist for us in the absence of those stimulus conditions that are known to produce their genuine sensory or perceptual counterparts, and which (4) may be expected to have different consequences from their sensory or perceptual counterparts. (Pp. 2–3)

Ryle's linguistic arguments would appear to gain some purchase against such reactivation or trace versions of the official theory of imagination for, though the terms 'vivid' and 'faithful' can be applied to reactivations such that our intuitions about imagination can be satisfied, the terms 'dim' and 'faint' also seem applicable to reactivations and this, says Ryle, does not accord with our intuitions about the nature of imagination.

What a trace theorist could, and should, I feel, say at this point, is that Ryle is just mistaken about our intuitions about imagination. It is not *prima facie* odd to say that one's image of a book is faint or that one can only dimly visualise one's aunt. Perky's experiments seem to support this response. His subjects did come to believe that the faint, blurred images projected on to the frosted glass were the images of their imagination.

Ryle's only criticism directed explicitly at the reactivation or trace theory seems quite innocuous: 'Addicts of the trace theory should try to fit their theory to the case of a tune running in someone's head. Is this a revived trace of an auditory sensation; or a series of revived traces of a series of auditory sensations?' (*CM*, p. 272) I can imagine a reactivation or trace theorist replying 'Does it matter?' That one might have difficulty in deciding whether recalling a tune is a reactivation of one single trace or many connected ones is about as easy and important as deciding whether hearing a tune in the first place is one single or many connected sensations.

I suspect that the greatest difficulty for the trace theorist is in explaining the nature of creative imagination, though such a difficulty is a difficulty for any theory of imagination for the simple reason that it is difficult to explain the nature of creativity anyway. But, since the reactivation theory explains the images of imagination in terms of embedded traces of past sensations, it may be said to have particular difficulty in explaining the production of images which are novel. How, for example, does the trace or reactivation theorist explain imagining a man from Mars or having breakfast with the Queen? The trace theorist would have to say that what one is doing is not merely reactivating a number of disparate traces but also putting them together in a novel way or extrapolating from images one has had to images one has never had. The trace theorist must give a more complex account of creative imagination than of imagination as recollection. But so what; perhaps creative imagination is a much more complex activity. After all, if it is genuinely *creative*, it must be going beyond just dredging up what we already have. But *a priori* there does not seem to be anything implausible in a trace theory accommodating such an account of creative imagination.

In his article 'Imagination' (*Mind*, Vol. 61, 1952), J. M. Shorter has defended the Cartesian model of imagination in terms of something very like creative assembling. Shorter suggests that the true analogy for a Cartesian is not between imagining and 'seeing' copies, or between imagining and reviving traces, it is between imagining and depicting. For both imagining and depicting are active, original performances whereas 'seeing' copies and reviving traces are more passive and unoriginal. They are just reseeing the originals or seeing copies of originals. 'Part of the answer to the very vague question "What is imagination?" has now been given. Visualising must be distinguished from other sorts of "seeing", and not confounded with them. Roughly to visualise is to *do* something, whereas to "see" snakes is not to do something.' (P. 536) But this theory of imagination as depicting, and the pure copy theory of imagination, are both defective in a way that the trace theory at least is not. Neither of these theories can tell us what these pictures, be they copies or original depictions, are made of or where they come from. The trace theory at least had an answer, they are sense data recalled. But if imagination is depicting or copying, how are the pictures or copies produced? What is it to visualise in the sense of depict? And, Ryle would ask, is the picture of a smell another smell or not?

Shorter gives two replies to this sort of demand. His first is simply that, '. . . if these questions are taken in one way, they are unanswerable.' (*Ibid.*, p. 537) You can no more describe what visualising is than describe what seeing is. It is just itself, a *sui generis* activity. His second answer is to say that

It is far better to say that there are mental pictures, and at the same time issue a warning against asking questions about them that can sensibly be asked only of real pictures. There remains the question 'What sorts of things are images?' The answer to this may be put briefly thus: 'They are the same sorts of things as pictures and descriptions. They are a sort of half-way house between pictures and descriptions.' This answer as it stands is of course very misleading, and its meaning is not obvious. (*Ibid*. p. 542)

Just so, I imagine, Ryle would say. Such a view avoids more questions than it answers. But it does stress one important aspect of imagination, namely that, in some of its modes, it is much more under the control and guidance of the subject than is sensation. In that sense imagining, especially creative imagining, does bear a resemblance to depicting.

Ryle would claim that none of these theories—the copy theory, the trace theory, or the depiction theory—explain away a very basic difficulty for theories which posit real images, namely, how can a *mental* image have *dimensions*. Presumably all these theories would hold that to imagine one's nursery would entail something like visualising one's cot to the right of one's potty and at a distance from the door, that is, visualising the nursery in at least two dimensions. But how can the mental have dimensions? The answer that any of these theorists could make to this sort of objection is that one need not hold to a Cartesian account of the mental. A trace theorist, for example, and I have suggested that the trace theory is the most plausible of these theories, would say that imagination is linked closely to sensation. So whatever the sense data or end-product of the causal process of sensation is, such that it includes perceiving in dimensions, so will be the end point of imagination, namely the images of imagination, for the images are reactivated sense data. Thus the problem is equally a problem for any theory of sensation as well, and primarily so, and it is not one peculiar to copy, trace, or depiction theories of imagination. If one adheres to some double-aspect account of the mental and the physical, then the problem is less severe, for the mental and the physical are posited as just two aspects of one and the same basic stuff which is known in these two modes or aspects. The mental is posited as basically inner, the product of the brain, but not posited as unable to interact causally with the physical or as incompatible with being produced by a physical causal sequence. It may be wrong, then, to presume that the mental is incompatible with having as its content, in imagination, dimensioned depictions. While consciousness itself may not have dimensions, its content can be dimensional.

Whatever view we may end up taking about Ryle's own account of imagination we cannot say that it avoids giving answers to the important questions. If you asked Ryle what mental images or mental copies or mental pictures are like he would say simply that there are no such things. To give an adequate account of imagination one need not posit such ghostly items. Ryle reduced imagination to narrating or describing, albeit non-linguistic narration or description, and so does not need to refer to any internal mental goings-on, for there is no need—as we saw in Chapter 3—to posit internal pictures or ghostly logical items such as propositions when giving an account of descriptive statements.

This account has an initial plausibility which makes it very attractive. It is especially plausible in the context of a boxer shadow-boxing and sparring while in training. The boxer's actions, says Ryle, are his way of telling us or describing to us what he would do in a real fight. His pulled upper-cuts and shadowed right crosses are pretended or imagined real upper-cuts and right crosses to an opponent. But Shorter makes the good point that this account of imagination as pretending or make believe, which in turn is the vehicle for describing, will not do for some very basic sorts of imagination. Visual imagination, for example, cannot be explained as sham or pretended seeing in the way that sparring is sham-fighting. While in sparring one goes through the motions of fighting without actually punching hard, in imagining one's nursery one does not pretend to see one's nursery when one does not or go through the motions of seeing one's nursery when one is not in fact doing so. Imagining is not stopping short of actually perceiving or pretending to perceive. 'Visualising is not sham-anything. It does not involve any form of pretence, or going through of any motions.' (Shorter, *op. cit.* p. 533)

Ryle's account of imagination, then, has particular difficulty in giving an account of someone imagining to himself without employing actions, gestures or any other external means. It is not merely that there is a difficulty in making sense of the idea of describing to oneself—for this is what Ryle would have to say about such cases—but that there is a difficulty in the whole idea of a description which is not a description in terms of anything at all. For Ryle's bold thesis, as we have seen, is that this sort of imagination—which, I have suggested, may best be accounted for in terms of reactivated seeing or sensa, or in the official copy theory version in terms of 'seeing' internal copies—is just dispositional and has no occurrent aspect

at all. Whereas the child is being imaginative by describing
in his actions what he thinks a bear looks and sounds like,
Ryle must say that when I am imagining my nursery or
running through a tune in my head, I am not in fact doing
anything in my head or anywhere else. Nothing is taking
place at all. I am just expectant or in a state of anticipation.
I am just being disposed to do something if called upon to
do so, something such as, presumably, describing in
words or gestures or drawings what my nursery was like
or, in the case of the tune, whistling it or putting it into
musical notation or playing it on a piano or humming it.
But if nothing is taking place, according to Ryle, one
might ask how it is possible to distinguish the two
quiescent states, listening for or anticipating notes not yet
played and not listening for them, or being in a state of
expectancy and not being so? Ryle, I think, cannot answer
this question, for, if he does, he must mention something
which has occurred between time t_1 when the description
'not listening for' is true, and time t_2 when the description
'now listening for' is true. Shorter is rather devastating
about this aspect of Ryle's account of imagination as well:
'How wrong it is to describe visualising as a sort of
abstaining. Rather visualising is a substitute for doing
something else. Similarly it is wrong to describe reading
to oneself as merely abstaining from reading out loud.
One way of doing this is not to read at all. (*Ibid.*
p. 534)

But the assimilation of imagination to anticipation,
when an account of imagining to oneself is called for, is
itself odd. Perhaps the clearest way of underlining this
oddness is to remark that imagination cannot be just
anticipation or expectancy of some sort, for one can
anticipate imagining something but one cannot anticipate
anticipating something. If I have answered an advertise-
ment in the Department of Experimental Psychology, and
find out that the advertised employment will consist in
sitting in a chair, with electrodes inserted into my skull,
and imagining scenes from my childhood, and learn that
this employment is to begin tomorrow, then today I might
speak of anticipation, eager anticipation, in regard to
imagining scenes from my childhood tomorrow. But I

would not—because it would not make sense—speak of anticipating a bout of anticipating.

The assimilation of imagining to oneself to a type of anticipation or expectancy is probably most plausible in the context of imagining what is going to happen to one or, in general, imagining the future. But it fits less well cases of imagining the past, particularly the past which was not experienced by me, or imagining what is purely fictional. As regards imagining the past unconnected to me, I might imagine what Aristotle was like. What could one be said to be anticipating here? Presumably Ryle would have to say that one is anticipating what he would look like, or what one believed he would look like, if he were still alive and was to appear before one's eyes. But, if this move were made, Ryle would be retreating to quasi-anticipating, for in such a case one clearly does not anticipate Aristotle's appearance or resurrection in any straightforward sense.

A great deal of imagining is neither of the past or future but 'purely imaginary'. In such a case the assimilation of imagining to anticipating or expecting proves to be not at all helpful. For example, if I have never thought about Martians before, but am suddenly called upon to imagine one, in what sense could I be said to anticipate a Martian? Indeed, what could be anticipated in such a case? Ryle tells us that imagining a tune is expecting the notes which would be heard if the tune were played. In imagining a Martian I can not be said to expect what would appear if Martians existed, because there is no agreement as to how Martians would appear. To imagine Martians is to be wholly creative. It is to imagine without previous expectations or presuppositions.

At other times Ryle seems to give up the account of imagining to oneself as anticipating and writes of imagining a tune as a 'utilization of knowledge of how the tune goes'. This version looks very like a mongrel-categorical account, an activation of a knowing how disposition. This version has the virtue of being able to answer the question, what is the difference between imagining to oneself and just abstaining altogether. Ryle can say that imagining involves an occurrence, the activation of a disposition. But this ver-

sion also runs into difficulties. What is this internal occurrence that counts as an activation or utilisation of knowing
how, say, knowing how a tune goes or how to whistle it, but
which goes on entirely in one's head? Does the tune run
through our head in some real sense? If so, is this a series of
real notes or copies or traces of real notes reactivated? In
short, to pursue this activation of a disposition account
forces Ryle into giving some account of the nature of these
internal notes which run through our head. It is not easy
to see how, in doing this, Ryle would be able to avoid
giving an account which makes him a copy theorist, a trace
theorist, or a depiction theorist, that is, the sort of theorist
he has been at pains to denounce as Cartesian and unacceptable.

I suspect that Ryle's talk of imagination as internal
utilisation was, if not just a momentary aberration, a
realisation that it is very difficult to avoid referring to
imagination in an occurrent way. To employ a typically
Rylean attack against Ryle, one might suggest that imagination must involve something occurrent if it is the case
that we employ adverbs and adverbial phrases about it. We
might say that we have difficulty in imagining our nursery
or that we can imagine our back yard clearly and vividly.
Further, Ryle himself has given an account of one form of
imagining as narrating or describing, and narration and
description are occurrent activities. If he is prepared to
give an occurrent account of one sort of imagining should
he not admit that the other sorts are likely to be occurrent
as well?

An account of imagination will always be peculiarly
difficult for an anti-Cartesian like Ryle precisely because it
does appear to be an irreducibly internal occurrence or
goings-on in its typical cases. One would have thought
that Ryle could capitulate concerning the occurrent nature
of imagination and still avoid Cartesian dualism by giving
an account of imagination as a purely physical goings-on,
say, in terms of brain states or activities. But this is one of
those spots where Ryle reveals his strong tendency always
to prefer a behaviour-oriented explanation in preference to
explanations in terms of internal events of any hue. If a
mental happening cannot be reduced to a piece of be-

haviour then Ryle usually suggests that it must be a
disposition to behave in a certain way, or else a mixture of
an external occurrence of behaviour and a disposition to
engage in such behaviour. So it is not surprising that Ryle
approached imagination via an account of a child's imaginative performance of a bear and a boxer's imaginative
sparring, that is, by taking external imaginative behaviour
as the clearest and the central account of imagination as
such, thus relegating imagination as fancying things in
one's mind to the role of pathological case. Imagination as
fancying is deliberately abstaining from imaginative behaviour. In much the same way as Ryle claimed that it
really takes an effort to engage in contemplation or silent
soliloquy or mutterings under our breath, that is, to
abstain from speaking our thoughts out loud, so I suspect
that he would say that the natural mode of imagination is
imaginative performance and that it really takes a special
effort to curb this performance and just anticipate it.

But Ryle's view on imagination has been influential and
others have sought to remedy its defects while maintaining its essentials. For example, the philosopher
Daniel Dennett has chosen some non-mental internal
goings-on to do the job of occurrently imagining to
oneself. In his essay 'Two Approaches to Mental Images'
(*Brainstorms*, Harvester Press, 1979), Dennett substitutes
a belief or 'belief manifold' for imagination and sees these
as caused by brain states. There are no intervening mental
items between the brain states and the subsequent beliefs
about what we would ordinarily call the content of our
imagining. But this version has its own difficulties which
are highlighted when one asks what exactly is going on
when one is imagining to oneself. Presumably Dennett
would say that one is entertaining a belief about the
content of one's alleged imagining plus a false belief that
one has mental images. But this looks odd. Beliefs are not
the sort of item to assuage our intuitions about imagining
and imagination. The logic of beliefs does not fit the logic
of imagination. For example, one can decide to imagine or
imagine on demand but one cannot decide to believe or
believe on demand. Then one can imagine that p but at the
same time not believe that p. One can imagine oneself as

having certain qualities while not believing for a moment that one really has them. Explaining imagining as believing only seems plausible with one particular linguistic usage about imagination, namely 'He imagined that p was the case.' It does not fit, 'He imagined p', though this seems to be what we ordinarily mean by imagination. Kimon Lycos has made this distinction between belief and imagining in the context of the imaginary (the object of fanciful imagining).

I am inclined to think, then, that our relation to the imaginary . . . is not one of belief in the sense in which our relation to the real can be one of belief. For the imaginary is dependent on me and the real is not. Hence my beliefs about the imaginary cannot be true or false in any straightforward sense. Nor is my relation to the imaginary simulated belief. In seeing the cloud as a figure in flowing robes I do not simulate a belief that it is. ('Images and the Imaginary', *Australasian Journal of Philosophy*, Vol. 43, 1965, p. 338)

A psychologist, Zenon Pylyshyn, had earlier suggested an account similar to those of Ryle and Dennett in his paper 'What the Mind's Eye tells the Mind's Brain: A Critique of Mental Imagery' (*Psychological Bulletin*, Vol. 80, 1973). He suggested that 'the representation corresponding to the "image" is more like a *description* than a picture: There is nothing in the representation corresponding to the notion of "appearance"', and so talk about images is metaphorical. (P. 22) But this account also has problems. For a start, one can imagine things but be unable to describe them. I can imagine the smell I experienced last night but be unable to describe it. If imagining was describing this should be impossible. Again, if one is imagining in a creative way, say, fantasising, what is one describing? Pylyshyn might suggest that what one is doing is forming fictional descriptions. But to make this move is to stretch the concept of description. Describing is reporting on what is the case, not creating a scenario. Finally, it is stretching the concept of description completely out of shape to explain the random, disconnected images of hypnagogic imagination as describing.

But, as I suggested in the chapter on consciousness, the most plausible way to extend a Rylean account is to say that imagining is not a conscious activity at all. When one imagines one's sensory brain traces are activated but that is all. We manifest this activity verbally in Cartesian terms. We talk of having had an inner image. But there is no such phenomenal image and the talk is not a report but an effect of the inner goings-on, the brain activity. The talk may be, and usually is, couched in the linguistic form suitable for reports and descriptions but it is strictly speaking neither. It could not be a report on the brain activity, if it turns out to be true that this is all that takes place, because we are not aware of brain activity as such. So imagination is a myth. Talk of it is merely a product of that activity, an automatic print-out which happens to be couched in Cartesian terms. There may be good reasons why we do manifest the brain activity in terms of a Cartesian myth. It may be simpler to do so, and so communication with others may be simpler in Cartesian terms. Cartesian language may be the best language for transmitting the products of higher brain activitiy.

At most this is a speculation thrown into the air; it may not fly. Ryle would not have wanted it, as he always refused to give explanations in terms of anything inner, even brain activity. Yet, that said, it seems to me to be one possible way in which a Rylean account can be extended. No doubt it leaves a lot unanswered. One obvious question will be how can it cope with creative imagination. From the brief sketch I have given it would seem to follow that creative imagination would be an unconscious activity. Is this plausible?

Towards the end of his life Ryle returned to the problem of imagination and produced a significant addition to his account in *The Concept of Mind*, subsuming it entirely under a general theory of thinking. This he did in his paper 'Thought and Imagination' which appears in the collection of his papers, published posthumously, under the title *On Thinking*:

We are all tempted to mark off imagination from thought by confining imagination to the realm of fiction, as if to use one's imagination were *ipso facto* to indulge in make-believe. Instead I have been trying to satisfy you that a man's imaginativeness shows itself in any of those moments of his thinking in which he innovates, when he invents, discovers, explores, essays, experiments, and so on, that is when he makes or attempts to make moves which are new in the sense of being undrilled, unrehearsed and (for him) unprecedented—for example making a new joke. (P. 61)

That is, Ryle is subsuming imagining under thinking by suggesting that to use our imagination is merely to think in an improvising and inventive way. The inventive make-believe of fiction or the child's imaginative performance are only some of the ways in which our thinking is inventive, involves make-believe and is novel. Writing history and producing scientific inventions also involve this same sort of thinking. So Ryle is passing the philosophical buck from his account of imagination to his account of thinking. 'Imagining is not something separate from thinking. . . . Make-believe is thought on a half-holiday.' (*Ibid*. p. 63) I shall be devoting a whole chapter to Ryle's accounts of thinking and, in particular, I will be discussing his final adverbial account of thinking. For it was to this account—produced towards the end of his life—that Ryle was assimilating imagining.

But it is in order here to say a little about this assimilation. Certainly there are linguistic uses which suggest the assimilation. 'Think of your childhood' could have been put as 'Imagine your childhood', and 'Imagine a blue book' could have been expressed as 'Think of a blue book'. But there are also linguistic usages which resist the assimilation. 'When you imagined a book was it coloured?' does not strictly translate into 'When you thought of a book was it coloured?' And this latter divergence gives us a clue as to why there are reasons for thinking that, while imagination is a cerebral activity and in that sense a species of thinking, the act of imagining some particular thing is different in kind from pure thought, such as thinking about the concept of justice. A Cartesian would say that the difference is that the former is done in pictures, or at least in sensory terms, while the latter is not or need not be. And a Cartesian would say that Ryle's assimilation of the two refuses to recognise our intuitive conviction that imagination is different in kind from pure thought, whether this difference be expressed in Cartesian terms or not.

How Ryle would have explained away these intuitions that imagination is different in kind from pure thought I do not know. I suspect that he would have denied that there was any difference and then suggested that our belief that there was stemmed from some such fact as that sight was the strongest of our senses so that, when we think of new scenarios, new inventions, new ramifications, then we feel that what we are doing is visualising these scenarios, inventions and ramifications. But what he would have said might become clearer in the chapter on thinking, for it was to this that he assimilated imagination.

Chapter 10
THE FATALIST DILEMMA

In *Dilemmas*, the published version of his Tarner Lectures delivered at Trinity College, Cambridge in 1953, Ryle informs us that he is going to discuss a series of problems in which there appear to be two or more equally good yet irreconcilable solutions or answers. In keeping with his view about the nature of philosophical problems, Ryle will argue that the dissolution of the dilemmas one finds oneself in when confronting these apparently irreconcilable answers will be a philosophical task and not one for empirical investigation and adjudication, for the dilemmas he has in mind are those which arise when answers to different questions are mistakenly taken to be answers to one and the same question. Bringing this confusion to light is a philosophical task because it involves showing that the purported answers to one and the same question cannot in fact be answers to one and the same question because they are of a different logical type or category. Towards the end of the chapter, 'Sensation and Perception', I discussed one of these dilemmas, namely, that which arises when the neuro-physiologist's account of perception, the philosopher's account and the ordinary man's view of perception are taken to be rival answers to one and the same question. In fact, as we have seen, they are answers to three different questions. The neurophysiologist's question is 'What are the mechanisms of perception?', the philosopher's is 'What is perception?', and the ordinary man's is 'What is perceived?'

In fact, some of the dilemmas which Ryle discusses in the lectures arise not from believing that answers to different questions are answers to one and the same question, but from misinterpreting some unproblematic and compatible proposition in such a way that it becomes a rival to the ordinary man's views on this matter.

Indeed, the first dilemma which Ryle discusses in his Tarner Lectures falls more readily into this second type of dilemma, for it is the dilemma which arises by considering the Fatalist interpretation of the dictum 'That whatever is, was to be', namely 'That for whatever takes place it was antecedently true that it was going to take place' (*D*, p. 15), as a rival to the ordinary man's view that whatever a person does, it was not inevitable that he or she do so, for 'there is plenty of room for precautions, planning and weighing alternatives.' (*D*, p. 16)

Ryle's solution to this dilemma is to argue that the Fatalist interpretation of the dictum 'whatever is, was to be' is a misinterpretation. There is clearly an interpretation of this dictum which is a truism, namely 'that for everything that happens, if anyone had at any previous time made the guess that it would happen, his guess would have turned out correct.' (*D*, p. 22) And it is clear that this truism is not in competition with the ordinary man's belief that he has some control over his actions. Now philosophical trouble starts, as well as the alleged rivalry between the dictum and the ordinary man's beliefs, when the dictum 'That whatever is, was to be' is interpreted as though propositions describing what takes place—propositions describing 'whatever is'—had been written down in some Book of Destiny, before the events described actually took place, such that 'a thing's actually taking place is, so to speak, merely the turning up of a passage that has for all time been written.' (*D*, p. 16) Indeed, the philosophical trouble and the rivalry are compounded if it is further suggested or assumed that there may be somebody around, such as God, who writes the Book of Destiny or at least reads it. For it is this latter suggestion which forms the basis for the theological version of Fatalism, the Doctrine of Predestination.

Ryle is not concerned with discussing the theological version of Fatalism, which he dismisses as 'quasi-historical, entirely without evidence and most likely just false'. (*D*, p. 17) But he is interested in showing how the Fatalist misinterpretation arises, for he believes that it arises from an important and easily-made category mistake. This mistake arises, he believes, from mistaking the nature of the term 'correct' in the innocuous interpretation of the dictum 'Whatever is, was to be', namely 'That for everything that happens, if anyone had at any previous time made the guess that it would happen, his guess would have turned out correct.' The use of the adjective 'correct' in this interpretation has led some philosophers into thinking that it is the label of some property, just as adjectives like 'white' and 'sweet' are. This in turn has led philosophers into the old mistake of supposing that 'correct' must be a term that labels a proposition, which, they explain, is a logical entity that exists or subsists timelessly, waiting around to be thought of or expressed by someone in sentences. From here it is not a large step to positing the existence, *before* events take place, of propositions correctly describing these events.

In Chapter 3, 'Employing Occam's Razor in the Logical Arena', we saw Ryle attack the tendency of logicians to reify propositions as special subsistent entities. Here, Ryle might have said, we see one of the results of not heeding his strictures. But, in fact, Ryle limits himself to rectifying the Fatalist's use of 'correct'. 'Correct', Ryle tells us, is not a label of some property but a 'merely obituary and valedictory epithet. . . . It is more like a verdict than a description.' (*D*, p. 20) To say that a proposition such as 'That tomorrow will be Friday' is correct, is not to make a statement like 'Refined sugar is sweet and white' but to make one like 'His guess was fulfilled.' Just as a guess, like a wish, is only fulfilled *after* the event wished for or guessed has taken place, so, strictly speaking, a proposition about the future is only correct after the event described in the proposition has taken place. A proposition about the future once made does not hover about full of correctness or incorrectness, any more than does a wish or guess when made, immediately attach to itself or give birth to a property of fulfilled or unfulfilled. And, after all, a proposition about the future is just a guess, and if we realise that the dictum 'Whatever is, was to be' is just talking about a guess, which, if it were made, would turn out to be correct, then all the alarming Fatalist nuances of the dictum dissolve.

Part of the trouble, Ryle suggests, may also stem from the Fatalist's thinking of the terms 'correct' and 'incorrect' as synonymous with 'true' and 'false'. 'True', for example, seems to have attached to it honorific connotations to the effect that a proposition pronounced 'true' is one which has been uttered or thought of with sincerity only after careful investigation. Thus, we do not speak of guesses as true or false, but only as right or wrong, correct or incorrect. In other words 'true' and 'false' are used as verdicts pronounced upon carefully-formulated propositions about past or present events, that is, events about which evidence can and has been gathered, while 'correct' and 'incorrect' are verdicts in a much looser sense and are applied to such things as guesses or predictions when they are eventually fulfilled. Thus, to assimilate 'correct' and 'incorrect' to 'true' and 'false' will lead to giving guesses the undeserved status of researched descriptions of past events, and so to interpreting 'was to be', not as a hypothetical guess which eventually turned out to be fulfilled, but as a proposition about the future which always was accurate from the moment it was formulated.

Ryle locates another source of the Fatalist's misinterpretation in his failure to realise that it is events which make propositions true and not propositions which make events come true. The Fatalist, of course, does not make this mistake when he analyses propositions about past events; why is it then that he makes this mistake when he analyses propositions about future events? Ryle suggests that 'A large part of the reason is that in thinking of a predecessor making its successor necessary we unwittingly assimilate the necessitation to causal necessitation. . . . We slide, that is, into thinking of the anterior truths as *causes* of the happenings about which they were true.' (*D*, p. 21) What Ryle is suggesting here is that since it is the case that we can argue from a proposition to an event—from, say, a proposition that there is a footprint on the sand to the fact that a foot must have trod on that piece of sand— and since we all know that causes come before effects, we can be led into thinking that propositions can cause events. This in turn softens us up for the Fatalist doctrine. We begin to think that perhaps a proposition that so-and-so will take place could cause an event to take place, especially if there seems to be some logical impulse which moves us from the proposition to the event, as seems to occur with noting that today is Monday and believing that Tuesday—if we can consider it an event—will take place tomorrow.

Of course propositions never do cause events to take place. When we argued from the proposition 'There is a footprint in the sand' to the fact that a foot must have trodden on the sand, we were drawing out the entailment of one truth by another, or one true proposition by another. We were making use of *logical* necessity not causal necessity. We argued from a proposition about the existence of a footprint to a *proposition* about the existence of a prior event. We didn't cause an event, a footfall, to happen by considering the implications of the proposition about the existence of a footprint, we merely drew out an entailment of it, and the entailment of a proposition is another proposition, not an event.

The Fatalist, says Ryle, is not merely assimilating logical necessity to causal necessity, but making logical necessity a particularly potent form of causal necessity, a sort of logically inevitable form. A mountaineer might speak of his being caught by an avalanche as inevitable because he was in its direct path. He meant that it was practically unavoidable that he be caught by the avalanche. A Fatalist is not merely claiming that events are practically unavoidable but that they have the same inevitability as the conclusion of a valid syllogism which has true premisses.

In a later chapter in *Dilemmas* Ryle sums up the false moves which led to the Fatalist imbroglio, in the following way:

The platitude that whatever happens would have fulfilled any prior guess to the effect that it would happen was a logician's platitude. It gave us no news about what happens, but it told us a truism about what it is for a statement in the future tense to come true. On the other hand, the platitudes that many things that happen are our fault and that there are some catastrophes which can and others which cannot be averted, these are not logicians' truisms, but truisms about the world and human beings. Very crudely, they are nursemaids' truisms. In attempting to harness the nursemaid's to the logician's truisms, we lost control and found ourselves ascribing to actions and happenings properties which can belong only to the stock in trade of logicians, namely statements or propositions. (*D*, p. 52)

This mistake in ascribing logical necessity to the causal chain of events was caused by a category mistake, namely that of analysing the term 'correct' as the label of a property rather than as a verdict term. This mistake led the Fatalist into believing that true propositions describing future events not merely existed for all time but determined events in the way that premisses determine conclusions.

One distinct worry about Ryle's solution to the Fatalist dilemma is that it seems to imply that no propositions about the future can be true, for his solution involved holding that 'true' and 'correct' are verdict terms which can only be used properly when all the evidence is gathered in and the propositional claim can be seen to be fulfilled, and so can only be used properly about the present or past. But such a position would seem to rule out our common contention that we can have adequate knowledge today, via well attested natural laws, that the sun will rise tomorrow or that a stone when thrown upwards by purely human power from planet earth will fall back down again. And one could argue that any move to suggest that this is not really knowledge but just guesses with an admittedly high probability of fulfilment was not only doing violence to our ordinary notion of knowledge but was liable to lead to a radical and impractical scepticism. This worry becomes even more pressing with knowledge about the future which seems even more certainly based than knowledge based on natural laws, that is with knowledge, for example, that, since today is Monday, tomorrow will be Tuesday.

R. D. Bradley, in his article 'Must the Future be What is Going to Be?' (in *The Philosophy of Time*, ed. R. Gale), suggests that one can both admit that propositions about the future have a definite truth value now, though no one might know what it is, and so admit the truth of logical determinism, but deny that it entails Fatalism. Bradley points out that, if properly understood, the thesis of logical determinism will be seen to be what it really is, an innocuous tautology with no empirical consequences. Strictly speaking, Bradley makes clear, logical determinism should really be called 'logical determinateness', for it amounts to the unastounding thesis that true propositions about the future, because their truth value is guaranteed by future events, must describe future events. The true propositions do not causally determine future events, rather the propositions themselves are rendered logically determinate (given a definite truth value) by future events.

Now to say that the future is logically determinate, i.e. that it will be what it is going to be, is not to say anything about whether it is also causally determined, i.e. whether it will be what it is going to be *because* of what happens before it. It may be but it may not be so determined. The inference from 'x is causally determined' to 'x is logically determinate' is a legitimate one but the reverse is not. Thus when we say that statements about the future are either true or false we are saying only that the future is logically determinate and this, by itself, does not warrant the further inference, on which the above argument depends, that it is causally determined. (P. 247)

Another criticism that might be levelled at Ryle's solution to the Fatalist dilemma is that it would not be a solution to all or even, perhaps, the most common forms of Fatalism. The more usual forms are those derived from theological, or at least epistemological considerations, or from determinism. As Richard Taylor puts it in his article 'Fatalism' (*Philosophical Review*, Vol. 71, 1962):

There are various ways in which a man might get to thinking in this fatalistic way about the future, but they would be most likely to result from ideas derived from theology or physics. Thus, if God is really all-knowing and all-powerful, then, one might suppose, perhaps he has already arranged for everything to happen just as it is going to happen, and there is nothing left for you or me to do about it. Or, without bringing God into the picture, one might suppose that everything happens in accordance with invariable laws, that whatever happens in the world at any future time is the only thing that can then happen, given that certain other things were happening just before, and that these, in turn, are the only things that can happen at that time, given the total state of the world just before then, and so on, so that again, there is nothing left for us to do about it. (Pp. 56–7)

If we called the sort of Fatalism which Ryle discussed 'logical Fatalism' because it is based on a suggestion of logical necessity holding between true propositions about future events and those future events, we might call the first type mentioned by Taylor 'epistemological Fatalism' because it is based on an alleged necessity holding between precognition and the future events allegedly known. The second type of Fatalism mentioned by Taylor might be dubbed 'causal Fatalism' as it is derived from considering the causal determinist thesis.

In dismissing Predestination from his discussion, Ryle dismissed from consideration epistemological Fatalism. This form of Fatalism, in a non-theistic version, would hold that if precognition were possible, then there would seem to be an inevitability of some sort existing between the fact that X knows that event E will happen, and the fact of E's happening. Precognition cannot be dismissed as just guessing which turns out to be correct, or as an oblique reference to hypothetical guessing which would have been correct. So a great deal of Ryle's dissolution of the Fatalist dilemma would be beside the point. This form of Fatalism would, of course, have to bring forward evidence both that precognition is possible and, given that it is possible, that it can determine the events it precognises. R. D. Bradley in his article 'Must the future be What it is Going to Be?', puts this point very cogently:

Predictive inference proceeding by way of our knowledge of causal laws, is not the only logically qualified candidate for the job of telling us what the future will be, for although the empirical evidence for the occurrence of precognition may be, as it undoubtedly is, still very weak, there are no fatal objections to it on purely logical grounds. Now all that is required for precognition to be possible is that the future which is to be precognised should be logically determinate—not that it should be causally determined. Thus, it is not hard to conceive of a world in which all events occurred purely at random, or without causes, and in which a being with the power of precognition could at any moment foretell what was to happen next: indeed, according to some theologians, this is what our own world is like, except, perhaps, that God, the precognising being, is not usually regarded as being in the world but rather as transcending it. Now the mere fact that such non-inferential knowledge of the future is logically possible means that we can conceivably know whether our statements about it are true or false even although it is not causally related to the present. That is to say, all that precognition demands is that there should be a determinate, not a causally determined, future to be precognised. (P. 248)

Arguably the most common form of Fatalism is causal Fatalism, namely the belief, not as with logical Fatalism that there exists in some timeless logical arena true propositions about future events which somehow necessitate those events, but that there exists in our ordinary space-time prior to any and every future event the fully determining cause of those events. That is, one common form of Fatalism is an offshoot of determinist theories rather than of logicians' or epistemologists' puzzles. If one believes that the causal chain which results in my sitting down to lunch tomorrow is already in motion now, and just needs the passing of time for its completion, then it is not difficult to imagine that my sitting down to lunch tomorrow is fully determined and so completely explained by, and so the inevitable result of the antecedent links in the causal chain leading up to this event.

The usual query about this form of Fatalism is directed at the jump from 'Event E is caused by antecedent conditions X and Y, and so completely explained by reference to X and Y' to 'Event E is therefore the inevitable result of X and Y.' One might admit that one's sitting down to lunch is both caused by and fully explainable by, and in that sense alone determined by certain social, psychological and physiological factors without feeling compelled thereby to admit that it was inevitable. 'Inevitable' means 'unavoidable', but my sitting down to lunch tomorrow might be avoidable. Some of the Xs and Ys that explain any event E may be or be subject to human inspiration, whims and wishes, which may not be wholly explainable in turn by reference to their antecedent conditions. My sitting down to lunch tomorrow, for example, is dependent on my personal wishes, so that if it is the case that a human's personal wishes are not inevitable (not the inevitable result of his or her psychological and physiological condition at the time) then the result of a wish—my sitting down to lunch—is not inevitable. It could turn out that other parts of nature, besides humans, also have the power to cause things in such a creative and so non-inevitable manner.

Chapter 11
PLEASURE

Arguably the most typically Rylean part of *Dilemmas* is Lecture IV on pleasure. Here we have Ryle in his most characteristic mood, using *reductio* arguments against an official theory. We can almost feel Ryle flexing familiar philosophical muscles. In *The Concept of Mind* the official theory was the Cartesian doctrine about minds, this time the official theory to be demolished is one that derives from nineteenth-century psychology, though, being still a Cartesian theory, it could have been put in the form of a Cartesian dogma. As Ryle puts it:

I begin by considering a piece of theoretical harness which some pioneers in psychological theory, with natural over-confidence, formerly tried to hitch on to the notion of pleasure. Thinking of their scientific mission as that of duplicating for the world of mind what physicists had done for the world of matter, they looked for mental counterparts to the forces in terms of which dynamic explanations were given of the movements of bodies. Which introspectible phenomena would do for purposive human conduct what pressure, impact, friction and attraction do for the accelerations and decelerations of physical objects? Desire and pleasure, aversion and pain seemed admirably qualified to play the required parts. . . . (*D*, p. 56)

As wasp-stings hurt us, and as the fear of such hurts is what commonly prompts us to keep clear of wasps, so, but in the opposite direction, pleasures were construed as feelings engendered by actions and other happenings; and the desire to have these feelings was construed as being what prompts us to perform or secure the things which produce them; and as pains differ in duration and intensity and are the worse the longer they last and the more intense they are, so, according to this dynamic theory, pleasures had to be analogous feelings or sensations, capable of analogous quantitative variations. Indeed it was commonly assumed that pleasure stands to pain as hot to cold or as rapid to slow, i.e. it is what occupies the opposite end of the very same scale. (*D*, p. 57)

So the official doctrine of pleasure was that it was just like pain, a feeling, but on the opposite end of the scale of feelings. Pain is the paradigm of the feelings we fear and seek to avoid; pleasure is the paradigm of the feelings we like and desire to experience.

The first of Ryle's barrage of arguments against this official doctrine is one that has become familiar to us from our discussions of *The Concept of Mind*. It is a linguistic argument in which Ryle argues that, if we take this official view of pleasure seriously, then we should be able to say about pleasure what we are accustomed to say about other feelings, but, when we do, we end up with absurdities. For example, says Ryle, while I might say that two minutes ago I had a pain, I would not say that two minutes ago I had a pleasure, for it sounds odd. Again, while I might say that my pain was the result or effect of eye-strain, I would not say that my pleasure was the result or effect of a smell of a rose. We might admit to gaining pleasure from smelling roses but we shy away from talking of pleasure as an effect caused by smelling a rose. That we do not have this same shyness with regard to pain, is some reason for thinking that pleasure may not be a feeling as pain is. This is reinforced when we reflect that we can locate pains and describe the characteristics of the feelings that they give us, but we cannot do this with pleasure. I can tell the doctor that the pain is in my leg, and that it is definitely a throbbing pain rather than a continuous ache or a short stretch of darting pain. It would seem odd and even absurd to locate pleasure in one's leg or even in one's head, says Ryle, and equally strange to try and decide whether the pleasure is a pulsating one or a steady one. So, Ryle concludes, 'Most of the questions which can be asked about aches, tickles and other sensations or feelings cannot be asked about our likings and dislikings, our enjoyings and detestings. In a word, pleasure is not a sensation at all, and therefore not a sensation on one scale with an ache or twinge.' (*D*, p. 58)

Ryle claims that analogous considerations confirm the conclusions drawn from these linguistic arguments. For example, if pleasure were the label of a particular sensation, then it would not be possible that, what you call pleasure, some people, although knowing the English language quite adequately, legitimately refuse to label 'pleasure'. But it is a fact that some people avow that the first gulp of scalding hot tea on a bitterly cold day is distressing while others say it is sheer delight or pleasure.

Another consideration, a non-linguistic one, which seems to indicate that pleasure is not a sensation or feeling, is the phenomenon that one can have a pain and then be so absorbed in something else that one forgets all about it. In the heat of battle I may forget about the pain caused by the shrapnel in my leg. But it is 'impossible, not psychologically but logically impossible', for a person to be enjoying something but be absorbed in something else. 'There is a sort of contradiction in describing someone as absent-mindedly enjoying or disliking something.' (*D*, pp. 58–9) More revealingly, one can be aware of a pain but unaware of its cause, but one cannot be aware of a pleasure but unaware of its cause. I can be aware of a pain in my foot but not know its cause, but I cannot be aware of pleasure—where does one locate it?—but not know that it was caused by my listening to music.

From these two considerations it can be concluded that pleasure is something we are all necessarily aware of and in some sense paying attention to. Pain can be isolated and attended to in isolation from anything else, pleasure cannot. Pleasure is an accompaniment of something we are doing or something that is happening, but it is not a separate happening, for, if it were, it could be isolated, 'separately clocked' and separately attended to. We cannot leave the concert in order to concentrate better on and enjoy the pleasure we were getting from listening to the music, because, in leaving the concert, we are cutting off the pleasure. Nor is it a separate process, for, while processes can be characterised as fast or slow, pleasure cannot.

Ryle puts this alleged demolition of the official doctrine about pleasure into the general context of the Tarner Lectures, namely, the solving or dissolving of dilemmas. This time the dilemma is not one caused by construing the answers to two questions as if they were answers to one and the same question, as happened in some philosophers' accounts of perception; or one caused by misinterpreting some unproblematic view because of some category error about a crucial concept in that view, as happened with Fatalism; but the dilemma is one caused by the rivalry which grew up in the nineteenth century between science and the ordinary, everyday account of the world. The nineteenth-century psychologists felt that they had to construe psychological items as entities or occurrences if they were to make psychology into a dynamic Newtonian science with proper mechanistic causal laws. It was this imposition of a Newtonian mechanistic straitjacket which led psychologists into the category mistake of thinking of pleasure as an isolatable sensation when it is not. But, says Ryle, it is not merely the construing of pleasure on a Newtonian model that causes category mistakes, for the older Platonic picture of pleasure as a passion, that is, as an uncontrollable emotional disruption subverting reason, like an unruly mob overthrowing the legitimate government, fares no better. For, as Ryle points out,

Terror, fury and mirth can be paroxysms or frenzies. A person in such a state has, for the time being, lost his head or been swept off his feet. If a person is perfectly collected in his deliberations and movements, he cannot, logically cannot, be described as furious, revolted or in a panic. Some degree of temporary craziness is, by implicit definition, an internal feature of passion, in this sense of 'passion'. But no such connotations attach to pleasure—though they do, of course, to such conditions as thrills, transports, raptures and convulsions. If a participant in a discussion or a game greatly enjoys the discussion or game, he is not thereby stopped from having his wits about him. Else the keener a person was on golf or playing the fiddle the less would be he capable of doing these things intelligently. . . . Complete calmness does not exclude great pleasure. (*D*, pp. 65–6)

Ryle's point is that, unlike the passions, pleasure does not subvert reason by putting the person undergoing the pleasure into some disruptive emotional state. One can enjoy calm intellectual things such that the pleasure in those activities does not subvert the engaging in those activities. We do not speak of having to control or suppress pleasure in the way we might suggest controlling or suppressing terror or hate or despair or even glee.

Summing up his demolition work—and it is mainly negative demolition work that Ryle enters on in his Tarner Lecture on pleasure—Ryle writes:

We can say that the concepts of enjoying and disliking have been wrongly alleged to be of the same category with having a pain; of the same category with the kinds of occurrences which rank as causes and effects of other occurrences; and of the same category with the passions of terror, disappointment, loathing or glee. (*D*, pp. 66–7)

Before going on to consider Ryle's second thoughts on the subject of pleasure, which he gave at a meeting of the Joint Session of the Mind and Aristotelian Societies in 1954, the year after his Tarner Lectures, it is well to cast a critical glance back at what he has achieved so far. His arguments against a Platonic picture of pleasure as one of the passions I find convincing, but I feel that, while his demolition work on the nineteenth-century doctrine of pleasure is on the whole justified, in the final analysis it removes too much.

Ryle is quite right to drive a wedge between pain and pleasure. Pain does seem invariably to involve immediate, localised sensations, though the term 'pain' does not seem to be the label of one *sui generis* sensation. 'Pain' seems to be a term we apply to a host of sensations which are produced via a fairly definite group of nerve endings and which we shrink from physiologically as well as psychologically. Empirical psychology and physiology have produced strong evidence that there are several nerve bundles (such as C-fibres and A-delta fibres) whose endings, if stretched or damaged, invariably cause—if the disturbance is transmitted to the brain—what we call 'pain'.

Over-strong stimulation of any sort will elicit pain from almost any part of the body. Hence it was long believed that pain was a special quality that resulted when any receptor was overstimulated. But certain lines of evidence, such as the fact that specific neural lesions will eliminate pain without disturbing touch, and vice versa, pointed to a separate pain sense. The discovery of pain spots in the skin gave strong support to this view. The receptors for pain are undoubtedly free nerve endings, which branch widely throughout the skin and other sensitive tissues. Stretching these endings results in pain. The resulting impulses travel in specific nerve bundles; the surgeon sometimes severs these nerves to remove persistent pain. There are even reports of people who have a congenital lack of pain, and often cut or burn themselves without knowing it. (Robert S. Woodworth and Harold Schlosberg, *Experimental Psychology*, Methuen, 3rd ed., Revised, 1955, p. 285)

There is another use of the term 'pain', such as is used in the sentence 'Your failure caused me great pain', which Ryle did not isolate nor discuss. This sense of pain is sometimes called 'cognitive distress' and seems to be a complex phenomenon made up of a belief about something regrettable and an emotional reaction of distress, including feelings, resulting from it. But this is not the prime meaning of the term 'pain', so I will not direct any attention to it.

It should also be pointed out that, while there are no special nerve endings for pleasure, there does seem to be in the brain a pleasure spot or centre—though, as yet at any rate, a not very well defined one—in much the same way that there is a pain centre.

Experiments, started by James Olds and Peter Milner in the early fifties, pointed to various parts of the brain stem as reward centres or 'pleasure centres', which might be involved in the reception of reinforcing messages. They discovered that if an electrode is permanently and painlessly implanted at any one of a vast number of points in a rat's brain, and it is connected up in such a manner that the rat can deliver a shock to the electrode by pressing a lever, the animal will do so, time after time, even to the total neglect of genuine bodily requirements, as if the normal actions associated with learning had been by-passed and the electrode had found the site of pure reinforcement. . . . The present evidence suggests that parts of the brain-stem where neurons use the substances noradrenaline and dopamine as their transmitter substances . . . may be the sites of reinforcement. There were hopes (or fears) that implantation of electrodes into the 'pleasure centres' of the human brain might become commonplace as treatment for the depressed or as titillation for the hedonistic. Fortunately it seems that the sensations produced by such stimulation in man are rarely intensely pleasurable, though the technique has been used on some patients in states of intense and incurable pain. (Colin Blakemore, *Mechanics of the Mind*, Cambridge University Press, 1977, p. 166)

This isolation of, an as yet vaguely defined, pleasure centre in the brain does not reinstate the claim that pleasure is a sensation in the more usual sense of the term because this centre is not connected with a definite set of nerve endings on the skin surface or to any sense organ. But it does incline one to the view that pleasure itself is a feeling or conscious event very like that which results from stimulating a sense organ or specialised nerve bundle.

At this point I should mention that some of Ryle's arguments that pleasure is not a sensation are defective, though I agree that pleasure, if it is a sensation, is not so in quite the same way that pain or a tingling on the soles of the feet are. On the other hand, I do not think that any of Ryle's arguments affect the view that pleasure might be a feeling though caused by a different sort of causal process than that which is characteristic of sensation.

For example, Ryle's argument that pleasure is not a sensation because the sensation one labels 'pleasure' can legitimately be labelled by another as 'pain', will not do. For this is characteristic of pain as well, which Ryle agrees is a sensation. I might find someone's tickling the soles of my feet painful, you might find it pleasurable. I might find the giddiness caused by the hurdy-gurdy pleasant, you might find it painful. What does emerge here is that neither 'pleasure' nor 'pain' are purely descriptive labels. They both contain an evaluative element. Thus, while to say that X is a pain implies that X is a sensation, it also implies that X is an unwelcome one, where 'unwelcome' is the subject's evaluation of the pain. With some pains, of course, 'unwelcome' is too weak a term. The sensation that is caused by the dentist's drilling on a raw nerve in one's tooth is not just unwelcome, it is insupportable. And, presumably, most pains of this sort are insupportable to everyone. In that sense, the awfulness of pain is objectively based. Indeed it is far easier to isolate sensations which everyone agrees are painful than to isolate sensations which everyone agrees are pleasurable. This is further evidence that the term 'pleasure' is not linked to the stimulation of fairly definite parts of the body in a definite way in the way that the term 'pain' is, or at least not with the same consistency.

Ryle's argument that pleasure is not a sensation because it is logically impossible for a person to be enjoying something but wholly absorbed in something else, will not do either, for this is also characteristic of pain, his acknowledged paradigm of a sensation. It is logically impossible to claim that one is in pain but wholly absorbed in something else, for the simple reason that it is logically impossible to have unfelt feelings or unsensed sensations. If I am in pain from a wound in the leg, but you hypnotise me and tell me that I am having a warm bath, and I come to believe that I am and experience its suffused pleasures, then I am no longer in pain. You have removed it by hypnosis. One might also have done it by just taking up my attention with, say, a superb film or even an exciting book.

Again Ryle argues that one can be aware of pain but not necessarily of its cause, but this dislocation is not possible with pleasure. But, though I own to being more hesitant here, this may be incorrect. If, unknown to you—say, while you are asleep—I inject you with a drug which puts you into a state of euphoria, you will awake in a state of euphoria, and declare how pleasant life is and how pleasurable even the most mundane tasks have become, yet be unable to state the cause of your pleasure. Again, unknown to you, I might plant an electrode in your brain and excite some part of your pleasure centre. However, it could be that administering such drugs or exciting the pleasure centre are only remote causes which make us more receptive to finding pleasure in proximate ones about us, our activities or sensations or experiences.

Finally, it is by no means indisputable, as Ryle claims, that one cannot locate and 'clock' some pleasures. For example, if one comes inside from working on the roads in freezing wet conditions and then puts one's wet and cold feet into a dish of warm water, it is not far-fetched to claim that one has a distinct pleasure located in one's feet beginning from the moment when one's feet were placed into the dish of warm water. And one can easily concentrate on this sort of pleasure to the exclusion of everything else. One just leans back and wallows in it. On the other hand it is true, as Ryle points out, that it does not make much sense to locate the pleasure of listening, say, to Richter playing the piano, or the pleasure gained from smelling a rose, in any particular part of the body, though one might be able to clock the beginning of these pleasures if not their precise ending. And it is true that it does not make much sense to speak of isolating and concentrating on the pleasure of listening to a great pianist while paying no heed to its cause, namely the performance of the great pianist, though this may only be because in normal circumstances it is impossible.

It may be that we cannot isolate and then concentrate on

the pleasure of listening to a great pianist, not because in such cases pleasure is not a sensation but because in such cases the sensation is mediated by the listening. If we divert our attention and so stop listening, the pleasure—which may be a sensation resulting from or accompanying it—would cease, and so for that reason we cannot direct our attention solely to the pleasure. To put it more succinctly, you cannot direct your attention directly to some pleasures (and they could be sensations) because they only result from giving attention more or less completely to certain events or activities.

It seems clear that pleasure can involve sensations at times and that, in doing so, it can be localised and of definite duration simply because its sensation component can. On the other hand, pleasure can involve other things besides sensations. It can involve activities or events. Watching Borg play tennis can give one great pleasure, so can fishing. So what is beginning to emerge from this discussion is that pleasure is a second-order phenomenon. It is parasitic on first-order occurrences such as sensations, activities and events.

Now it is time to look at Ryle's second thoughts on pleasure which he first gave at the Joint Session of the Mind and Aristotelian Societies in 1954 under the title 'Pleasure', and which were subsequently printed in the Proceedings (and reprinted in Ryle's *Collected Papers*, Volume 2), for these thoughts do put forward a second-order account of pleasure.

After mounting against the feeling-sensation model of pleasure, and the emotion model of pleasure, a selection of the arguments which we have already discussed, Ryle introduces a third model which has often been used to explain pleasure, but which is also, he argues, unsatisfactory. This model is that of moods. Someone might be tempted to construe pleasure as a mood or frame of mind, but this, says Ryle, would be a mistake. For pleasure differs from its nearest related mood, feeling cheerful, in a crucial way. Feeling pleasure is associated with a particular object, but a mood need not be. One might have got up and felt cheerful and the mood may have lasted all day. Pleasure on the other hand is connected with particular

objects and happenings, smelling roses, attending con-
certs or taking walks. Just as one might be depressed by
nothing in particular but by 'the Scheme of Things in
General' so one might be cheerful about 'the Scheme of
Things in General', but one cannot take pleasure in 'the
Scheme of Things in General'.

While I think that Ryle is correct in separating pleasure
from moods, his first argument for this distinction is not
the strongest, particularly if we bear in mind that Ryle
often uses the term 'enjoying' as a synonym, whether as a
rough one or not is not clear, for 'pleasure'. For one can
speak of enjoying life which does look a little like enjoying 'the Scheme of Things in General'. One can, of course,
be in a mood directed particularly, say, at a certain person
or episode, in much the same way as enjoyment is. I can
be irritable with you, all day even. Or my son might sulk
all day because I stopped him playing with his train during
a meal time. If asked why he is sulking, at any time during
the day, he might refer to my taking the train from him at
breakfast. But Ryle would not deny this, his point is that
moods *sometimes* are, while enjoyment *never* is, free-
floating.

The most interesting part of Ryle's Joint Session paper
on pleasure comes towards the end of the paper, where he
makes a beginning on a positive account of pleasure. Ryle
suggests that the central notion of pleasure is enjoyment
and that central to this is the notion of attention. Attention
is a necessary but not a sufficient condition for pleasure.
To enjoy something entails attending to it. But it would
be wrong to construe this attention as necessarily of a very
positive form, that is, as if it were like switching some
mental torch beam on to some object or episode. Attention
can be more like something impressing itself on me than I
directing myself upon it. It can be the noticing such as
occurs when my attention is drawn to a smell of dead fish
in the corner, or when I fall over something and realise
that it is a piece of barbed wire. A third sort of attention is
that of doing something carefully or attending to tasks,
such as a car driver does or should do when he or she
drives. A fourth sort of attention is that of the spectator at a
football match. Such a person is not engaging himself to

do something carefully, like the car driver; nor switching on his attention for a short spell, like the student in a lecture; nor having his attention gradually or more swiftly drawn by something such as by a bad smell or something one trips over; but he is drawn to attend to something by interest in it and so the attention is maintained without effort. This latter sort of attention is more like that of blotting paper soaking up ink than of a torch being switched on and directed at something. This sense of attention is, roughly, being interested in, and it is, says Ryle, the sense of attention which is part of the analysis of pleasure as enjoyment.

> To be, at a particular moment, interested in something is certainly to be giving one's mind to it. . . . Now to say that someone has been enjoying a smell or a walk at least suggests and maybe even implies that he has been interested in the smell or in the exercise and the incidents of the walk—not that he gave his mind to them in e.g., the sedulous way, but rather that his mind was taken up by them in a spontaneous way. This is, of course, not enough. Alarming, disgusting and surprising things capture my attention. . . . So do pains and tickles. (*CP* 2, p. 332)

And Ryle is right. As an account of pleasure as enjoyment, it is not enough to say that it entails being interested in what one is enjoying. But this is as far as Ryle gets in his positive account of pleasure. As Ryle puts it in his very last sentence of his Joint Session paper, 'the real work remains to be done.'

It is tempting to speculate that Ryle did not treat of pleasure in *The Concept of Mind* because he did not have more than the barest outline of a positive account to give. While convinced that the nineteenth-century Cartesian psychological account of pleasure as a sensation would not do, Ryle was not clear about what to substitute in its place. In *Dilemmas* and his Joint Session paper Ryle endorsed an account of pleasure as involving attention in the sense of taking an interest in something. As he gives a purely dispositional account of other heed concepts (in *The Concept of Mind*, Chapter V) it seems fair to say that he was inclining towards a dispositional account of pleasure or, as he seemed to hold as more or less synonymous, enjoyment. That he did not lean whole-heartedly in that direction may be an indication that he had doubts about the success of such an analysis.

Terence Penelhum in his classical critique of Ryle's views on pleasure, in his paper 'The Logic of Pleasure' (I shall be referring to its reprinted version in *Essays in Philosophical Psychology*, ed. Donald Gustafson), certainly takes it that Ryle's final view was a dispositional account of enjoyment or pleasure, and argues that it will not do for the important reason that pleasure is irreducibly occurrent and internal. He suggests that, while rightly holding that pleasure is not a sensation, and that it cannot occur in the absence of any first-order event or episode which could be connected with it, he wrongly inferred from this that pleasure was in no respect occurrent or episodic. For Penelhum mounts a series of sharp arguments to show that pleasure is occurrent or episodic and internal. His main argument is that 'if enjoyment were a disposition, my knowledge that I was enjoying myself would be inferential, just like my knowledge that others are doing so' (p. 241), for the usual way of working out that someone has a disposition is to watch their behaviour. But I do not have to watch carefully my own behaviour to work out that I am enjoying something, I am immediately aware of it when I am enjoying something.

I am less convinced by Penelhum's contention that 'there is no sense to the claim that I feel I am enjoying something but may be mistaken' (p. 242), therefore enjoyment is an occurrence about which we are directly aware. For I can imagine finishing a game of tennis, and being asked whether I enjoyed it or not, and not being able to decide or, having decided that I did, later want to withdraw the claim. As Anthony Manser puts it in his paper, 'Pleasure' (in the *Proceedings of the Aristotelian Society*, Vol. 61, 1960–61)

This [that one is in a privileged position about one's own enjoyment] does not mean that there are not cases where I am in doubt whether I enjoyed something, or even that I may decide that I was wrong in saying that I enjoyed it. The first case could be illustrated by the man who said of lychees that he had to go on eating them 'to see if he did like them' and could never quite decide. Such a doubt frequently arises where some taste or other physical sensation is experienced for the first time. (P. 235)

This does not show that the enjoyment itself is not occurrent but only that, if it is, in reporting about it or interpreting it, one can misreport or misinterpret. This may be so, even if there are certain pleasures which are so immediate—say, putting one's feet in warm water after coming in from the cold—that one cannot be in doubt or mistaken about them. For it might be the case that the occurrence which is pleasure is so vivid on occasion that it compels awareness of its enjoyableness while in other cases and on other occasions this is not so.

Penelhum endorses Ryle's account of enjoyment as a form of attention, a passive form, as Ryle suggested in his final account of pleasure as a form of having one's interest aroused by something. His chief point of difference with Ryle is in insisting that pleasure is irreducibly occurrent. Now, if we take it that Penelhum is correct in insisting on the occurrent nature of enjoyment, what we end up with is that pleasure is a second-order or second-level internal occurrent state which is usually aroused when one is aware of activities, one's own or those of others, or events. The suggestion that there are pleasure centres in the brain implies that, in untypical laboratory circumstances, this second-order state can be directly aroused by sending currents through electrodes. This suggests that enjoyment or pleasure could be isolated and concentrated on in isolation, though in normal circumstances it cannot (perhaps for the good evolutionary reason that, if we could, we might do nothing else!). Thus enjoyment may ultimately be best accounted for in a way that is closer to the Cartesian account than to the Rylean account. It may be an internal state of euphoria which, in normal circumstances, is only aroused by activities or events, and so is normally euphoria *at* or *in* something, and very hard to separate from attention to or engagement in that thing. This euphoria would usually be psychosomatic, with both cognitive and bodily aspects. It would include pro-evaluations and beliefs directed towards activities or events, and agreeable bodily feelings which are not necessarily localised. But it still remains true that the available evidence points to the fact that pleasure is a sensation or something very like it. Perhaps it should be called a second-order sensation, for it is not aroused directly by contact of some sort but by activities, mental and, especially, physical. It has a reinforcing role, namely to get us to repeat those activities which arouse pleasure. It is a well attested fact that 'the most responsive pleasure centres—thalamus, hypothalamus, basal ganglia, etc.—are in the upper brainstem and associated mid-line region of the brain, which serve also as centres for controlling sexual, digestive, excretory, and similar basic organic processes.' (Roland Puccetti, 'The Sensation of Pleasure', *British Journal for the Philosophy of Science*, Vol. 20, 1969, p. 243)

Puccetti has suggested that Ryle's neglect of research in empirical psychology on pleasure—such as that undertaken by Olds, Milner, and others on the pleasure centres —is a good example of the limitations of a purely linguistic analysis account of psychological phenomena.

In retrospect it seems obvious from the above discussion that any philosophical method relying solely on ordinary language for the investigation of concepts accepts severe limitations on what it can achieve. For one thing, ordinary language reflects ordinary experience, and it is not part of ordinary experience to have wires sunk into one's brain and one's pleasure centres artificially stimulated. (*Ibid.* p. 245)

As I shall endeavour to support in more detail in a later chapter, I think Puccetti is right. While Ryle was one of the most ingenious, fertile, creative and important philosophers working in the field of philosophical psychology, he seemed to set up two artificial barriers to the ultimate success of his work. One was his neglect of empirical psychology, the other was his refusal to seek answers to problems in philosophical psychology in terms of inner states or episodes of any variety. We have already seen these artificial barriers blocking Ryle's way in other areas and topics, but nowhere do they seem more in evidence than in his work on pleasure.

Chapter 12
TECHNICAL AND UNTECHNICAL CONCEPTS

In the previous chapter we discussed Ryle's examination of the concept of pleasure and saw how he suggested that the category mistake enshrined in our view of pleasure—that of construing it as a sensation when it is more like a special way of attending to something—was the result of nineteenth-century psychologists trying to force a Newtonian theory of dynamics on to psychological occurrences, and that this mistake led to a marked gulf between the ordinary man's biographical way of speaking about pleasure and other psychological items, and the psychologist's way of speaking about them. In the latter part of the Tarner Lectures Ryle concentrates in a more general way on this rivalry between science and the everyday world, and between technical and untechnical concepts. In *Dilemmas*, Lecture V, 'The World of Science and the Everyday World', Ryle writes that,

When we are in a certain intellectual mood, we seem to find clashes between the things that scientists tell us about our furniture, clothes and limbs and the things that we tell about them. We are apt to express these felt rivalries by saying that the world whose parts and members are described by scientists is different from the world whose parts and members we describe ourselves, and yet, since there can be only one world, one of these seeming worlds must be a dummy-world. Moreover, as no one nowadays is hardy enough to say 'Bo' to science, it must be the world that we ourselves describe which is the dummy-world. (*D*, p. 68)

In short, Ryle is saying, many of us feel that there is not merely a rivalry but a feud between the scientific account of the world and the ordinary man's account, and that, all appearances to the contrary, it is the scientific account which is the true one. In particular it is the accounts of the world given by fundamental or nuclear physics and, though to a lesser extent, the physiology of perception, which makes us feel that our ordinary view of the world is erroneous. 'Where theologians used to be the people to tell us about the creation and management of the cosmos, now these physicists are the experts.' (*D*, p. 73) And the truths propounded and expounded by these new experts seem to leave no room for the truths of daily life.

But this feeling we have, says Ryle, is mistaken. Fundamental physics is not in competition with the ordinary man's view of the world any more than is an auditor's accounts for some college in competition with a student's account of the same college. While it is true that the auditor's accounts cover every aspect of college life, for they list everything that happens or pertains to the college —the buildings, tuition, books, meals and so on—they do not, so to speak, cover every aspect of every aspect.

He [the student] cannot question the accuracy, comprehensiveness or exhaustiveness of the accounts. He cannot complain that they cover five or six sides of college life, but do not cover the other sixteen sides. All the sides that he can think of are indeed duly covered. . . . Yet the accounts were silent about what had been taught and the auditor betrayed no inquisitiveness about what progress the student had made. . . . Nothing had been said about him personally at all. He has not been described, though he has been financially accounted for. (*D*, p. 76)

The auditor's view of a college is purely from one perspective or with one interest in mind, the financial. The buildings of the college, its tuition, books, meals, and even students themselves, will only appear in his report in so far as they can be costed and a monetary debit or credit put alongside them. The auditor is not interested in what the buildings are used for, or what are in the books, or whether the meals are nourishing, or whether the students learn anything.

Now, says Ryle, there are some important similarities between the relation of the auditor's accounts for the college to the student's account, and the relation of the physicist's account of the world to that of the ordinary man's. 'I do not want to press the analogy beyond a certain point . . . but only that it [a scientific theory] is like a balance-sheet in one important respect namely that the formulae of the one and the financial entries of the other are constitutionally speechless about certain sorts of matters.' (*D*, pp. 77–8) The physicist's account and the ordinary man's are two different but complementary ways of giving information of very different sorts about roughly the same area. A nuclear physicist neither truly nor falsely describes chairs or tables because he does not set out to describe them at all, even though his account of the nature of matter applies to all matter, including chairs and tables. The ordinary man is not wrong to describe a deck chair as made of wood, canvas, nails, glue and paint, nor is this account rendered false by the physicist's account of matter —including wood, canvas, nails, glue and paint—as made up of neutrons, protons, electrons and so on.

In Chapter VI of *Dilemmas*, 'Technical and Untechnical Concepts', Ryle continues his account of the apparent clash between the scientific view and the ordinary man's view. He urges us to return again to his analogy where he contrasted the auditor's view of a college with a student's view. He reminds us that he has already argued that these accounts are not rivals, but accounts of different aspects of the same items. The auditor or accountant sees all the items under one aspect alone, the financial, and describes all those items by means of a very specialised and at least semi-technical notation, namely in the monetary terms of accounting. Now the second point he wants to bring out from this analogy is that the description given by the auditor is not merely compatible with the description given by the student but presupposes it. For example, a book would not have a price expressible in monetary terms unless it had some value to a student or someone similar. Unless people wanted to study or at least read the contents of books, or put them to some such use, they would not be worth anything expressible in terms of a price.

Precisely this is the way that we had, I think, to construe the silence of the college accounts about the contents of the books bought for its library. Only book-prices were mentioned, but this restriction was not merely compatible with the books that were bought for these prices having other properties than these prices, it was actually incompatible with books being nothing more than the vehicles of purchase-prices. An object could not be merely something costing half-a-crown. (*D*, p. 84)

Though Ryle is not very explicit about how this aspect of the analogy is to be cashed out in the contrast between the physicist's view of the world with the ordinary man's, I think he is suggesting that, in a related though different manner, a physicist's description of a chair's composition in terms of protons, neutrons and electrons, and their properties, implies that there must be a less fundamental macro set of properties. To say these are the fundamental particles implies that there are less fundamental aggregations of those particles, which in turn implies properties of these aggregations which will be different from the properties of the particles making up those aggregations. For example, fundamental particles do not have taste, colour or smell. They are too small to impinge on our senses. The only things that can have secondary or sense qualities are things large enough to impinge on man's senses. Thus, only things in the everyday world could be described in terms of secondary qualities. Besides, fundamental physics, and physics in general, deals only with primary qualities such as mass, extension and motion, for these, unlike secondary qualities, are measurable and quantifiable.

But the analogy does not work very well, for subatomic particles do not have the properties they have in virtue of the macro secondary qualities in terms of which humans describe objects. The properties of subatomic particles are not evaluative properties supervenient on descriptive ones in the way that prices or values on books are supervenient on other, more fundamental, properties of books. Conversely, macro, secondary qualities, while they do exist partly in virtue of there being micro, subatomic particles which effect our senses, do not bear the relation to the properties of subatomic particles of values placed upon them. We are not even directly aware of these properties, though they cause various effects in us. But perhaps Ryle did not mean the analogy to be pressed so closely.

Another way, Ryle suggests, in which scientific or technical concepts and theories are not hostile rivals to the concepts and theories of the ordinary man, can be shown by means of another analogy. A child might be perplexed that one and the same card can be described as 'the Queen of Hearts' as well as 'a trump card'. A child is perplexed because he or she thinks that being Queen of Hearts and being a trump are on the same level, such that if the card is the one, say Queen of Hearts, *ipso facto* it could not be the other as well. But, of course, we know a card can be both Queen of Hearts and a trump card at the same time, for we know that the term 'Queen of Hearts' applies to a definite card in every pack of cards, no matter what game the pack is being used for, and that this card is indeed the Queen of Hearts can be checked by just looking at the face of the card. But the term 'trump card' only applies to a Queen of Hearts, or to any other card in the pack, if it is part of a pack being used for a game like bridge, and if the particular card in question is one from the suit which has been selected as trumps by a turn of a card in accordance with very specific rules of the complex and sophisticated card game of bridge. In short, a trump card not merely possesses a face-value property, say of being a Queen of Hearts, it has gained a further complex property by being part of a game for which the cards are being used.

In a somewhat similar way, a chair which has the simple face-value, untechnical property of being red, can also gain the further highly complex property of being partly made up of, say, electrons, by being viewed in connection with a sophisticated theory propounded by nuclear physicists. And to think that these two properties are incompatible rivals is as foolish as thinking that a card cannot be both Queen of Hearts and a trump.

But again there is something not quite right about this analogy. While a card is to be called the 'Queen of Hearts' in virtue of the properties of the drawing on one side of it, and it is to be called 'a trump' in virtue of the conventional rules of the game in which the card is pressed into service, it is not the case that, while a chair has a simple face-value of being red, it has the property of being made of electrons only because it is employed in some game governed by conventional rules. A physicist would say that a chair's being made up of electrons is a matter of natural laws. Being made up of electrons is just as much a face-value property as being red. The former is a property of its subatomic or micro face, if you like, while the latter is a property of its macro face.

In the last chapter of *Dilemmas*, Chapter VIII, 'Formal and Informal Logic', Ryle tells us that this rivalry, between the scientific, technical view and the non-technical non-scientific view, has even invaded and divided philosophy itself. The formal logician accuses the philosopher who does not employ his technicalities on all occasions as amateurish, and the philosopher replies by suggesting that the technical moves of the formal logician are just empty formalities which solve no real problems.

Like all such feuding Ryle believes that the hostility is unfounded. The formal logician and the philosopher are engaged in two different tasks. 'Neither is doing what the other is doing, much less is either doing improperly what the other is doing properly.' (*D*, p. 119) The formal logician is working within a system like the pure mathematician. He works with constants, such as logical quantifiers (e.g. some, all) and connectives (e.g. and, or) that have been carefully defined and are topic neutral. What he is interested in is new connections between these constants and between propositions relating these constants to one another. The philosopher, on the other hand, is investigating variables, the ordinary, everyday slippery concepts with which we try to express what we want to say, concepts such as sensation, perception, pleasure and thinking. Of course the two endeavours do overlap. Formal logic instills and sets the standards of rigour which the philosopher or informal logician tries to emulate in his investigations of the uncharted and undefined concepts of ordinary thought and discourse. Philosophical problems will never be reducible to standard moves in some deductive system devised and charted by the formal logician, for philosophical problems crop up precisely in those areas uncharted by any technical system, or grow out of the overlap of two charted areas. As Ryle puts it, 'where there is virgin forest, there can be no rails.' (*D*, p. 126) But, very often, some steps through the forest can be bolstered by the technical aids of formal logicians.

Ryle's division of labour between the formal logician and the philosopher is probably uncontroversial, but I have a suspicion that many would consider that Ryle is being curiously overprotective towards the ordinary man's untechnical view of the world and is exaggerating the lack of rivalry between science and the everyday world. In particular, I feel that Ryle is being somewhat naïve in thinking that the ordinary man's unscientific view of the world is limited to descriptions of the world about him in terms of secondary qualities. Ordinary language and the ordinary man's view of the world is theory laden, and the theories that impregnate ordinary language are often yesterday's scientific castoffs or descredited philosophical or theological views. After all Ryle himself, for a great deal of his philosophical life, was at pains to purify ordinary language of its Cartesian category mistakes, and these Cartesian views were the scientific and philosophic orthodoxies of their day.

If we feel that there is a rivalry between science and the ordinary man's views, I think that it is not primarily because of the findings of nuclear physics, but because of the propounding and confirmation of theories in astronomy, biology and, increasingly, psychology. For example, Western man's belief in his uniqueness is cast in doubt by the astronomer's suggestion that our solar system, with its planets that have atmospheres which can support life, seems very likely to be duplicated many times throughout the universe. Christian man's belief that God directly created him was cast in doubt by biology's theory of the evolution of man by genetic mutation. And throughout this century psychology has undermined the realist, ordinary man's view of perception.

Ryle might reply to the above by saying that, even if he has misplaced the source of the rivalry between science and the ordinary man's view of this world, he is at least right in saying that there should not be any rivalry between fundamental physics and our ordinary view of objects in the world. But Ryle cannot even retreat to this position, for as J. J. C. Smart has pointed out in his essay 'Ryle in Relation to Modern Science' (in *Ryle*, ed. Wood and Pitcher) the theories of fundamental physics can clash with our ordinary views about things in the world at a number of points. To adapt one of Smart's examples, anyone who has lived through a long, dry but fiercely cold winter, such as one experiences, say, in Alberta, will notice that, when one combs one's hair, it stands on end, and that one receives frequent shocks from car door handles and aerials and other metal parts. To proffer an explanation of these phenomena without mentioning electrons and static electricity would be at least inadequate and at most mistaken. Of course, because such phenomena are common, the correct physicist's explanation may now be known by the ordinary man in the street and be part of his world view. But this makes my point, for the ordinary man must have adopted the correct view in place of a rival incorrect or inadequate view at some stage.

To adapt another of Smart's examples, nowadays the ordinary man in the street comes across X-rays more or less as a matter of course. He sees X-ray machinery and the pictures it produces in his doctor's and dentist's surgery, and his conception of the machinery and the pictures would be either inadequate or incorrect if he had no conception of what X-rays were, and to have such a conception he must get to know something about electromagnetic radiation. A full understanding would, of course, go much further. I suspect that the ordinary man's view of X-rays is most often not a rival to the scientific view because he has no view at all. But this would lend no comfort to the Rylean view that the ordinary man's and the scientific account of the world are never in contention.

In putting forward his view that science does not clash with the everyday view of the world, Ryle seems to have argued from the claim, which he believed everyone would admit, that there is no clash between an account of matter in terms of fundamental particles and an account of a material object such as a chair in terms of secondary qualities, to the conclusion that the scientist's and the ordinary man's accounts *never* clash. Such an argument is about as valid as arguing from the fact that there is no clash between a doctor's account of someone's fainting in terms of brain lesions, loss of blood, and so on, and a reporter's account of the same happening in term's of the victim's slipping from his chair and, in falling, breaking a precious Ming vase belonging to the Tate Galley, to the fact that doctors' and reporters' views could never clash. Of course they could clash. If the reporter includes in his reports speculations about the causes of the fainting, then he is putting up an account which is a direct rival to the doctor's account. Similarly, when the ordinary man speculates about such things as the origins of the universe or of man, and about the nature of static electricity or X-rays, or the linguistic analyst speculates about perception, imagination and pleasure, he is putting forward views which are rivals to the empirical scientist's.

But what of Ryle's initial claim, which he believes everyone would admit, that there is no clash between an account of matter in terms of fundamental particles and an account of a material object such as a chair in terms of secondary qualities? It would depend entirely on *what* account of secondary qualities an ordinary person would give. An account of secondary qualities which denied scientific facts about perception would be just plain wrong.

It is no use complaining that when the ordinary man does speculate about the origins of the universe or something like that, he is not really giving an ordinary man's account, but momentarily and forgetfully straying into the scientist's back yard without permission; for, notoriously, the ordinary man has always had views about his and the universe's origins and nature, and about the explanation for natural phenomena which he witnesses. The ordinary man's view of the world is shot through with discarded and discredited philosophical and scientific theories, and it was just this point which made Bertrand Russell so hostile to Linguistic Analysis as he felt that many of its practitioners made appeals to ordinary language as if to a touchstone of truth.

I am tempted to speculate that Ryle's stark separation of scientific views from the ordinary man's views is some sort of cousin to his lifelong belief that philosophers, except presumably philosophers of science, need not know any science. This latter belief of Ryle's was underlined when, in his conversation with Ryle about his work—in a BBC radio series of 1970–71—Bryan Magee mentioned that *The Concept of Mind* ignored well-known psychological theories with which its thesis was incompatible. Ryle replied, 'Well, here I don't feel very penitent. I'd never studied any psychology . . . I don't know the ground so I don't want to step on it.' (Bryan Magee, *Modern British Philosophy*, p. 131) When Magee countered by mentioning that Russell, in his review of *The Concept of Mind*, suggested that Ryle ought to have known the ground for he had already stepped on it, for 'it was pointless to write about matters like sensation and perception if you weren't thoroughly familiar with what neurologists, opticians, psychologists and other empirical observers had said about them; in short that there was no point in doing this kind of philosophy at all if you don't know a lot of science', Ryle replied dismissively to Magee that 'Russell thought one ought to know a lot about, say, the rods and cones in the eye, and I don't pretend to know anything about them, and, if I may speak a bit rudely, I don't want to.' (*Ibid.* pp. 131–2)

Recently Norman Malcolm, in a paper entitled 'The Myth of Cognitive Processes and Structures' (in *Cognitive Development and Epistemology*, ed. T. Mischel) mounted a Rylean type of attack—though Malcolm invariably traces his inspiration to Wittgenstein—on, among other things, cognitive processes such as remembering and recognising, to which contemporary psychologists refer. He suggests that these psychologists erroneously construct theories and models in terms of inner cognitive processes and structures because they wrongly infer that there must be something else happening to humans besides their behaviour when they claim, for example, to recognise someone. They fail to find any direct evidence for such processes yet they fail to see, said Malcolm, that recognition is not something underlying the visible behaviour but is just that behaviour in certain specifiable circumstances. In a reply in *Analysis*, 1972–3, Michael Martin argued that such attacks do not even come to grips with the theories of contemporary psychologists because, unlike nineteenth-century psychologists, they do not hold that such processes are introspectible or directly observable in any other way. Their postulation of such processes is on a par with the postulation by physicists of electrons. The acceptance or rejection is in terms of their 'predictive power and explanatory capacity'. Moreover, contemporary psychologists would not claim that their concepts are or ought to be consonant with the concepts embedded in ordinary language. 'It seems unlikely that psychologists are particularly interested in . . . giving a philosophical analysis of the commonsense or ordinary meaning of 'pattern recognition' or 'remembering'. Psychologists, like all scientists, redefine terms to suit their theoretical purposes.' (P. 85)

Ryle would not claim that the ordinary man's view could impugn the scientific picture of something, indeed he would claim that they do not even overlap, but he would claim that philosophers have sufficient data from a mere consideration of ordinary, everyday human activities, without aid from specially controlled laboratory conditions or special apparatus, to impugn certain scientific theories. Ryle, for example, put forward in just such a way a theory of pleasure in opposition to the nineteenth-century psychologist's views. But it is probably no accident that Ryle, unlike Malcolm, did not cross swords with contemporary psychologists. I suspect he realised that the concepts and theories of contemporary empirical psychologists are of a completely different order from the concepts of the ordinary man, the ordinary language philosopher, and nineteenth-century science. But what Ryle failed to realise is that, while the ordinary language philosopher's and the ordinary man's view of the world will not impugn the contemporary scientist's view, the reverse is not true. There is overlap, and when there is, it should be acknowledged that, since the scientist has to hand both the data available to the ordinary man and ordinary language philosopher, as well as his own data gained through controlled experiments and with the help of special apparatus, his theory will be the more comprehensive. One of the uses of philosophy is that its theories are often about areas still untapped by the scientists and so useful as preliminary ground clearing and theory formation. Often a philosopher can show that certain unscientific theories are incoherent or mistaken given even the ordinary data available, and a philosopher's theory is often the initial impetus to send scientists off to design experiments and to begin theorising of their own in the light of such experimental work. As Russell put it in his review of *The Concept of Mind* (in the *Journal of Philosophy*, 1958):

A great many philosophical questions are, in fact, scientific questions with which science is not yet ready to deal. Both sensation and perception were in this class of problems, but are now, so I should contend, amenable to scientific treatment and not capable of being fruitfully handled by anyone who chooses to ignore what science has to say about them. (P. 9)

One suspects that Ryle's pleading that the ordinary man's view of the world does not overlap with the scientific view of the world is less a naïvety on Ryle's part than a case of special pleading on behalf of doing philosophy, particularly philosophical psychology, while confining one's factual data to the sort of data that supports the ordinary man's view of the world but not, as many later practitioners of Linguistic Analysis did, to that view of the world which is enshrined in ordinary language. One cannot help speculate that these chapters in *Dilemmas* are also the expression of Ryle's growing uneasiness and consequent defensiveness about doing philosophy, however brilliantly, with such self-imposed tunnel vision. As Russell bluntly put it:

Professor Ryle's attitude to science is curious. He no doubt knows that scientists say things which they believe to be relevant to the problems he is discussing, but he is quite persuaded that the philosopher need pay no attention to science. He seems to believe that a philosopher need not know anything scientific beyond what was known in the time of our ancestors when they dyed themselves with woad. It is this attitude that enables him to think that the philosopher should pay attention to the way in which uneducated people speak and should treat with contempt the sophisticated language of the learned. (*Ibid.* pp. 8–9)

Russell is wrong to suggest that Ryle paid special attention to or had an undue reverence for the way uneducated people speak—for, as we have seen, Ryle saw Linguistic Analysis as by and large a corrective to the category mistakes hidden in ordinary language—but he is right to complain that Ryle confined his fact gathering, which formed the basis of his theories, to the sort of data which is available to the man in the street.

Chapter 13
RYLE'S THREE ACCOUNTS OF THINKING

In one of the more loosely constructed chapters in *The Concept of Mind*, Chapter IX, 'The Intellect', Ryle gives us his first account of the notion of thinking in the sense of thinking out the answers to puzzles, problems or difficulties, that is, thinking in the sense of pondering, deliberating or theorising. Epistemologists, though not the laity, he tells us, give a Cartesian 'wires and pulleys' explanation of pondering, that is, they tell us about internal unrecordable private mental acts of judging, inferring and abstracting, and posit these as the ingredient causal components of the chain reaction which produced the end-product, a theory.

Ryle suggests that the Cartesians have been led into this epistemological myth-making because, 'Finding premisses and conclusions among the elements of published theories, they postulate separate, antecedent, "cognitive acts" of judging; and finding arguments among the elements of published theories, they postulate separate antecedent processes of moving to the "cognising" of conclusions from the "cognising" of premisses.' (*CM*, p. 291) In short, Cartesians have argued from the existence, in the written or spoken exposition of theories, of items describable as premisses, conclusion and inference to the existence of parallel mental cognitive episodes of thinking about the premisses and drawing conclusions, which must have occurred in the construction of those theories.

Leaving aside Ryle's emphasis on the fact that no one ever reports the actual occurrence at any particular time of any of these alleged episodes, and the fact one gets a strong feeling of oddness when one discusses these 'episodes' as if they were really episodes, his main argument that these 'episodes' are mythical is that they are not needed as part of the explanation of what has happened. If I announce an inference, say, 'Tomorrow cannot be

Sunday, unless today is Saturday', all that has taken place beforehand is 'just a soliloquised or muttered rehearsal of the overt statement itself.' (*CM*, p. 29)

Of course, when one is stating the inference to oneself, one is not just reciting it by rote, one is saying it with understanding. But,

> To say something significant, in awareness of its significance, is not to do two things, namely to say something aloud or in one's head and at the same time, or shortly before, to go through some other shadowy move. It is to do one thing with a certain drill and in a certain frame of mind, not by rote, chattily, recklessly, histrionically, absent-mindedly or deliriously, but on purpose, with a method, carefully, seriously and on the *qui vive*. Saying something in this specific frame of mind, whether aloud or in one's head, *is* thinking the thought. (*CM*, p. 296)

So Ryle's first account of thinking in the sense of pondering is that it is a mongrel-categorical. Thus, its full description will include first of all a reference to an occurrence, namely to the actual stating of a conclusion or theory and the premisses which ground it, either spoken out loud or to oneself. Secondly, it will include a mention of a disposition, namely a frame of mind whereby one is disposed to purposefully, methodically, carefully, seriously and attentively do whatever one does in this frame of mind, in this case, state a theory and the grounds for it. Part of the characterisation of this frame of mind, Ryle suggests, should probably be the addition of the adverb 'didactically', for most pondering is done as part of the process of instructing oneself.

Perhaps all of this is seen most clearly, says Ryle, by considering another paradigm example of Cartesian pondering, namely entertaining an abstract idea. Take the case of the abstract idea of geographical height or contour, as symbolised by contour lines on a map. We say a person knows what contour is, not by believing his introspective report about the presence of an abstract idea labelled 'contour' within his mind, but by seeing him use the contour lines on his map to pin-point which hill is the best vantage point and so on. To acquire the abstract idea, contour, is to learn how to use or to instruct oneself in the use of the abstract symbol, contour lines on a map.

In general, then, in *The Concept of Mind* Ryle held that thinking in the sense of pondering and deliberating is doing something, in one's head or on paper, in a certain frame of mind, namely 'on purpose, with a method, carefully, seriously and on the *qui vive*'. This frame of mind is not a second, parallel or connected occurrence, but a disposition or propensity which has been activated and is displayed in the activity which is going on in one's head or on paper.

Now there are two separate difficulties with such an account of thinking. First, there is the difficulty that seemingly anything that one can do in one's head, out loud or on paper is going to count as thinking, given that it is done carefully, and so on. But this was not the difficulty which led Ryle to change his mongrel-categorical account into, first the rather negative polymorphous account, and then finally into an adverbial account, for Ryle not merely retains this catholicity as regards what can count as the occurrent part of thinking but extended it still further. So I shall leave discussion of this aspect till later when I come to discuss the final adverbial account.

The second difficulty or set of difficulties with this mongrel-categorical account of thinking was connected with the disposition aspect of this account. In the first place it is odd to speak of doing something carefully, seriously and so on, where the carefulness and seriousness are not occurrent in any way, though they are what make the occurrence one of thinking. Thus, this account explains that X is an example of thinking solely because X stems from a disposition to do X in a thoughtful way. But this begins to be a rather mysterious sort of explanation, for how does one know that the X, say someone's humming a tune, stems from a disposition to hum that tune thoughtfully rather than from a disposition to hum it without thinking anything about it?

Ryle would reply that the difference between 'S—a subject or person—is humming thoughtfully' and 'S is humming unthinkingly' is revealed in the occurrent humming itself. In the first case, the humming will show care and seriousness, say, by not being done while S is doing something else, by including repetitions till the humming accurately follows some known tune, and so on. In the second case it will not.

One might reply that, if doing X in a certain way is the thinking, then a machine could be programmed to do X in a certain way and so must, on Ryle's account, be said to be a thinking machine. To put this another way, a machine, or for that matter a person, could be trained to do something accurately and methodically—say, assemble a transistor radio—in such a way that it now does it unthinkingly. However, on Ryle's account, if the assembling is done in a manner which still reveals that it is done on purpose, with method, carefully and seriously, though now automatically, it is still a case of thinking. Ryle might reply that this is only a case of thinking on his view if it is also done 'on the *qui vive*'. But how can this be dispositional? How can actual alertness and attention to something here and now be dispositional?

Another difficulty with the mongrel-categorical account of thinking is that it seems to allow as thinking only those activities which one has a disposition to do. This seems to make it impossible to explain how one can do some original thinking—say, propose an original method of brain surgery—for original thinking is precisely venturing where no one has ever been before. On the mongrel-categorical account it would appear that one can only go over old ground, for one can only do X and have X count as thinking if one has a certain disposition or propensity to do X in a certain way. The X is thinking, on Ryle's view, only because it reveals practised or dispositional carefulness, seriousness and method.

Ryle might attempt to explain such original thinking by suggesting that the X—the new method of brain surgery —reveals, not that one has a disposition to employ such a method in a methodical, serious and careful way, but that one has a disposition to approach problems—in brain surgery or elsewhere—methodically, seriously and carefully.

But shifting the X back from the emergent new method of brain surgery to the problem about surgery will not help Ryle, for approaching a problem is not a doing of a tangible Rylean sort, or need not be. Thus, often it will not turn out to be, for Ryle, an acceptable filler for the X which reveals the disposition to be careful, serious and methodical. For it looks very like, at least on many occasions, something internal and non-behavioural, something redolent of Cartesianism. Secondly, Ryle will also be landed with the problem of giving an account of the upshot of such problem-solving—the new theory—when this is still at the in-the-mind stage. This too looks very like something internal and mental. Further, both the stage of approaching a problem and the resulting formulation of a theory seem to be occurrent happenings. Ryle seems to account for all such internal theorising, as we shall see later on, by saying that it is speaking under one's breath, that it is, in other words, a real piece of behaviour on a par with speaking out loud. But, as we shall also see, this is notoriously one of the tender spots in behavioural analyses.

Ryle, of course, did see that this early account of thinking in terms of an occurrent-dispositional mix could not give a convincing account of original or creative thinking. In several later papers, such as 'Thinking and Self-Teaching' (1972) and 'Improvisation' (1976) in particular, Ryle was at pains to demonstrate that thinking is very often speculative and exploratory in nature. But he was only able to accommodate this sort of thinking after he had given up the mongrel-categorical account.

At any rate it was difficulties such as these which prompted Ryle to return to the notion of thinking after *The Concept of Mind* had been published. As Ryle put it in the Introduction to Volume 2 of his *Collected Papers*:

Like plenty of other people, I deplored the perfunctoriness with which *The Concept of Mind* had dealt with the Mind *qua* pensive. But I have latterly been concentrating heavily on this particular theme for the simple reason that it has turned out to be at once a still intractable and a progressively ramifying maze. (P. viii)

Thus, in the quarter century since he wrote *The Concept of Mind*, Ryle had been engaged mainly in the analysis of thinking and had produced a long series of articles on this theme, to which series he was adding right up to the time of his death in October 1976. The early papers in this long series tend to cover some of the ground already worked over in *The Concept of Mind* and also result in an account —the polymorphous account—which he discards in later papers in the series. There is also clear evidence that Ryle was never very satisfied with the view which appeared in the later papers in the series, the adverbial account of thinking, for in one of a series of BBC radio talks with philosophers during the winter of 1970–71 (published as *Modern British Philosophy*, by Bryan Magee) Ryle made clear his own dissatisfaction with his positive account of the notion of thinking, though by this time he had published several papers which propounded the adverbial account.

In one of the early articles in the series, 'A Puzzling Element in the Notion of Thinking' (1958), Ryle tells us that while the verb 'to think' is used 'both for the beliefs and opinions a man has, and for the pondering and reflecting that a man does', he is concerned with the latter use at this point. And in his article 'A Rational Animal' (1962), Ryle tells us that he is mainly interested in separating off 'thought in the near-professional or near academic sense' from 'thinking in the general sense of the word', for while the latter general notion is 'what is partly constitutive of all specifically human actions and reactions' the former specialised notion is what we usually mean by intellectual activity proper. The difference in these two senses of thinking is, in the main, that intellectual activity proper is thinking that involves effort and 'essentially embodies the element of self-correction', because it involves 'some specialist training' and 'standards of its own'. He then goes on to link this specialist sense of thinking with Theoretical Reason as contrasted with Practical Reason, and with our notions of 'rationality, reasonableness and reasons'. In short, the sort of thinking he is especially concerned with could be summarised as saying that it is what Rodin's *Le Penseur* is doing as he sits there with his chin supported by his hand, namely reflecting.

His first conclusion in this series about the nature of thinking as reflecting took the form of saying that there was no general answer which could be given to the question 'What is thinking?' for the concept of thinking turns out to be many different things which have no common ingredient of any sort. In 'Thinking and Language' (1951), Ryle suggested that 'there is no general answer to the question "What does thinking consist of?"' for 'the concept of *thinking* is polymorphous.' That is, 'there are hosts of widely different sorts of toilings and idlings, engaging in any one of which is thinking.' And in 'Thinking' (1953) Ryle glossed this account of thinking as polymorphous by connecting it with the Wittgensteinian concept of family resemblance by means of the example usually found in connection with this concept, namely games, for he wrote that 'to look for some common and peculiar ingredient of all thinking is like looking for an ingredient common and peculiar to cat's-cradle, hide-and-seek, billiards, snap and all the other things which we call "games".' And in his article 'A Puzzling Element in the Notion of Thinking' (1958) Ryle suggested that another way of putting this view that there is no answer to the question 'What is thinking?' is to realise that we cannot really fill the gap in the phrase 'no thinking without . . .' in the way in which we can fill in the gap in the phrase 'no singing without . . .' with the word 'noises', for thinking does not have any 'proprietary implements or materials'.

But in this article 'A Puzzling Element in the Notion of Thinking' there were already signs that Ryle was unhappy with this answer, that one could give no answer, for he suggests towards the end of the article that 'we could stretch our slogan, if we hanker for a slogan, to read "No thinking without adverting to something or other, no matter what", but then it would be as empty as the slogans "no eating without food", "no buildings without materials" and "no purchases without commodities".'

Then Ryle revised this answer as well, telling us that there was indeed an answer to the question 'What is thinking?', and so a filler for the gap in the phrase 'no thinking without . . .', but that the answer was not in terms of a common ingredient but in terms of a common modification. This view first appears, in embryo, in the article 'A Puzzling Element in the Notion of Thinking'—perhaps the most important one in the series—as the comment that 'the verbal noun "thinking" does not, as we knew in our bones all along, denote a special or proprietary activity in the way in which "singing" does. Thinking is not one department in a department store. . . . Its proper place is in all the departments.'

Ryle then went on to argue that, not merely is thinking not a ghostly inner activity, it is not even an ingredient common to a variety of activities, it is merely an adverbial-like modification of activities. Thus, to think is to do practically anything you like with one's wits about you or 'with initiative, care, patience, pertinacity, and interest'. Different kinds of thinking can be distinguished by having regard to whether this doing something or other *wittingly* (in the Rylean sense of that word) is detached from the circumstances, or genuinely the result of personal initiative, or free of 'apparatus' such as words or symbols or material objects, or the opposite, or depends on some special training, or is self-correcting, or is the result of some permutation or combination of these circumstantial additives.

In his article 'Thinking and Reflecting' (1969) Ryle argues that both the reflecting which *Le Penseur* is doing and the thinking which the thoughtful attentive tennis player engages in are adverbial. Indeed, thinking in the sense of 'doing x, such as playing tennis, attentively' is the basic notion. Just as the verb 'to hurry' is misleading and should really be understood as 'to do x hurriedly', so 'to think' is misleading and should really be understood in all its senses as 'to do x "vigilantly, pertinaciously, etc."' The only difference between the thinking which the tennis player does and which *Le Penseur* engages in, is that the tennis player's thinking is involved with what is going on around him while the latter's thinking is 'circumstance-detached and apparatus-free', and more or less initiated intentionally and voluntarily by himself. The x which the tennis player does thinkingly is play tennis; the x which *Le Penseur* does is utter words to himself or under his breath or compose music out loud or in his head, or something of that sort.

In 'Some Problems about Thinking' (1970) Ryle filled out the adverbial concept of thinkingly or wittingly in terms of doing something or other 'with initiative, care, patience, pertinacity, and interest' or, in a shorter version, 'with attention, intention and control'. There are a number of other papers in the series—some of which were published for the first time in the posthumous collection *On Thinking*—but they add little of substance to the central idea of this adverbial account. But what they do add is a growing awareness on Ryle's part, and a growing uneasiness on the reader's part, of the difficulties inherent in this account.

While Ryle has realised that to analyse away mental activities, he must show that there is no inner core-activity common to all the activities we call 'thinking', he also realises that he cannot say that there is nothing at all which is common to all the activities we call 'thinking' otherwise why call them all 'thinking' rather than 'drinking' or 'winking'. His way out of this dilemma, his way of attempting to show that the inconsistency is only apparent, is to say that what is common to all activities termed 'thinking' is not an activity-factor or ingredient but a qualification-of-an-activity-factor. Hence his thesis that thinking is basically not an activity but a way of qualifying it. Somewhat as 'swiftly' or 'with swiftness' can modify many activities which could then all be called 'swift' or 'examples of swiftness', and 'predictably' can specify activities which could then all be labelled as 'examples of predictable things', so 'with attention, intention and control' is a way of specifying or qualifying or modifying many activities which could then all be called 'thoughtful' or 'examples of thinking'.

An initial objection to Ryle's view might be that he makes cases such as 'walking the treadmill with attention, intention and control' to be examples of thinking, a contention that is certainly at variance with common usage and our intuitions about the nature of thinking. But Ryle might reply that the treadmill walker is in keeping with his tennis player example for it does come under his basic paradigm of thinking as doing X, if not thinkingly, at least wittingly. Admittedly Ryle would probably have added that it is a very attenuated example. But one might reply to Ryle that perhaps we only let in the tennis player example as being a case of thinking or doing something wittingly because it requires 'nous' of some sort to decide where to place your volley and what sort of second serve to use against a player who thrives on top spin. You really do have to attend to what you are doing and make choices about what to do. It requires on the other hand no such 'nous' to walk the treadmill, though one might still be said to be doing it with attention, intention and control. But I do not think that this is a very damaging criticism as Ryle could easily maintain that, in so far as the treadmill walker does have to attend and control matters, then he can be said to be doing it in a thoughtful way.

Another more basic objection is that, if thinking is, as Ryle says, just an adverbial modification of activities and not itself an activity, how is it that some thinking is laborious and some easy, some fast and some slow? In short, if thinking is itself a modification, it ought not to be subject itself to modification. Swiftly cannot be laborious or easy, only the activity which is done swiftly can. In the same way, on Ryle's view, it should be impossible that thinking be laborious or easy, fast or slow. Yet it clearly can. A mathematical problem may require ten moves. One student can work through these moves, in his head, in twenty seconds, another in ten. Ryle might reply that what was done swiftly or slowly was not the thinking but the going through the moves on paper or in one's head, thinkingly. Yet we would say, perhaps, to the slower student, try to think faster so you can finish all the questions on your maths exam paper and so be more likely to gain a pass. We do not say 'Try to make your moves thinkingly but much faster' for this implies that to go faster in regard to mathematical problems has nothing to do with one's ability to think, which seems odd.

Earlier I brought forward an example of 'doing X with attention, intention and control', namely walking the treadmill with attention, intention, and control, which fits in with the Rylean conditions for something being a case of thinking while seeming to strain our credulity. Now I want to suggest a case of thinking which does not lend itself to the Rylean analysis yet most of us would consider to be a clear case of thinking, that is, the reverse sort of counter-example. Such a case, I suggest, would be that of thinking in an indeliberate and unstructured way as, for example, when someone says 'Come what may, I could not stop myself thinking of the ordeal that would begin tomorrow.' This suggests that the thinking which is going on is uncontrolled, unwanted and indeliberate. It is thinking which is not done with intention and control, and not done with the same sort of attention as is required for solving, say, problems in mental arithmetic. Another such example might be the uncontrolled teeming thoughts an artist or impressionist poet might deliberately, if not foster, at least not discipline.

Ryle did take account of something like this difficulty in a later paper 'Adverbial Verbs and Verbs of Thinking' (probably written around 1971 but published posthumously in *On Thinking*): 'Even *Le Penseur* need not be in harness all day long. He may, like us, sometimes be pleasantly engaged in just going over the incidents of yesterday's football match, or the lines of a well-known poem. . . . He is voluntarily and pleasantly strolling.' (P. 28) But, in enlarging his account of thinking to take account of the sort of objection I put forward (about unstructured thinking), Ryle now lands himself in a new difficulty. All the stuffing in Ryle's adverbial account of thinking is in the carefully defined, adverbial modification. *Le Penseur* is thinking in so far as he is x-ing with attention, intention and control. But if, in order to sidestep an objection that this account is too narrow, Ryle now suggests that x-ing without attention or control, that is just idling or strolling about one's thinking, must also be included in his account of thinking, then his account has become diffuse and unfocused. What, one might ask Ryle, is common to x-ing with attention, intention and control, and x-ing with intention but without attention or control? It looks as if it is just intention. But to give an account solely in terms of doing *x* intentionally is clearly not a good account of thinking.

Ryle will be forced to give a disjunctive account of thinking, namely thinking is x-ing with attention, intention and control, or with intention but without attention or control. But one of my original counter-examples concerning these matters was one where even intention was missing. Thoughts were being forced upon the thinker. To accommodate this Ryle would have to add another disjunction. But to do this would make his account even more diffuse. Indeed, it would not be an account but a defeated one.

Another area of doubt about the Rylean account of thinking as basically adverbial arises in the following way. If we allow that in deciding to think about, say, the disposition-occurrent distinction, one is deciding to mutter under one's breath thinkingly, the muttering under one's breath appears to be only a metaphorical not a literal muttering, at least at times. But Ryle—and according to his theory he must—takes it literally. In 'Adverbial Verbs and Verbs of Thinking' Ryle wrote:

There really are, in these cases, some positive, concrete *per se*, non-adverbial, things that *Le Penseur* is doing, perhaps even audibly doing, in composing, translating and counting, which are such that he might have audibly done these self-same things non-translatingly and non-enumeratingly, that is, as Behaviourists would relish them. (Pp. 26–7)

Except for his occasional use of the term 'sub-vocal' with its Behaviourist connotations, Ryle never tells us explicitly what is going on inside *Le Penseur* when he is thinking inaudibly, that is, he never tells us explicitly what is the *x* which he is doing thinkingly. J. B. Watson held a view on thinking which was similar to Ryle's but he—more bravely or more unwisely?—was explicit about what was going on when *Le Penseur* was thinking inaudibly. In his paper 'Is Thinking merely the Action of Language Mechanisms?' (1920) Watson suggested that thinking should be defined as 'our general term to cover all subvocal behaviour', and the term 'subvocal behaviour' in turn referred to laryngeal processes or, as in the case of the deaf and dumb, some muscular substitute for them.

The difficulty for such a view is plain. Quite simply the view is unsupported by the empirical evidence available. As Woodworth and Schlosberg point out (in *Experimental Psychology*) the empirical evidence suggests that there are clear cases of thinking where both no overt behaviour, such as talking out loud or writing or signalling with one's hands, or covert behaviour such as subvocal muscular movement of the vocal chords or some other muscular substitute, takes place. 'As to speech *movements*, the evidence for their always being present during thinking is not convincing . . . Some active thinking apparently occurs without *any* sort of internal speech.' (P. 817) They drew this conclusion after reviewing the evidence from experiments designed to monitor muscular movements in the vocal chords and other parts of the body, both by mechanical means and by means of the electrical discharges during muscular movements.

In his paper 'Thought and Soliloquy' (*c.* 1971) Ryle tackled this problem once again, and seemed to believe that he had got around the difficulty of spelling out what is going on when *Le Penseur* is thinking inaudibly by saying that, while he may be uttering things to himself in English or French words, he cannot be said to be thinking in those words. For the words are the result of the thinking not the thinking itself. But for Ryle to make this move is really to do nothing more than throw out one answer to the difficult question 'What is *Le Penseur* occurrently doing such that its being modified in a certain way makes it a case of thinking?' Ryle has not given us an answer to that question. He never did give us a satisfactory answer, any more than anyone else of a Behaviourist persuasion has.

At any rate, whether we are convinced or not by Ryle's account of thinking, Ryle was right to be very concerned about this topic, as thinking is clearly occurrent and so does not lend itself to his usual reductionist move of making what others believe to be occurrent activities into dispositions. Ryle himself seems convinced that reflecting is basically occurrent and that thinking in general is so as well. But Ryle also realised that, if he was to avoid the Cartesian account of occurrent thought as inner mental activities, he must find some middle ground as an alternative to these two sorts of analyses, that is, some middle ground between dispositions and activities. Thus his chosen middle ground was adverbial analysis of what seems to be irredeemably occurrent happenings which have a claim to be mental, for adverbs modify occurrences yet are not themselves occurrences.

The nature of thinking, in the sense in which Ryle discussed it, is a topic on which psychology so far has had very little to say of a positive kind, or of a positive kind which has stood the test of time. About the only thing on which all schools of thought are agreed is that in explaining thinking one must posit something which is both inner, or 'covert' as psychologists generally say, and occurrent. Behaviourists (or Peripheralists as they are sometimes called in this context) try to discover internal muscular activities, such as laryngeal ones or eye movements, which can be correlated to a high degree with paradigm cases of unaccompanied thinking such as silent reading or doing mental arithmetic. The opponents of the Behaviourists (or Centralists), on the other hand, try to discover brain cell activity which might be found to occur invariably with these paradigm cases. The evidence favours the Centralists, as we have ordinary experimental evidence that people who are paralysed or have damaged laryngeal muscles or who have lost their eyes can still think, and we have sophisticated experimental data which comes to the same conclusion, and the more thinking in the sense of reflecting is linked with autonomous brain activity—as it is according to available evidence—the less viable is any theory, such as an adverbial one, which works from the premiss that thinking is not an occurrent activity.

So, while Ryle's theorising about thinking was not successful, and he realised it was not, it signalled a belated move away from behavioural dispositions as his chief weapon for demolishing Cartesianism. Ironically, I believe that this was a wrong move. With a more complex account of dispositions—a true genetic account which acknowledged their categorical base—Ryle would have been able to generate much more powerful rival accounts to the Cartesian ones. But he would have needed to overcome his lifelong philosophical aversion to explanations which included reference to something internal, even though this might be something as unCartesian as a brain state or activity or some complex interaction of these.

Chapter 14
CONCLUDING REMARKS—RYLE'S BEHAVIOURISM

In the final chapter of *The Concept of Mind* Ryle denied that he was a Behaviourist. I think that his denial is in order but not for the reason that he gave. Ryle maintained that he was not a Behaviourist because Behaviourism is a mechanistic doctrine, that is, it explains human behaviour, or seeks to, not merely solely in causal terms but in causal terms of a mechanistic type. Its goal is to explain behaviour in terms of matter and motion, that is, to apply Newtonian mechanics to behaviour, and it was from this goal which Ryle wished to dissociate himself.

But I think Ryle is wrong in his suggestion that Behaviourism is or has been committed to a mechanistic explanation of human behaviour. At least one brand of classical Behaviourism explains human behaviour on a stimulus-response model, which need not be mechanistic. Watson, for example, wanted to find and isolate patterns in human behaviour, especially patterns in physiological reactions, and to correlate these with stimuli in the environment: 'By pattern-reaction we mean that the separate details of response appear with some constancy, with some regularity, and in approximately the same sequential order each time the exciting stimulus is presented.' (*Psychology from the Standpoint of a Behaviorist*, Lippincott, 1919, p. 195) B. F. Skinner's Behaviourism was not couched in terms of a simple stimulus-response model but in terms of patterns to be found in operant behaviour or, in non-Skinnerian language, behaviour that produces a desired result and so tends to be repeated because of this. The stimulus, if one could call it that, is not merely or even mainly the environment but a very complex interplay, namely the consideration of and deliberation in the light of the results which one's tentative or 'experimental' behaviour happened to produce last time when confronted by that environment. One behaves in manner X in environment Y because one recalls that last time X was performed in

Y, it produced desirable result Z which was more desirable than the results produced by any other form of behaviour in those circumstances.

But in neither Watson's nor Skinner's Behaviourism is there any commitment or necessity to make a commitment to explaining the interaction between environment and person in purely Newtonian mechanistic terms. The causal processes, whereby in Skinner's account the environment 'twigs' the memory, and then the intellect, to compute the best possible results from various possible courses of action —where the items memory and intellect are physiologically conceived—need not be mechanistic. They might be causal processes which are to be cashed out in terms of non-mechanistic powers or interactions which the physiologist may one day explain in non-mechanistic terms. As Skinner himself puts it: 'What an organism does will eventually be seen to be due to what it is, at the moment it behaves, and the physiologist will some day give us all the details.' (*About Behaviourism*, Cape, 1974, p. 249) Even Watson did not commit himself to a mechanistic account of his simpler stimulus-response picture. He would also have replied that it was not the task of the psychologist to give an account of the causal interaction between physiology and environment, and *a fortiori* not prudent for the psychologist to jump to the conclusion that the causal interaction will turn out to be mechanistic.

But even though I think Ryle's grounds for his plea that he is not a Behaviourist are mistaken, I still think that he should not be characterised as a Behaviourist. To put the point in a Rylean way, psychological Behaviourists and Ryle are answering two quite different sorts of question, and so the theories which they propound in answer to these questions fall into quite different categories. To confuse Ryle's theories with those of the Behaviourists is to commit a category mistake. The Behaviourists were asking the question 'What causes me to behave in manner X?' and gave answers such as 'Environment Y', or 'My computing of the probabilities concerning the most desirable results my behaviour could produce in environment Y'. Ryle was asking the question 'What is the correct logical form or category of concept X?' and tended to ask the question of what traditionally were termed mental concepts such as the will, the intellect, mental images, and so on, and thus in reply often said 'A disposition to behave in manner P and not an internal mental entity or activity' or 'A behavioural occurrence S seen in the light of a disposition to behave in that and related ways'.

Of course, Ryle and the Behaviourists do come close together in that, in answering their different questions, they end up with similar accounts of certain traditional mental concepts. Thus a Behaviourist might describe vanity in terms of either a reflex or operant behaviour pattern, while Ryle would describe it as a disposition to behave in a certain way in certain circumstances. Thus Ryle and the Behaviourists might give roughly similar accounts of such things as emotions, moods, personality traits and temperaments. But where they would differ greatly would be in the explanation of such items as pondering, dreaming, wishing, and willing. A Behaviourist would probably say that, being internal, they are the province of the physiologist and are probably to be cashed out as brain-states or brain-processes. Ryle would have none of that, and gave us a dispositional or mongrel-categorical account of them which refers to behaviour but makes no mention of anything internal at all. As J. J. C. Smart writes in 'Ryle in Relation to Modern Science':

It looks as though he [Ryle] cannot see a third possibility beyond either behaviourism or Cartesian dualism. He seems strangely reluctant to allow the identification of 'mental' causes with structures or processes in the central nervous system, whether these are described neurophysiologically or functionally. Neglect of this possibility indeed clouds his whole concept of a mental disposition. Thus vanity can naturally be taken as the structure which explains typically vain behaviour. No adequate translation into hypotheticals about behaviour can be produced. . . . This strategy of identifying dispositions with physical structures is as efficacious as Ryle's in disposing of 'ghosts' and it avoids obvious difficulties in Ryle's account. (In *Ryle*, eds. Wood and Pitcher, p. 304)

So those who label Ryle a Behaviourist are not foolish. He is, throughout most of his philosophy, a behaviourist with a small 'b', for he is a behaviourist in the sense that he is one who tends to explain his bogeys, Cartesian 'entities' and 'activities', in terms of dispositions to behave in certain ways. As J. L. Austin wrote in his review of *The Concept of Mind*:

Professor Ryle holds that we should contrast not mind with body but intelligent behaviour with unintelligent behaviour: behaviour is intelligent when executed 'in certain frames of mind' or 'from certain dispositions', by which phrases we introduce a reference, not to entities and episodes different in kind from behaviour, but to past and future and possible behaviour in addition to actual present behaviour. (In *The Times Literary Supplement*, 1950; reprinted in *Ryle*, eds. Wood and Pitcher)

Ryle is not a Behaviourist in the psychologists' sense because he is not concerned with the question their theories are designed to answer. If one were to propose a label for Ryle's philosophy one might suggest 'Informal Logic' or, more narrowly, 'category correcting'. For, after all, though his philosophical psychology was the major part of his life's work and that for which he is best remembered, it is by no means the whole of it. Indeed, it could be argued that his early papers in the philosophy of logic, such as 'Negation', 'Are There Propositions?', 'Systematically Misleading Expressions' and 'Imaginary Objects' are among his finest work. What I tried to make clear was that they were seminal papers, in that it was in these early papers that he developed the logical weapons with which he later belaboured the Cartesian doctrines. It was his initial puzzlement about the nature of philosophy and his answer that philosophy was the activity of correcting our category muddles, that led him into attacking the Cartesian category muddles. Ryle could complain that his behaviourism should definitely have a small 'b' for, after all, it was not so much a theory which he proposed, much less a theory about the causes of human behaviour, but simply the outcome of a programme of replacing our category habits with category disciplines. In a sense, it is quite secondary that this programme, when applied to the orthodox Cartesian view of the mind, suggested that mental concepts should be put into the category, disposition, which category makes reference to behaviour patterns.

Towards the end of his life, as we have seen, Ryle moved away from behaviourism even with a small 'b'. He attempted to give an account of thinking of the speculative, ruminative sort neither in terms of a piece or pattern of behaviour nor in terms of a pure or impure disposition to behave. He attempted an account of thinking in terms of a modification or adverbial mode of some activity or piece of behaviour. But this, I argued and Ryle himself seemed to realise, was not very successful. But, given his marked reluctance to allow that the answer might lie in something internal, though non-Cartesian, it may be no wonder that his attempts to escape his own Behaviourist past were not very successful.

Ryle was a philosophers' philosopher. His problems and puzzles were generated by what philosophers said. Indeed, his whole approach to philosophy, and his single-minded and singular prosecution of it was a result of the impact of Positivism. If the Positivists were right, Ryle thought, then philosophy was obsolete. As he did not believe that philosophy was obsolete, he had to define clearly, for himself and others, what was left for philosophy to do. The upshot was that he declared that philosophy did not have an area of its own but a level. It was a meta-occupation, whereby the philosopher sought to correct category errors and clarify the logical geography of concepts wherever they occurred, whether they be in science, psychology, theology or philosophy itself.

Though the major influence on his philosophy was Positivism, Ryle never embraced it or even flirted with it. But, like so many philosophers in this century, he was unavoidably tinged with it. While Ryle never subscribed to the Verification Principle* or any version of it, he was tinged with the Positivists' Occamizing, anti-metaphysical, pro-Behaviourist spirit. Yet the influence of Positivism on Ryle was chiefly negative. It forced him to clarify what it was he thought he was doing in philosophy. On the other hand his work did come close at times to the early Positivist work of Wittgenstein, for they both saw philosophy as conceptual clarification of sorts, though Ryle would not have consigned philosophy to being just the handmaiden of science. But Ryle's anti-Cartesianism

---

* The Logical Positivists' principle setting out the manner in which a statement might be tested for meaningfulness. As this was to be done in terms of the statement's verifiability, it became known as the Verification Principle.

would have pleased the Positivists for, while he at no time embraced or even wrote about materialism, and explicitly rejected mechanistic materialism, his work in *The Concept of Mind* might be seen as paving the way for materialism.

In the 'Introduction' to his *Collected Papers*, Volume I, 'Critical Essays', Ryle wrote:

A Kant, a Hume or an Aristotle seeks to eradicate *one* briar-patch—which necessarily consists of a multiplicity of briars. To elucidate the thoughts of a philosopher we need to find the answer not only to the question 'What were his intellectual worries?' but, before that question and after that question, the answer to the question 'What was his overriding Worry?'

The particular briar patch which Ryle himself sought to clear was philosophy of mind. The briars which particularly troubled him were Cartesian dualism and its tendency to make philosophy of mind into a spurious branch of internal Newtonian psychology. So the particular direction which philosophy of mind has taken in the second half of the twentieth century, and the vigour and interest which are shown today in that department of philosophy are due in no small measure to Ryle.

When Ernst Mach and his followers dethroned philosophy from its position of metaphysical matriarch of the sciences, it was first Wittgenstein and then Ryle who proffered solutions to the question of what place, if any, there was left for philosophy. And if one were asked what Ryle's great worry was, one would have to answer that it was about the nature of philosophy itself. And Ryle's resolution of this problem, at least to his own satisfaction, has had an enormous influence on both the subject matter and techniques of twentieth-century philosophy. If philosophy in the English-speaking world has taken a heavily linguistic turn, then Ryle is one of the major causes. For, Ryle proclaimed, 'Science talks about the world, while philosophy talks about talk about the world.' (From 'Logic and Professor Anderson' in *Collected Papers*, Vol. I, 'Collected Essays' p. 247)

BIBLIOGRAPHY—Major References plus Further Reading

Chapter 1—'A Short Biography of Gilbert Ryle'
Gilbert Ryle, 'Autobiographical', *Ryle*, eds. O. P. Wood and G. Pitcher, 'Modern Studies in Philosophy' Series ed. Amelie Rorty, Macmillan, 1970.
— 'Introduction', *The Revolution in Philosophy*, A. J. Ayer *et al.*, Macmillan, 1963.
— 'Fifty Years of Philosophy', *Philosophy*, Vol. 51, 1976.
— 'Graduate Work in Philosophy at Oxford', *Universities Quarterly*, Vol. VI, 1952.
J. L. Austin, 'Intelligent Behaviour', Review of *The Concept of Mind*, *The Times Literary Supplement*, 7th April, 1950; reprinted in *Ryle*, eds. O. P. Wood and G. Pitcher.
Stuart Hampshire, 'Critical Review of *The Concept of Mind*', *Mind*, Vol. 59, 1950; reprinted in *Ryle*, eds. O. P. Wood and G. Pitcher.
W. Kneale, 'Gilbert Ryle, 1900–1976', *Archives de Philosophie*, Vol. 40, 1977.
G. E. L. Owen, 'Gilbert Ryle', *Proceedings of the Aristotelian Society*, Vol. 77, 1976 – 77.
G. J. Warnock, 'Gilbert Ryle's Editorship', *Mind*, Vol. 85, 1976.
B. Williams, 'Ryle Remembered', Review of *On Thinking*, *The London Review of Books*, Vol. 1, No. 3, 1979.
Obituary for Gilbert Ryle, *The Times*, 7th October, 1976.

Chapter 2—'Ryle and the Nature of Philosophy'
Gilbert Ryle, 'Introduction', 'Systematically Misleading Expressions', 'Taking Sides in Philosophy', and 'Philosophical Arguments' (Inaugural Lecture), *Collected Papers*, Vol. 2, 'Collected Essays: 1929–1968', Hutchinson, 1971.
— 'Introduction', *The Revolution in Philosophy*, A. J. Ayer *et al.*
L. Addis and D. Lewis, *Moore and Ryle, Two Ontologists*, Martinus Nijhoff, 1965.
J. L. Austin, 'A Plea for Excuses', *Philosophical Papers*, eds. J. O. Urmson and G. J. Warnock, Clarendon Press, 1961.
A. J. Ayer, *Language, Truth and Logic*, Pelican Book, 1971 (reprint of 2nd ed., 1946), Prefaces, Chs. 1, 2, 3.
— 'Philosophy and Language', An Inaugural Lecture, Clarendon Press, 1960.
— 'The Vienna Circle', *The Revolution in Philosophy*, A. J. Ayer *et al.*
Isaiah Berlin, 'An Introduction to Philosophy', *Men of Ideas: Some Creators of Contemporary Philosophy*, Bryan Magee, BBC, 1978.

Graham Bird, *Philosophical Tasks: An Introduction to Some Aims and Methods in Recent Philosophy*, Hutchinson, 1972, Chs. 1, 2.

Keith Graham, *J. L. Austin: A Critique of Ordinary Language Philosophy*, Harvester Press, 1977, Chs. I, II.

Bryan Magee, *Modern British Philosophy*, Paladin Books, 1973, Ch. 6.

Ved Mehta, *Fly and the Fly-Bottle: Encounters with British Intellectuals*, Weidenfeld and Nicolson, 1963, Chs. 1, 2.

Kai Nielsen, 'On Philosophic Method', *International Philosophical Quarterly*, Vol. 16, 1976.

A. M. Quinton, 'Contemporary British Philosophy', *A Critical History of Western Philosophy*, ed. D. J. O'Connor, Macmillan—The Free Press, 1964, Section entitled 'The Philosophy of Ordinary Language'.

P. F. Strawson, 'Construction and Analysis', *The Revolution in Philosophy*, A. J. Ayer *et al.*

J. O. Urmson, *Philosophical Analysis: Its Development between the Two World Wars*, Clarendon Press, 1956, Pt. III.

G. J. Warnock, *English Philosophy Since 1900*, Oxford University Press, 2nd ed., 1969.

L. Wittgenstein, *Notebooks 1914–1916*, eds. G. H. Von Wright and G. E. M. Anscombe, trans. G. E. M. Anscombe, Blackwell, 1961, Appendix 1.

— *Tractatus Logico-Philosophicus*, trans. D. F. Pears and B. F. McGuinness, Routledge and Kegan Paul, 1963, Sections 3.323–3.325, 4.002–4.0031, 4.1122–4.12, 5.61–5.62, 6.53.

— *Philosophical Remarks*, ed. R. Rhees, trans. R. Hargreaves and R. White, Blackwell, 1975, I, 1–3.

— *Philosophical Investigations*, eds. G. E. M. Anscombe and R. Rhees, trans. G. E. M. Anscombe, Blackwell, 1958, Sections 109–133.

Chapter 3—'Wielding Occam's Razor in the Logical Arena'

Gilbert Ryle, 'Are There Propositions?', 'Imaginary Objects', and 'The Theory of Meaning', *Collected Papers*, Vol. 2.

— 'Thinking and Saying', *On Thinking*, ed. K. Kolenda, Blackwell, 1979.

Simon Blackburn, 'The Identity of Propositions', *Meaning, Reference and Necessity: New Studies in Semantics*, ed. S. Blackburn, Cambridge University Press, 1975.

R. Cartwright, 'Propositions', *Analytical Philosophy*, First Series, ed. R. J. Butler, Blackwell, 1966.

Richard Gale, 'Propositions, Judgments, Sentences and Statements', *Encyclopedia of Philosophy*, ed. P. Edwards, Collier–Macmillan, 1967, Vol. 6.

B. Russell, 'On Propositions: What They Are and How They Mean', *Proceedings of the Aristotelian Society*, Vol. 19, 1919; reprinted in Bertrand Russell *Logic and Knowledge: Essays 1901–1950*, ed. R. C. Marsh, George Allen and Unwin, 1956.

Jenny Teichmann, 'Propositions', *Philosophical Review*, Vol. 70, 1961.

L. Wittgenstein, *Notebooks 1914–1916*, Blackwell, 1961.

— *Tractatus Logico-Philosophicus*, Routledge and Kegan Paul, 1963.

— *Philosophical Investigations*, Blackwell (2nd edit. revised) 1958, part I, §120.

Chapter 4—'Category Mistakes and Dispositions'
Gilbert Ryle, 'Categories', *Collected Papers*, Vol. 2.
— *The Concept of Mind*, Hutchinson, 1949, Introduction, Chs. I, V.
W. J. Alston, 'Dispositions and Occurrences', *Canadian Journal of Philosophy*, Vol. 1, 1971.
D. M. Armstrong, *A Materialist Theory of the Mind*, Routledge and Kegan Paul, 1968, Ch. 6, Section VI.
Margaret Boden, *Purposive Explanation in Psychology*, Harvard University Press, 1972, pp. 290–98.
Everett Hall, 'Ghosts and Categorial Mistakes', *Philosophical Studies*, Vols. 7–9, 1956–8.
H. D. Lewis, *The Elusive Mind*, George Allen and Unwin, 1969, Ch. I.
William Lyons, 'Ryle and Dispositions', *Philosophical Studies*, Vol. 24, 1973.
D. H. Mellor, 'In Defense of Dispositions', *Philosophical Review*, Vol. 83, 1974.
John Passmore, *Philosophical Reasoning*, Duckworth, 1961, Ch. 7.
U. T. Place, 'The Concept of Heed', *Essays in Philosophical Psychology*, ed. D. Gustafson, Doubleday, 1964.
J. E. R. Squires, 'Are Dispositions Causes?', *Analysis*, Vol. 29, 1968–9.
L. Stevenson, 'Are Dispositions Causes?', *Analysis*, Vol. 29, 1968–9.
T. D. Weldon, 'The Concept of Mind', *Philosophy*, Vol. 25, 1950.

Chapter 5—'Knowing How and Knowing That'
Gilbert Ryle, 'Knowing How and Knowing That', *Collected Papers*, Vol. 2.
— *The Concept of Mind*, Ch. II.
D. G. Brown, 'Knowing How and Knowing That, What', *Ryle*, eds. O. P. Wood and G. Pitcher.
C. A. Campbell, 'Ryle on the Intellect', *Philosophical Quarterly*, Vol. 3, 1953.
J. Hartland-Swann, 'The Logical Status of "Knowing That"', *Analysis*, Vol. 16, 1955–6.
H. D. Lewis, *The Elusive Mind*, George Allen and Unwin, 1969, Ch. II.
Jane Roland, 'On "Knowing How" and "Knowing That"', *Philosophical Review*, Vol. 67, 1958.
Israel Scheffler, 'On Ryle's Theory of Propositional Knowledge', *Journal of Philosophy*, Vol. 65, 1968.

Chapter 6—'The Myth of Volitions'
Gilbert Ryle, *The Concept of Mind*, Ch. III.
D. M. Armstrong, 'Acting and Trying', *Philosophical Papers*, Vol. 2, 1973.
Bruce Aune, 'Prichard, Action and Volition', *Philosophical Studies*, Vol. 25, 1974.

A. Danto, *Analytical Philosophy of Action*, Cambridge University Press, 1973, Ch. 4.

Lawrence Davis, *Theory of Action*, 'Foundations of Philosophy Series', Prentice-Hall, 1979, Ch. 1.

A. Goldman, 'The Volitional Theory Revisited', *Action Theory*, eds. M. Brand and D. Walton, Reidel, 1976.

John Ladd, 'Freewill and Voluntary Action', *Philosophy and Phenomenological Research*, Vol. 12, 1951–2.

H. D. Lewis, *The Elusive Mind*, George Allen and Unwin, 1969, Ch. II.

H. McCann, 'Volition and Basic Action', *Philosophical Review*, Vol. 83, 1974.

— 'Trying, Paralysis, and Volition', *Review of Metaphysics*, Vol. 28, 1975.

A. I. Melden, 'Willing', *Philosophical Review*, Vol. 69, 1960.

— 'Willing and the Will', *Philosophy and Phenomenological Research*, Vol. 31, 1970–71.

B. O'Shaughnessy, 'The Limits of the Will', *Philosophical Review*, Vol. 65, 1956.

W. Sellars, 'Volitions Reaffirmed', *Action Theory*, eds. M. Brand and D. Walton.

G. N. A. Vesey, 'Volition', *Philosophy*, Vol. 36, 1961; reprinted in *The Philosophy of Action*, ed. A. R. White, Oxford University Press, 1968.

L. Wittgenstein, *Philosophical Investigations*, Part I, 611–647.

Chapter 7 — 'The Bogey of Consciousness'

Gilbert Ryle, *The Concept of Mind*, Ch. VI.

D. M. Armstrong, *A Materialist Theory of Mind*, Routledge and Kegan Paul, 1968, Ch. 6, Sections IX, X, and Ch. 15.

Colin Blakemore, *Mechanics of the Mind*, Cambridge University Press, 1977, Ch. 2.

Margaret Boden, *Purposive Explanation in Psychology*, Harvard University Press, 1972, Ch. VIII.

Daniel C. Dennett, 'Toward a Cognitive Theory of Consciousness', *Brainstorms*, Harvester Press, 1978.

J. C. Eccles, *Facing Reality: Philosophical Adventures by a Brain Scientist*, Longman, 1970.

E. P. Frost, 'Cannot Psychology Dispense with Consciousness?', *Psychological Review*, Vol. 21, 1914.

M. S. Gazzaniga, 'The Split Brain in Man', *Scientific American*, Vol. 217, 1967.

N. K. Humphrey, 'Nature's Psychologists', *Consciousness and the Physical World*, B. Josephson and V. S. Ramachandran, Pergamon Press, 1980.

Wm. James, *The Principles of Psychology*, Macmillan, 1890, Vol. I, Ch. IX.

— 'Does Consciousness Exist?', *Essays in Radical Empiricism*, Harvard University Press, 1976 (orig. 1921).

K. S. Lashley, 'The Behavioristic Interpretation of Consciousness I' and 'The Behavioristic Interpretation of Consciousness II', *Psychological Review*, Vol. 30, 1923.

G. Mandler, *Mind and Emotion*, Wiley, 1975, Ch. III.

Thomas Nagel, 'What Is It Like to Be a Bat?', *Philosophical Review*, Vol. 83, 1974.

T. Natsoulas, 'Concerning Introspective "Knowledge"', *Psychological Bulletin*, Vol. 73, 1970.

Curt Rosenow, 'Behavior and Conscious Behavior', *Psychological Review*, Vol. 30, 1923.

R. W. Sperry, 'The Great Cerebral Commissure', *Scientific American*, Vol. 210, 1964.

J. B. Watson, 'Psychology as the Behaviorist Views It', *Psychological Review*, Vol. 20, 1913.

B. Williams, *Descartes: The Project of Pure Enquiry*, Penguin, 1978.

Chapter 8 — 'Sensation and Perception'

Gilbert Ryle, *The Concept of Mind*, Ch. VII.

— *Dilemmas: The Tarner Lectures 1953*, Cambridge University Press, 1954, Lecture VII.

— 'Sensation', *Contemporary British Philosophy*, Third Series, ed. H. D. Lewis, George Allen and Unwin, 1956.

A. J. Ayer, *The Central Questions of Philosophy*, Penguin Books, 1976, Ch. IV.

D. W. Hamlyn, *The Psychology of Perception: A Philosophical Examination of Gestalt Theory and Derivative Theories of Perception*, Routledge and Kegan Paul, 1957.

R. J. Hirst, *The Problems of Perception*, George Allen and Unwin, 1959.

R. J. Hirst (ed.), *Perception and the External World*, Macmillan, 1965.

A. M. Quinton, 'Ryle on Perception', *Ryle*, eds. O. P. Wood and G. Pitcher.

Chapter 9 — 'Imagination'

Gilbert Ryle, 'Imaginary Objects', *Collected Papers*, Vol. 2.

— *The Concept of Mind*, Ch. VIII.

— 'Thought and Imagination', *On Thinking*, ed. K. Kolenda, Blackwell, 1979.

Daniel C. Dennett, 'Two Approaches to Mental Images', *Brainstorms*, Harvester Press, 1979.

E. J. Furlong, *Imagination*, George Allen and Unwin, 1961.

Alastair Hannay, *Mental Images—A Defence*, George Allen and Unwin, 1971; reprinted by Harvester Press, Ch. II.

Peter Haynes, 'Mental Imagery', *Canadian Journal of Philosophy*, Vol. 6, 1976.

Hidé Ishiguro, 'Imagination', *Proceedings of the Aristotelian Society*, Supplementary Volume, 1967; and in *British Analytical Philosophy*, eds. B. Williams and A. Montefiore, Routledge and Kegan Paul, 1966.

S. M. Kosslyn, 'Information Representation in Visual Images', *Cognitive Psychology*, Vol. 7, 1975.

Kimon Lycos, 'Images and the Imaginary', *Australasian Journal of Philosophy*, Vol. 43, 1965.

A. R. Manser, 'Images', 'Imagination', *Encyclopedia of Philosophy*, ed. P. Edwards, Vol. 4.

Gareth B. Matthews, 'Mental Copies', *Philosophical Review*, Vol. 78, 1969; reprinted in *Ryle*, eds. O. P. Wood and G. Pitcher.

Ulric Neisser, 'Changing Conceptions of Imagery', *The Function and Nature of Imagery*, ed. P. W. Sheehan, Academic Press, 1972.

C. W. Perky, 'An Experimental Study of Imagination', *American Journal of Psychology*, Vol. 21, 1910.

Zenon Pylyshyn, 'What the Mind's Eye Tells the Mind's Brain: A Critique of Mental Imagery', *Psychological Bulletin*, Vol. 80, 1973.

Norvin Richards, 'Depicting and Visualising', *Mind*, Vol. 82, 1973.

Alan Richardson, *Mental Imagery*, Routledge and Kegan Paul, 1969.

Peter W. Sheehan, 'Mental Imagery', *Psychology Survey*, No. 1, ed. B. M. Foss, George Allen and Unwin, 1978.

J. M. Shorter, 'Imagination', *Mind*, Vol. 61, 1952; reprinted in *Essays in Philosophical Psychology*, ed. D. Gustafson, and in *Ryle*, eds. O. P. Wood and G. Pitcher.

J. R. Smythies, 'On Some Properties and Relations of Images', *Philosophical Review*, Vol. 67, 1958.

J. E. R. Squires, 'Visualising', *Mind*, Vol. 77, 1968.

Chapter 10 — 'The Fatalist Dilemma'

Gilbert Ryle, *Dilemmas*, Lecture II.

Aristotle, *De Interpretatione*, 18a–19b.

Winston Barnes, 'Tangles Unravelled', Critical Review of *Dilemmas*, *Philosophical Quarterly*, Vol. 5, 1955.

R. D. Bradley, 'Must the Future be What It is Going to Be?', *Mind*, Vol. 68, 1959; reprinted in *The Philosophy of Time*, ed. Richard Gale, Macmillan, 1968.

Steven M. Cahn, 'Fatalistic Arguments', *Journal of Philosophy*, Vol. 61, 1964.

Richard Taylor, 'Fatalism', *Philosophical Review*, vol. 71, 1962; reprinted in *The Philosophy of Time*, ed. R. Gale.

Chapter 11 — 'Pleasure'

Gilbert Ryle, *Dilemmas*, Lecture IV.

— 'Pleasure', *Collected Papers*, Vol. 2.

D. E. Berlyne and K. B. Madsen (eds.), *Pleasure, Reward and Preference: Their Nature, Determinants, and Role in Behavior*, Academic Press, 1973.

Colin Blakemore, *Mechanics of the Mind*, Cambridge University Press, 1977, Chs. 2, 6.

Margaret Boden, *Purposive Explanation in Psychology*, Harvard University Press, 1972, Ch. V, Section entitled 'Hedonistic Psychology'.

Alan E. Fuchs, 'The Production of Pleasure by Stimulation of the Brain: An Alleged Conflict between Science and Philosophy', *Philosophy and Phenomenological Research*, Vol. 36, 1975–6.

J. C. B. Gosling, *Pleasure and Desire: The Case for Hedonism Reviewed*, Oxford University Press, 1969.

A. R. Manser, 'Pleasure', *Proceedings of the Aristotelian Society*, Vol. 61, 1960–61.

Ronald Melzack, *The Puzzle of Pain*, Penguin, 1973.

Gerald Myers, 'Ryle on Pleasure', *Journal of Philosophy*, Vol. 54, 1957.

J. A. Olds, 'Pleasure Centers in the Brain', *Scientific American*, Vol. 195, 1956.

J. A. Olds and P. Milner, 'Positive Reinforcement Produced by Electrical Stimulation of Septal Area and other Regions of the Rat Brain', *Journal of Comparative Physiology and Psychology*, Vol. 47, 1954.

Terence Penelhum, 'The Logic of Pleasure', *Philosophy and Phenomenological Research*, Vol. 17, 1956–7; reprinted in *Essays in Philosophical Psychology*, ed. D. Gustafson.

Roland Puccetti, 'The Sensation of Pleasure', *British Journal for the Philosophy of Science*, Vol. 20, 1969.

— 'The Great C-Fiber Myth: A Critical Note', *Philosophy of Science*, Vol. 44, 1977.

Warren S. Quinn, 'Pleasure—Disposition or Episode', *Philosophy and Phenomenological Research*, Vol. 28, 1968.

L.-M. Russow, 'Some Recent Work on Imagination', *American Philosophical Quarterly*, Vol. 15, 1978.

C. C. W. Taylor, 'Pleasure', *Analysis*, Vol. 23, 1963.

B. Williams, 'Pleasure and Belief', *Proceedings of the Aristotelian Society*, Supplementary Volume 33, 1959; reprinted in *Philosophy of Mind*, ed. S. Hampshire, Harper and Rowe, 1966.

Robert S. Woodworth and Harold Schlosberg, *Experimental Psychology*, Methuen, 3rd ed., Revised, 1955, Ch. 10.

Chapter 12 — 'Technical and Untechnical Concepts'

Gilbert Ryle, *Dilemmas*, Lectures, V, VI, VIII.

Winston Barnes, 'Tangles Unravelled', *Philosophical Quarterly*, Vol. 5, 1955.

Bryan Magee, *Modern British Philosophy*, Paladin, 1973, Ch. 6.

Norman Malcolm, 'The Myth of Cognitive Processes and Structures', *Cognitive Development and Epistemology*, ed. T. Mischel, Academic Press, 1971.

Maurice Mandelbaum, 'Professor Ryle and Psychology', *Philosophical Review*, Vol. 67, 1958.

Michael Martin, 'Are Cognitive Processes and Structure a Myth?', *Analysis*, Vol. 33, 1972–3.

B. Russell, 'What is Mind?', *Journal of Philosophy*, Vol. 55, 1958.

Aaron Sloman, *The Computer Revolution: Philosophy, Science and Models of Mind*, Harvester Press, 1978, Ch. 3.

J. J. C. Smart, 'Ryle in Relation to Modern Science', *Ryle*, eds. O. P. Wood and G. Pitcher.

Chapter 13 — 'Ryle's Three Accounts of Thinking'
Gilbert Ryle, *The Concept of Mind*, Ch. IX.
— 'A Puzzling Element in the Notion of Thinking', 'A Rational Animal', 'Thinking and Language', 'Thinking', 'Thinking and Reflecting', *Collected Papers*, Vol. 2.
—'Some Problems about Thinking', *Mind, Science and History*, eds. H. Keifer and M. Munitz, SUNY Press, 1970.
—*On Thinking*, ed. K. Kolenda, Blackwell, 1979.
B. Aune, 'Thinking', *Encyclopedia of Philosophy*, ed. P. Edwards, Vol. 8.
A. J. Ayer, '"Le Penseur": Thinking about Thinking', *Encounter*, Vol. 53, December, 1979.
Andrew Burton and John Radford (eds.), *Thinking in Perspective*, 'Psychology in Progress' Series, Methuen, 1978.
W. J. Ginnane, 'Thoughts', *Mind*, Vol. 79, 1960.
Gilbert Harman, 'Modes of Meditation', Review of Ryle *On Thinking*, *The Times Literary Supplement*, 20th June, 1980.
Bryan Magee, *Modern British Philosophy*, Ch. 6.
F. J. McGuigan (ed.), *Thinking: Studies of Covert Language Processes*, Appleton–Century–Crofts, 1966.
F. N. Sibley, 'Ryle and Thinking', *Ryle*, eds. O. P. Wood and G. Pitcher.
J. O. Urmson, 'Polymorphous Concepts', *Ryle*, eds. O. P. Wood and G. Pitcher.
Robert S. Woodworth and Harold Schlosberg, *Experimental Psychology*, Methuen, 3rd ed., 1955, Ch. 26.

Chapter 14 — 'Concluding Remarks — Ryle's Behaviourism'
Gilbert Ryle, *The Concept of Mind*, Ch. X.
— 'Logic and Professor Anderson', *Collected Papers*, Vol. I, 'Critical Essays'.
J. L. Austin, 'Intelligent Behaviour', Review of *The Concept of Mind*, *The Times Literary Supplement*, 7th April, 1950; reprinted in *Ryle*, eds. O. P. Wood and G. Pitcher.
William McDougall, 'Purposive or Mechanical Psychology?', *Psychological Review*, Vol. 30, 1923.
B. H. Medlin, 'Ryle and the Mechanical Hypotheses', *The Identity Theory of Mind*, ed. C. F. Presley, University of Queensland Press, 1967.
B. F. Skinner, *About Behaviourism*, Cape, 1974.
J. J. C. Smart, 'Ryle in Relation to Modern Science', *Ryle*, eds. O. P. Wood and G. Pitcher.
Jenny Teichmann, *The Mind and the Soul: An Introduction to the Philosophy of Mind*, Routledge and Kegan Paul, 1974, Chs. 4, 5.
J. B. Watson, *Psychology from the Standpoint of a Behaviorist*, Lippincott, 1919.
M. Weitz, 'Professor Ryle's "Logical Behaviorism"', *Journal of Philosophy*, Vol. 48, 1951.

INDEX